Struggling to Surrender

Dedication:

"To Jameelah, Sara & Fattin"

Also, I would like to thank **amana publications** and its
production and editorial staff for their kind and enthusiastic
support and for their many very valuable suggestions.
Special thanks to Br. Jay Willoughby for his careful editing
of the book and to Br. Alī R.Abūzaʻkūk for his careful
reading and critique of the original manuscript.

Jeffery Lang

Struggling to Surrender:

Some Impressions
of an American Convert to Islam

Jeffery Lang

Second Revised Edition

amana publications
Beltsville, Maryland, USA

First Edition
(1415 AH / 1994 AC)

Second Edition
(1416 AH / 1995 AC)

Third Printing
(1417 AH / 1998 AC)

Fourth Printing
(1421 AH / 2000 AC)

Fifth Printing 1422 AH / 2000 AC
Sixth Printing 1424 AH / 2003 AC

Library of Congress Cataloging-in-Publications Data

Lang, Jeffrey, 1954 (1373) —
Struggling to Surrender: Some Impressions of an American Convert to Islam / by Jeffrey Lang, 3rd Printing.
    p. 244 cm. 23
    Includes bibliographical references
    ISBN 0-915957-26-4
    1. Lang, Jeffrey.
    2. Muslim converts—United States.
    I. Title.
    BP170.5.L36   1995
    297'.42—dc20   94-29827
    [B]   CIP

Printed in the United States of America by
International Graphics
10710 Tucker Street, Beltsville, Maryland 20705-2223 USA
Tel: (301) 595-5999 • Fax (301) 595-5888
E-mail: ig@igprinting.com

Contents

PREFACE

Almost everything of their beauty could be traced to northern Europe—the delicate angularity of their features, their fair complexions, their long, luxuriant golden-brown hair—but not their eyes: large, flashing dark brown eyes, the type you might steal a glance from at an outdoor market or on a village street in Arabia, the type that sees right through you and lingers in your memory for a long time.

"Why did you become a Muslim?" asked one of my two interrogators. What answer would their innocence comprehend? Both gazed up at me dispassionately, as if they had all eternity to wait for an explanation. Maybe they were not meant to understand but only to ask, to initiate the process of self-examination.

No, I thought, their question was more personal than that. I remember when I asked my own father why he had become a Catholic. It was not due to curiosity alone but a result of my own search for self-definition.

When I became a Muslim, I did not consider how many choices I was making, not just for myself but for my three daughters and their children and their descendants. Of course they needed to know why I made that decision, because it had been made for them as well and they would have to come to terms with it for the rest of their lives.

The prophet Muhammad said of his youngest daughter: "Fatimah is a part of me and I am a part of her. Her happiness is my happiness and her pain is my pain." A father finds special fulfillment in his relationship with his daughters. Through their feminine nature, he can reach beyond the limits of his gender and is opened to a greater range of feelings and emotions than his public life allows. They complement and counter-balance him, not just as females but as his children, because he sees the completion of himself in their personalities. "Why did you become a Muslim?" holds an entirely different significance for me when it comes from my daughters, for it originates in me. It is my completory voice, in its still untainted truthfulness, cross-examining me.

I explained it to them briefly and as well as I could, but not in a way that finalized the matter, as I wanted to be sure the door was left open for further inquiry. Their question is the impetus behind this book, which began as nightly reflections on their question.

If you are not honest with your daughters, you are being untrue to yourself. For that reason, I did my best to tell it as sincerely and honestly as I could: to "tell it like it is," as we used to say. This meant including all the various highlights and lowlights, discoveries and doubts, answers and questions. Thus, this is in no way an authoritative book on Islam in the United States. My daughters know that their father is not a scholar of Islam and Muslim scholars will easily recognize this as well. I therefore offer this remark as a caution to those with lesser knowledge of the religion. For those who wish to understand mainstream Islam in the United States today, I may suggest Gamal Badawi's excellent Islamic Teaching Series.

The work before you might be best described as my experience of or reaction to Islam, something like a diary or personal journal, that will most likely be of interest to a certain type of audience. As I could not include every personal reflection or question I have ever had, I confined myself to topics that seemed to be of general concern to converts, as voiced in American Muslim newsletters and magazines. In addition, I have relied on personal communications with fellow converts, some of whose recollections appear throughout this book.

Some themes (i.e., the signs of the Qur'an and science) became of interest to me through association, while others (i.e., questions about divine mercy and justice) were intrinsic to my own search for spirituality. The first two chapters are reflections on becoming a Muslim: the first chapter highlights the decision to convert and the second focuses on the part played by the Qur'an. Although I have done my best to interpret these topics, there is so much contained within them that still remains a mystery to me. The last three chapters, which form the major part of this work, are, in reality, an appendix to these subjects. They deal with the difficulties encountered after conversion and the struggle to participate in Muslim community life.

The American Muslim convert is most often of Christian or Jewish background, which means that he or she has rejected one prophetic tradition and one version of history in favor of another, closely related one. As this entails rebellion against the prior religious tradition, it should come as no surprise that converts are often skeptical of Islamic tradition, particularly when dealing with the sayings and reports concerning Prophet Muhammad. Tradition, Muslim scholarship, popular feeling, history, and Western criticism all collide to create what appears to be irreconcilable confusion. This is the subject of chapter three.

The Muslim congregations in the United States are made up of a vast array of cultures and customs, many of which have a religious basis. The majority are from traditional and more conservative societies. The shock that they face upon their arrival in this country, like all immigrants before them, is perplexing and frightening. The convert also experiences this pain, for he/she finds himself/herself in the unaccustomed position of being a minority within the Muslim religious community. This aspect of conversion to Islam is taken up in chapter four, with special emphasis on the changing roles of the sexes. The last chapter deals with some of the difficulties of being a Muslim in a non-Muslim family and society.

I have been fighting with myself for some time over whether or not I should publish this book. My hesitation was not due to any fear of causing controversy but rather because of its very personal character. Without doubt, it is a very American interpretation of Islam, for how could it be otherwise? I cannot (and should not be expected to) extricate myself from the first twenty-eight years of my life. I continue to follow a strategy that I used when I was an atheist: I study what scholars inside and outside of a religion say about it. Insiders often overlook or brush aside sensitive questions, whereas outsiders have their own prejudices. Through cautious comparison and contrast, I hope to offset the two tendencies. Thus, my understanding of Islam has been influenced by non-Muslim scholars.

Nevertheless, it was the encouragement of fellow Muslims that finally prompted me to publish this book. I was reminded of my own opinion that the many questions and issues that now face American Muslims need to be explored openly and patiently; for the unity of the community is at stake. This book, then, represents my very small contribution to the growth of Islam in the United States. Like Muslim writers of old, I attribute what is good therein to the mercy and glory of God, and seek His forgiveness for that which is not.

Note: It is a long established and cherished tradition among Muslims to follow the mention of a prophet's name by the benediction, "May peace be upon him." In time, this practice was adopted in writing, although the most ancient extant manuscripts show that this custom was not adhered to rigidly by Muslim writers in the first two centuries. To avoid interrupting the flow of ideas, especially for non-Muslim readers, I have not followed the customary practice. I will simply take this occasion to remind the Muslim reader of this tradition.

Note: It is quite a problem to decide upon the best transliteration system for Arabic words. The most common solution is to use the system followed by the Library of Congress as outlined in Bulletin 91. For the sake of simplicity, to make my own life easier, I have adopted the spellings of this system but omitted the superscriptal and subscriptal dots and dashes. Experts should still be able to discern the corresponding Arabic words, and it should not, I hope, pose a disadvantage to nonexperts.

CHAPTER 1

The *Shahadah*

Then Satan whispered to him, saying, "O Adam, shall I lead you to a tree of eternity and a kingdom which does not decay?" (20:121)[1]

It was a tiny room with no furniture, and there was nothing on its grayish-white walls. Its only adornment was the predominantly red-and-white patterned carpet that covered the floor. There was a small window, like a basement window, above and facing us, filling the room with brilliant light. We were in rows; I was in the third. There were only men, no women, and all of us were sitting on our heels and facing the direction of the window.

It felt foreign. I recognized no one. Perhaps I was in another country. We bowed down uniformly, our faces to the floor. It was serene and quiet, as if all sound had been turned off. All at once, we sat back on our heels. As I looked ahead, I realized that we were being led by someone in front who was off to my left, in the middle, below the window. He stood alone. I only had the briefest glance at his back. He was wearing a long white gown, and on his head was a white scarf with a red design. And that is when I would awaken.

I was to have this dream several times during the next ten or so years, and it was always that brief and always the same. At first it made absolutely no sense but later I came to believe that it had some kind of religious connection. Although I shared it with persons close to me on at least one occasion, possibly two, it did not appear to be worth any further consideration. It did not trouble me and, as a matter of fact, I would feel strangely comfortable when I awoke.

It was at about the time of that first dream, either a little bit before or after, that I was expelled from religion class. Before that semester, I had never had any misgivings about my faith. I had been baptized, raised,

---

[1]For the most part, I have relied on 'Abdullah Yusuf 'Ali's *The Holy Qur'an: Text, Translation and Commentary* (Brentwood, Maryland: Amana, 1983). This source was republished in 1992 under the title of *The Meaning of the Holy Qur'an: New Edition with Revised Translation and Commentary.*

schooled, and confirmed a Catholic. It was "the one true religion"—at least in southern Connecticut. All my friends, neighbors, relatives, and acquaintances, with the exception of a few Jews, were Catholics. But one thing just led to another.

It was the beginning of my senior year at Notre Dame Boys' High School, and our religion teacher, a truly fine priest, decided that we needed to be convinced that God exists. And so he proceeded to prove it by arguing from first causes. I was a pretty good mathematics student and enamored of mathematical logic, so I could not resist the urge to challenge his conclusions.

My position was simply that an explanation is not a proof. The existence of a Supreme Being, if given the right attributes, could explain our existence and our deeper perceptions of guilt, right and wrong, and so on, but there are alternative explanations, such as those—admittedly imperfect—that we learn from science. While religions are still struggling with their own conflicts with reason, science appears to be making steady progress toward complete solutions. The ontological argument is hardly a proof, since one can argue that widespread belief in God may have its origins in widespread ignorance and fear. Perhaps the more secure we are in our knowledge, the less we will adhere to religion. This is the case with modern man, especially those in academia.

For the next few weeks we would argue in circles, and I was winning several classmates over to my point of view. When we reached a critical impasse, the Father advised me and those who agreed with me to leave the class until we could see things differently. Otherwise we would receive an F for the course.

Several nights later at dinner, I thought I had better explain to my parents why I was going to fail religion. My mother was shocked and my father was angry. "How can you not believe in God?" he screamed. Then he made one of those predictions of his that always have had a way of coming true: "God will bring you to your knees, Jeffrey! He'll bring you so low that you'll wish you were never born!" But why? I thought. Just because I could not answer my questions?

There I was, an atheist in the eyes of family, friends, and schoolmates. The strange thing was that, at this point in time, I had not abandoned my belief in God but instead was only pursuing a line of argument largely for the sake of argument. I had never stated that I disbelieved. What I **had** said was that I found the proofs presented to our religion class inadequate. Nonetheless, I did not reject this new designation because the altercation did have a profound effect on me. I came to realize that I was not sure what I believed or why.

In the months to come I would continue to challenge, in my mind, the existence of God. It was the spirit of our time to doubt our institutions, even religious ones. We were a generation raised on mistrust. In grade school we use to have air raid drills, during which we would run to the basement in anticipation of nuclear fallout. We stocked our cellars with provisions in case of such an emergency. Our heroes, the Kennedy brothers and Martin Luther King, Jr., were being assassinated and replaced by leaders who would eventually be forced into political exile and disgrace. There were race riots, burning and looting, especially in industrial towns like mine. Every night on television there were the body counts. There was a lingering fear that at any time you might be harmed by someone, and for something of which you had no knowledge. The idea that God had made us/it this way and, on top of that, that He was going to punish all but a few of us in the end, was more terrible and haunting than not to believe at all. I became an atheist when I was eighteen.

At first I felt free, for my new view liberated me from the phobia that Someone was tapping into my thoughts and fantasies and condemning me. I was free to live my life for myself alone; there was no need to worry about satisfying the whims of a superhuman Power. To some extent, I was also proud that I had had the courage to accept responsibility for who I was and to assume control of my life. I was secure, for my feelings, perceptions, and desires were entirely mine and did not have to be shared with any Supreme Being or anyone else. I was the center of my universe: its creator, sustainer, and regulator. I decided for myself what was good and evil, right and wrong. I became my own god and savior. This is not to say that I became completely greedy and self-indulgent, for now I believed more than ever in sharing and caring. But my reason for so doing was not to attain a future reward: I felt a real genuine human love. We hold love to be the highest human emotion. Whether this is due to evolution, chance, or some eco-biological utility hardly matters, for it is as real as anything else and it makes us happy. When you give out love, you really do receive in return, here and now.

Going away to college is not the same as leaving home: you are simply not living with your parents any more. It is a transition between dependence and independence, a time and place when it is still safe to test your views. I learned very quickly that no one knows loneliness like an atheist. When an average person feels isolated, he can call through the depths of his soul to One who knows him and sense an answer. An atheist cannot allow himself that luxury, for he has to crush the urge and remind himself of its absurdity. He may be the god of his own universe but it is a very small one, for its limits are determined by his perceptions and it is continuously shrinking.

The religious man has faith in things that are beyond what he can sense or conceive, while an atheist cannot even trust those things. Almost nothing is truly real for him, not even truth. His concepts of love, compassion, and justice are always turning and shifting on his predilections, with the result that both he and those around him are victims of instability. He has to be absorbed in himself, trying to hold it all together, to balance it, to make sense of it. Meanwhile he must contend with outside powers that rival his, those human relationships that he cannot control and that intrude upon his universe. He needs simplicity, solitude, and isolation, but he also needs to extend himself beyond himself.

We all desire immortality. The religious man imagines a solution, whereas an atheist has to construct one right now. Perhaps a family, a book, a discovery, a heroic deed, the great romance, so that he will live on in the minds of others. His ultimate goal is not to go to Heaven but to be remembered. Yet what difference does it make after all?

Mankind aspires to perfection; it is an inner craving that whips us into action. Shall I become the great mathematician, runner, cook, humanitarian, or parent some day? For an atheist, nothing satisfies the need, because his creed is that there is no perfection and no absolute. The next best thing is stability. I followed the tested social patterns not because I valued them but because they were functional and serviceable.

After finishing my studies at the University of Connecticut, I got married. My wife and I moved to West Lafayette, Indiana, so that we could enroll in Purdue University's graduate school. Although newly married, we agreed that our marriage was not a permanent commitment and that it would end amicably if better opportunities arose. But for the moment, it had some practical advantages. We were certainly friends but there was no passion, and, as expected, we divorced three years later on good terms.

To my surprise, I was stricken with sorrow. It was not that I had lost the love of my life or someone I could not live without; it was that I was afraid to face myself alone again. But when I really thought about it, I knew that I was always alone, whether I was married or not. Through three years of matrimony, I had always hoped for this moment. My wife was a wonderful person but I just had no room for anyone else in my life. The day she left—and she had initiated the divorce—I came to the harsh realization that my universe had become a prison, a place to hide. But I had no idea what I was running from. It was not so easy being a god, after all!

At that point I so intensely wanted to break out. I wanted to be all things to all people and it mattered how others saw me, even if I insisted to myself that it didn't. We all have this need to justify our existence, and if no one else valued my life, then of what value was it? If it had no value, why live at all? But at least I had my mathematics, and so I concentrated on finishing school. I had a few brief romances over the next two years, just long enough to experience love but not long enough to effect a bond. Then something very strange happened.

I had just defended my Ph.D. thesis and was waiting outside the room while my committee was coming to a decision. It was five years of intense devotion to my subject that had brought me to that day and I was emotionally exhausted. The door opened and I was greeted with the words, "Congratulations, Doctor Lang!"

But as I wandered back to my apartment, my joy began slipping away. The more I tried to recover it, the more I was overcome by melancholy, disappointment, and bitterness. It reminded me of when we outgrow Christmas, when we try so hard to retrieve the excitement of our childhood but cannot because we are no longer children. Maybe life is a series of television ads, I thought, and this is why we become so desperate for the most frivolous things. We cheat ourselves into believing that our goals have some real value when, in truth, we are only another kind of animal trying to survive. Is this what life is all about—one artificial victory after another? I started to rethink it all.

It was December 1981 when I graduated, and I stayed on as an instructor for another semester while I searched for a job. West Lafayette was made for contemplation; there was nothing else to do there. It was the type of college town that becomes a ghost town when the students leave for vacation. It had several fast food restaurants, a couple of movie theaters, a few churches, three laundromats, and some large grocery stores. You did not have to go very far before you were out in the rural farming areas. I walked several miles each day along the roads, crunching through the deep snow. It was the coldest winter I had ever known. The sea of white was invitingly peaceful as I sifted through my thoughts.

I could not forget the young lady who had come to my office for help. When I opened the door, there was this mysterious, presumably Middle Eastern woman facing me. She was completely covered in black from head to toe, although her hands and face were visible. She needed help in field theory, she said, and her professor had recommended me.

I agreed to help her, and my preconceptions about Arab women were very quickly shattered. She was a graduate student in mathematics and I supposed that, since she shared an office like mine with other teaching assistants, she must be a teaching assistant as well. But I simply could not imagine her standing in front of a class of Indiana natives of Germanic descent dressed like that. At the same time, she had such poise and dignity that I felt a little ashamed of myself next to her. I found myself trying not to stare at her, although her face was radiantly and unintentionally beautiful.

Although I only tutored her twice, I felt that I needed to talk to her again. I was not sure whether it was curiosity or infatuation—probably both. There was a gentle inner strength and beauty in her that I had to know. Several times I came close to knocking at her office door, but I never actually did it.

I now acquired a heightened interest in other religions. I began to have close foreign student friends from Egypt, India, Pakistan, Japan, and China. Up to that point, I had always considered the panorama of different religious systems as one more evidence against monotheism. But I now saw that the essential beliefs were very similar and that only the symbols, rituals, and deities varied. Maybe there was some universal power or soul, a vital force, that permeated our beings, I thought. The symbols for expressing that awareness would naturally be determined by the culture from which it grew. This would account for the diversity of ideas. Since we both shape and are shaped by our cultures, I thought that I might now return to my religious roots.

I went home to Connecticut for six weeks during the summer. My mother was excited, although not completely surprised, when I asked if I could join her and my father for the Sunday church service. There had been enough signs in my letters and telephone calls to indicate that I was searching.

I would stand at the back of the church, as my father always did, listening intently to the sermon. However, the words did not reach me, for the priest seemed to be talking to someone else, to those who already believed. And even **they** did not appear to be listening, just as they had never done so, as far as I could remember. They must have been getting something out of the Mass, however, or else why would they attend?

But that was not the case with me. When we would go out for pancakes after church, my parents would share their personal experiences, dissatisfactions, and doubts with me. I knew they were trying to help me and I loved them for it. And I attended church on the next three Sundays.

It was hard for me to tell my mother on the fourth Sunday that I would not be going with them. I could not even face her and kept my back to her when she came to wake me. "It's just not for me, mom," I told her.

There was a short pause. Perhaps she was thinking of a way to encourage me. Maybe she was going to tell me that I should give it more time, that it was naive to assume that three Masses would be enough. "All right, son," my mother said at last. Her words were sunk in despair and resignation, suspended in that parental pain and love that digs so deeply when you have a suffering child and there is little you can do to help. I wanted to get out of bed and hug her, to tell her that I was sorry. But I could not even turn around. She stood silently by my bed a moment longer, and then I heard her footsteps leave the room.

San Francisco was a chance to begin anew, for new places provide new opportunities. You can do something different or unexpected because of your anonymity. My professors encouraged me to work elsewhere but I chose the University of San Francisco.

I was not sure why. It was not a research school, and I had never liked big cities. At the start of the semester, my personal life was already exciting and chaotic. I had decided to live for the moment and not to dwell so much on the future or the past. It was wonderful to be earning a real living instead of the graduate student stipend I was used to.

I was about to begin my first lecture when this extremely handsome, regal-looking Arab fellow walked in the rear door of the classroom—or, I should say, made his entrance. He was tall, slim, and dressed in a style that reflected impeccable taste. The entire class turned to view him; I thought they might even stand up. Everyone obviously recognized him, and he was acknowledging members of his audience with smiles and polite quips that had them laughing as he made his way to his seat. The mood of the group had actually changed!

My lecture had some relation to medical research, and I asked the class if anyone had any insights to share. Who should raise his hand from the back of the room but the young man whom I had assumed was a prince? In perfect English tinged with a slightly British accent and with great self-assurance, he elucidated the entire matter for the class.

"What's your name?" I asked.

"Mahmoud Qandeel," he responded.

"You seem to know quite a lot about medicine. Is that your area of study?"

"No," he replied. "I happened to read a magazine article on this subject the other day."

"Well, thank you for sharing it with us, but I think you should consider a career in medicine. Hereafter, I'll refer to you as Doctor Qandeel." He smiled graciously in response.

Mahmoud was five years younger than I and light-years more worldly. He took it upon himself to introduce me to San Francisco. Everyone knew him (**adored** might be a better word): the mayor, the police chief, rock stars, drug dealers, street people. He was excessively generous and could make the humblest person feel important. At the same time he was completely open and self-effacing.

You did not have to hide things from Mahmoud, for he accepted you as you were. His greatest skill was with people. He could discover your hurts and make you forget them, at least temporarily. He was charming, fun, and impossible to keep pace with. Women greeted him with kisses on the cheek everywhere we went—and we went everywhere! It was a world I had never seen before, one that consisted of the finest cars, clothes, jewelry, restaurants, delicacies, yachts, dignitaries, diplomats, call girls, champagne, and discotheques, in which wealthy middle-aged women would ask you to come home for the night—"for breakfast," they would say.

It glittered and glamored in every direction—like ice! Conversations were cold, lifeless, and led nowhere. We were poor actors playing roles for which we were poorly suited. Everyone was desperately absorbed in having a good time, preoccupied with being "in" and "with it" and "exclusive". There was no joy or happiness, only empty laughter. I had never before felt so much hurt in one place and at one time. I did not fit in with that society, nor did I ever want to.

Although he had mastered the game, Mahmoud did not really belong to it either. Intrinsically, he was a simple, humble, generous man. His attraction was his innocence, his honesty, his boyishness, all of which had miraculously survived San Francisco only slightly tarnished. And I was not the only one who was missing something: Mahmoud had his own agony. He could not have relieved the pain of so many others if he had not. And I hoped so badly that he would find what he had lost.

He introduced me to his family. It was not clear immediately who had adopted whom, but they surely gave more of themselves than I. Mahmoud was the eldest son, which is a position of responsibility in a Saudi family. His brother Omar was a very bright physics student at the University of California—Berkeley. Omar was tall and muscular and a second degree black-belt in Tae Kwon Doe. His eyes were so intense that, when he was not smiling, you thought that he might be angry. But when he smiled, as he frequently did, it was the most gentle and comforting smile.

Their sister Ragia, also a student at the University of San Francisco, was pure goodness and kindness. Her large brown eyes were her whole story; they were caring, warm, penetrating, and passionate. She was exotically and ethereally beautiful, difficult to define and impossible to forget.

Hawazin was Mahmoud's pretty young bride-to-be. She was intelligent, perceptive, witty, and loved to laugh. Mahmoud's father had died when they were children, and it was clear from their reminiscences that the emotional wounds still had not healed. His mother lived alone, surrounded by several servants, in Saudi Arabia.

The times we spent together picnicking and touring the Bay area or eating dinner at their apartment were the best I had had in a long time. We did not discuss religion very much and when we did, it was almost always in response to my questions. I did not push it, for I did not want it to interfere with our friendship. My understanding was that they felt the same way. And so I was astonished when I was given a translation of the Qur'an and some books about Islam. I knew they had an attachment to their faith, but their lives were not **that** religious, and I had not seen them taking such an interest in anyone else.

I wondered who thought of it. Omar certainly had the spirituality, Ragia the compassion, and, of course, Mahmoud knew me so well. Was it so obvious that I was unhappy? In any case, I received it as a gift, a sharing of something personal. In return, I would read it and try to understand.

You cannot simply **read** the Qur'an, not if you take it seriously. You either have surrendered to it already or you fight it. It attacks tenaciously, directly, personally; it debates, criticizes, shames, and challenges. From the outset it draws the line of battle, and I was on the other side.

I was at a severe disadvantage, for it became clear that the Author knew me better than I knew myself. Painters can make the eyes of a portrait appear to be following you from one place to another, but what author can write a scripture that anticipates your daily vicissitudes? The Qur'an was always way ahead of my thinking; it was erasing barriers I had built years ago and was addressing my queries.

Each night I would formulate questions and objections, and somehow discover the answer the next day as I continued on in the accepted order. It seemed that the Author was reading my ideas and writing in the appropriate lines in time for my next reading. I had met myself in its pages, and I was afraid of what I saw. I was being led, working my way into a corner that contained only one choice.

I had to talk to someone—but not the Qandeels—to someone who did not know me, so that there would be no expectations. That Saturday, while I was in Golden Gate Park and heading back to Diamond Heights after my daily walk, I settled on a solution: I would go to the local student-run mosque on Monday.

St. Ignatius Church, located at the peak of Golden Gate Boulevard, is a source of great pride to the University of San Francisco. The university catalogue includes several shots of it from different angles. I have seen more majestic churches, but when the fog rolls in and descends over it, its steeples appear to be reaching into Heaven.

One clear, breezy Wednesday afternoon I stood outside the Harney Science Center, where my office was located, and stared at the church. To the rear of the church in its basement was the mosque (actually, it was a small room that the Jesuits were letting the Muslim students use). Contrary to my earlier plan, I had not yet visited the mosque. I was even beginning to wonder whether my decision to visit it had been too hasty. Finally, I decided to go ahead with my plan now, reassuring myself that I was only going to ask a few questions.

I rehearsed my introduction as I headed across the church parking lot. The stairway down to the mosque was up ahead and to the left of the statue of St. Ignatius. An American student had pointed it out to me several weeks earlier, with the joking comment: "The rumor is that they keep corpses down there!"

I arrived at the top of the stairs and eyed the door below. The writing on it was definitely Arabic. I could feel my heart racing as I stood there hesitating, allowing my anxiety to grow. Then I thought I should ask somebody in the church if this was the right place.

I went around to the side entrance. It was quite dark inside, and the stained glass sent down bold pillars of colored light. To the left of the altar I spied what had to be a janitor. As I darted over to him, I passed in front of the crucifix without genuflecting. It's amazing how those lessons get ingrained in you.

"Can you tell me where the mosque is?" I asked. I must have looked as unbalanced as I felt, for his expression was a combination of surprise and indignation. I did not wait for an answer.

When I got outside, I drew a couple of deep breaths. What a relief it was to be out in the sun again! I just needed to relax for a few minutes. Then I circled the church to see if there were any other possible entrances to the mosque. There was one, but the door was locked. And so I ended up where I had begun, in front of the stairs by the statue.

I was anxious and felt a little nauseated as I started down them. Midway to the door, my chest tightened and my heart was pounding. Quickly I turned around and climbed back up the stairs.

"Wait a minute!" I scolded myself. "You go in and out of doors every day at this university. There are only students in there, for goodness sake!"

I took another deep breath and started back down the stairs. The midway point was worse this time. When I reached the bottom, I felt constricted and sick. My legs, which carried me seven miles each day on my walk, were weakening. I reached for the doorknob. My hand was shaking, I was shaking, I was sweating. I ran for the top of the stairs.

I froze there, with my back to the mosque. I did not know what to do. I felt embarrassed and defeated. I considered returning to my office. Several seconds passed. I was gazing at the sky. It was vast, mysterious, comforting. I had fought the urge to pray for ten whole years. But now my resistance was spent and I just let the feelings rise. "O God, if you want me to go down those stairs, please give me the strength!"

I waited. Nothing; I felt nothing! I was hoping the ground might shake, a bolt of light might surround me—at least goose bumps. But I did not feel anything. I made a 180 degree turn, walked down the stairs, put my hand on the doorknob, and pushed open the door.

"Are you looking for something?"

I had interrupted their conversation. They were standing directly ahead of me near the left wall. They were both barefooted and considerably shorter than I. One was dressed in what appeared to be traditional Eastern clothing, with a round white cap on his head. The other wore Western clothing.

I had forgotten my lines. "Is Omar, Mahmoud here?" I managed to say. I was getting nervous again.

"What's their last name?" The one without the cap looked suspicious.

"Qandeel?" I tried. But it did not help.

"There's nobody else here. Just us."

This was not going to work. "I'm sorry. I must be in the wrong place." I started to turn around.

"Do you want to know about Islam?" the one with the cap called out.

"Yes, yes, I do!" I took a step toward them.

"Would you please take off your shoes? We pray here," he explained. The traditional fellow was doing the talking. The other had evidently decided merely to observe something which was, judging from his expression, unusual.

We sat on the floor in the left-hand corner. They let me choose the place, and I positioned myself so that I was facing the door with my back to the wall. There was a small washroom off to my right and a closet-sized room for ladies off to my left.

Abdul Hannan, a student from Malaysia, was the young man with the white cap. Muhammad Yusuf, the other student, was from Palestine. I told them what I knew about Islam, and they were pleasantly surprised. We talked for about fifteen minutes.

I asked some superficial questions, but nothing was as I had expected. Abdul Hannan began saying something about angels beating the souls of dead disbelievers and the tortures they would be subjected to in the grave. I only pretended to listen. I said that I had an office hour to get to (I didn't, but that always works) and I thanked them for their time.

11

I was about to stand up to leave when the doorknob turned. It was now late afternoon and the setting sun was stationed somewhat behind the door. The lighting in the room was dim, so when the door opened the entrance was engulfed in light. Standing there was this silhouette of a man with a scraggly beard, ankle-high robe, sandals, turban, and a cane. He looked like Moses returning from Mount Sinai; he was biblical and fascinating. I had to stay.

He entered quietly and did not seem to notice us. He was whispering what must have been a supplication with his head raised slightly and his eyes almost shut. His hands were near his chest, his palms turned upwards as if waiting for his share of something. When he finished, he asked Muhammad something in Arabic and then walked unassumingly into the washroom.

"That's Brother Ghassan." They were revived and optimistic. "He's the imam. He leads the prayers."

I knew from my reading that Muslims had no official clergy. "Anyone can lead," Muhammad offered; Abdul Hannan, myself, anybody." A moment later Ghassan came into the room. His head was lowered meekly as he came over to us. He had a slight, Ghandi-ish kind of frame. His complexion was fair and his eyes and face were simultaneously peaceful and desolate, as if he had resigned himself to some great personal tragedy.

As the other two students made room for him, he sat down next to me. He put his hand on my knee.

"What's your name?" He was the first to ask and, unlike Abdul Hannan and Muhammad, he wanted to talk casually at first, apparently to reduce the tension. I appreciated his attempt to put me at ease. His voice was low-toned and strong, and had a certain special resonance that gave him an aura of inspiration. His accent told me he was from Arabia. He was somewhat shy and tried not to look straight into my eyes.

"Jeff Lang."

"Are you a student at USF?" he asked. I looked much younger than my age; in fact, earlier that semester, I had been asked to leave a teachers' meeting because everyone thought I was a student.

"No, I'm a professor in the math department."

His eyes widened and he glanced at the others. We spoke for a few minutes, and then Ghassan asked me politely if I would excuse them while they prayed the afternoon prayer. It was the first time I had seen Muslims praying together. I used the break to stretch my legs, which by now were stiff from sitting on the floor.

When they were done we returned to our former places. Ghassan resumed the conversation. "So how did you become interested in Islam?"

I wondered if he knew the Qandeels but I said only, "I've been reading about it." Apparently that answer sufficed. We continued for a while discussing mostly technical matters, but we were not really communicating. I was running out of questions and he was running out of comments. We were both disappointed, and I thought of getting back to the math department.

"Do you have any other questions?"

"No, not really." But then something popped into my mind. "I do have one question."

I paused, not sure how to formulate it. "Can you tell me what it feels like to be a Muslim? I mean, how do you see your relationship with God?"

I could already see that Ghassan had the fantastic charisma and intuition so indispensable for a spiritual leader. I would later discover that he had a huge following, both here and abroad. Like Mahmoud, he was acutely sensitive to your inner pain, but unlike Mahmoud, he would not let you ignore it. He would magnify it in front of you and force you to focus on it. This is a tremendous power that few possess. Every great religious leader must have it, however, and, along with it, the accompanying tremendous responsibilities and dangers.

His eyes met mine but he did not answer immediately. Maybe he was surveying the source and the intent of the question. Then he lowered his head, as if praying, summoning his spiritual energy. Slowly moving his head from side to side, as people do when they want to indicate a negative response, he began to speak.

The first word he said was both a prayer and a call: "Allaaahh!" He paused and took a deep breath. "Is so great! And we are nothing compared to Him, we are less than a single grain of sand." As he spoke, his thumb and index finger squeezed tightly a nonexistent speck of sand, which he lowered to the floor and then released to reveal nothing, making his symbol all the more effective. "And yet, He loves us more than a mother loves her baby child!"

He was fighting back his feelings; his eyes were nearly closed and his head still lowered. From this point on, until he finished his words, I would see a spirit that was burning with fear, hope, and desire. Each remaining sentence would be a wave of emotion, rising and then receding.

"And **nothing** happens except by the will of Allah! When we breathe in"—he put his hand to his chest—it is by His will. And when we breathe out, it is by His will. When we lift our foot to take a step, it is by the will of Allah, and we would never be able to put that foot back on the ground except by His command! When a leaf falls from a tree and twists and turns on its journey to the ground, no segment of that journey takes place except by Allah's will. And when we pray and put our nose on the ground, we feel a joy, a rest, a strength that is outside this world and that no words could ever describe. You have to experience it to know."

He remained quiet for several seconds, letting the words sink in. How much I wished that he and I could change places, if only for a few minutes, so that I could feel the desire, the passion, the anguish, the yearning for his Lord! I wanted to know the serenity and the torment, the trust and the fear, rising from insignificance, aspiring for surrender. I yearned to be resuscitated from this spiritual death.

"So, would you like to become a Muslim?"

His words cracked the air, exploding in my consciousness. Why did he have to say that? That wasn't why I'd come here! I could see myself trying to explain it to my family, colleagues, and friends. I was working at a Jesuit university. What about my job?

Faces and voices crowded my mind: my ex-wife, old acquaintances, a couple of them even dead, while I stumbled over excuses. I felt panicked again; my lower back and the back of my neck were hot, my palms were wet. What business was it of his, anyway? Why not just leave it alone and let us both walk out of there? He wasn't going to lose anything. I did my best to conceal my anxiety and alarm. I suffocated all that turmoil and spoke calmly: "No, not today, anyway. I really just wanted to ask a few questions."

How I hoped that would end it! I needed to get to my office. What was I even doing here? My body was locked in tension, braced for the next attack. I knew I would have to be firmer this time. But a part of me was straining to hear him say it again. Groping! Reaching! Pleading! Begging! Praying! "Don't leave me, not after having come this far!"

Ghassan had been through this before and he knew better than to give up easily. He tried again softly. "But I think you believe in it. Why don't you try?"

The voices and faces were gone. There was no need to get so upset. I did not owe anything to anybody—not to Ghassan, my friends, no one. The decision was mine alone. Then I remembered my parents and all those lessons about being "German" that they had taught my four brothers and me (every culture has the same lessons that it identifies as its own), and I remembered one in particular: if you feel that something is right, then pursue it, regardless of what other people think. "Follow your feelings," my mother would say. The first time I had applied that philosophy was when I had changed undergraduate majors. In retrospect, that was so comparatively easy. I looked at the three of them and nodded my head up and down. "Yes, I think I'd like to become a Muslim."

Their faces celebrated in jubilation and relief. They reminded me of the NASA engineers after the successful moon landing. I wondered what all the fuss was about; you'd think that **they** had converted to Islam. Anyway, I had not officially converted yet. I still had to make the profession of faith.

The doorknob turned again. There was another bolt of light, another silhouette, and another prophetic image standing at the door in a robe, turban, and beard. He was a little bigger and heavier than Ghassan.

"Mustafa!" Ghassan called. "This brother wants to become a Muslim."

Mustafa's big, gentle, fatherly face (he looked a little like Burl Ives) beamed gleefully. He ran over to hug me.

"Mustafa!" Ghassan interrupted. "He still has to say the *Shahadah!*"

He retreated softly, as if he had discovered something fragile and precious. But Ghassan did not want to deprive him of his participation or excitement: "Teach the brother what to say, Mustafa."

Mustafa rehearsed the *Shahadah* in English for me so that I would understand what I was about to say. His voice was hushed, as if he were talking to a newborn. He then pronounced the *Shahadah* in Arabic, a word or two at a time, which I repeated after him.

"*Ashhadu,*" said Mustafa.

"*Ashhadu* (I testify)," I repeated. I was struggling with the pronunciation, trying to get it right. It was like learning how to talk again.

"*An la ilaha,*" said Mustafa.

"*An la ilaha* (that there is no god)," I repeated. My entire adult life up to that day was a learning and confirmation of this fact. "There is no God." I had come to know firsthand the awesome truth of it and its terrible emptiness and other consequences.

"*Illa,*" said Mustafa.

"*Illa* (except)," I repeated. *Illa* is a conjunctive, pointing to something overlooked. A tiny word that had stood between me and the filling of that emptiness, the tremendous vacuum that was my life, that had distanced me from the reality I was always seeking.

"*Allah,*" said Mustafa.

"*Allah* (God)," I repeated. The words were like drops of clear water being slowly dripped into the scorched throat of one who has nearly died of thirst. I was regaining strength with each of them. I was coming to life again.

"*Wa ashhadu anna,*" said Mustafa.

"*Wa ashhadu anna* (and I testify that)," I repeated. I was joining a fellowship of prophets and followers of all periods of history, of all races and

15

colors by extending my hand in discipleship to one who had called to mankind fourteen centuries ago.

"*Muhammadan*," said Mustafa.

"*Muhammadan* (Muhammad)," I repeated. This was more than a mere acknowledgment: it was a commitment to a way, time-honored and universal, preached from the lips of the very first human message-bearers and sealed in the revelation through Muhammad.

"*Rasul*," said Mustafa.

"*Rasul* (is the Messenger)," I repeated. I felt protected, secure, and liberated. I could love again and be loved by the One whose giving knows no limits. I collapsed into the mercy that flowed from the supreme love. I had come back home again!

"*Allah!*" said Mustafa.

"*Allah* (of God)," I repeated.

Two days later, I experienced my first Friday congregational prayer. It was a beautiful warm sunny Indian summer day (in San Francisco that's the only summer there is). We were in the second of the two cycles of prayer. Ghassan was reciting the Qur'an in his unique and distinctive style. Most Qur'anic recitation is slow, melodic, and controlled, but Ghassan released it from the deepness of his needs. He was an abandoned child calling for his parents. He would pound out his pleas in a tense rhythmic chant. We stood shoulder to shoulder, foot to foot behind him.

"*Allahu akbar* (God is the Most Great)!"

On hearing the command, we bowed with hands on knees, backs perpendicular to our legs. I whispered the divine praise, "*Subhana rabbi al 'azim* (Glory to my Lord, the Almighty). Thank You for bringing me here."

"*Sami' Allahu li man hamidah* (God hears those who praise Him)."

We all stood straight and responded, "*Rabbana wa laka al hamd* (Our Lord, and to you is the praise)."

Now, standing in rows in tight formation, we had been moving as a single body. I had prayed four of the prayers in the mosque on Thursday but not with so many people. Now there must have been eighty worshippers packed into the tiny room, young men from all over the world, representing maybe twenty countries, celebrating our brotherhood.

"*Allahu akbar!*"

Fluidly and gracefully, we lowered ourselves to the floor, first to our knees, then to all four limbs, and then we put our faces onto the carpet. I recited quietly, "*Subhanah rabbi al 'ala* (Glory be to my Lord, the Most High)," repeating it several times. "Never let me turn away!"

"*Allahu akbar!*"

We sat back on our heels in our rows, following Ghassan. I was in the third row.

"*Allahu akbar!*" We bowed down in prostration with our faces on the red-and-white carpet. It was serene and quiet, as if the sound had been turned off. And then we sat back on our heels again.

As I looked ahead, I could see Ghassan, off to my left, in the middle, below the window that was flooding the room with light. He was alone, without a row. He was wearing a long white gown and on his head was a white scarf with a red design.

The dream! I screamed inwardly. The dream exactly! I had forgotten it completely, and now I was stunned and frightened. Am I dreaming? I wondered. Will I awaken? I tried to focus on what was happening to determine whether I was asleep. A rush of cold flowed through my body, making me shudder. My God, this is real! Then the coldness subsided, succeeded by a gentle warmth radiating from within. Tears welled up in my eyes.

"*Al salamu 'alaykum wa rahmat Allah* (Peace be upon you and the mercy of God)." We turned our heads to the right side as we said the words.

"*Al salamu 'alaykum wa rahmat Allah* (Peace be upon you and the mercy of God!)," we repeated with our heads turned to the left.

The prayer had finished. I sat on the carpet studying the grayish-white walls, trying to make sense of it all. Dreams are very strange and there is so much that we do not know about them. But whatever the mechanism behind them is, through **this** one I saw the pieces of my life—things I had done, people I had met, opportunities I had had, choices I had made that at the time did not make sense—leading to this prayer and culminating in that prostration. I perceived that God was always near, directing my life, creating the circumstances and opportunities to choose, yet always leaving the crucial choices to me. I was awestruck by the realization of the intimacy and love that reveals, not because we deserve it, but because it is always there and all we have to do is turn to Him to receive it. I cannot say with certainty what the meaning of that vision was, but I could not help seeing in it a sign, a favor, and a new chance.

CHAPTER 2

The Qur'an

It were a bold assertion that the Koran is any less studied than it used to be, or that its haunting rhythms have lost their power over men's minds.[2]

This appraisal, made by the orientalist Gibb in 1950, holds even more true today. The Qur'an, in the minds of many Muslims, has met and risen above the challenge of the West and is the driving force behind a world-wide Muslim awakening. It continues to be, for approximately one billion believers, "the ultimate manifestation of God's grace to man, the ultimate wisdom, and the ultimate beauty of expression: in short, the word of God."[3]

But what about the Western convert to Islam, who is far removed from the cultures, traditions, and languages that this scripture helped to shape and preserve—what does he or she find compelling about the Qur'an?

This is not an obvious or necessary question, for not every religion's converts are familiar with its scriptures. It probably would not be asked so readily of converts to Buddhism or Hinduism or Christianity, for example. Yet practically every Western convert to Islam speaks of the primacy of the Qur'an in his or her life.

In reality, the common believer's reliance on the Qur'an is built into the religion because its recitation in the original Arabic is a compulsory part of the five daily prayers. As a result, all new Muslims learn several passages and their interpretation very quickly. This daily contact with the Qur'an opens the way to further study, and large numbers of newcomers report that they read some portion of the Qur'an in translation each day, apart from reciting parts of it during the prayer. Many go on to learn a good deal of Arabic, which, for Americans is quite atypical, and a few have even produced new and original Qur'anic commentaries and inter-pretations.[4] Therefore, since the Qur'an is such an integral part of a Mus-

---

[2]H. A. R. Gibb, *Wither Islam* (New York: A. M. S. Press, 1932), 350.
[3]Muhammad Asad, *The Message of the Qur'an* (Gibraltar: Dar al Andalus, 1980), ii.
[4]Ibid.; Thomas B. Irving, *The Qur'an: The First American Version* (Brattleboro, VT: Amana Books, 1985); Marmaduke W. Pickthall, *The Meaning of the Glorious Qur'an* (New York: The Muslim World League, 1977).

lim's personal religious experience, even though we would obtain a wide range of answers to our initial question, at the same time we would expect some prevalent responses.

Although Islam is spreading very rapidly in the West, its presence is still something quite new. The number of Western Muslim authors remains quite small. Some of the better known are Muhammad Asad, Marmaduke Pickthall, Martin Lings, Maryam Jameelah, and Hamid Algar.[5] Today, there are numerous European and American Muslims who are spreading their faith to others, and we are seeing an increasing number of Western writers who are sympathetic to Islam.[6] In their impressions, one discovers oft-repeated themes. In this chapter, my aim is to highlight some of these and also to describe, based on my own experience and the many discussions that I have had with others, how these pieces might fit and work together in guiding one to accept the message of the Qur'an. In other words, I will attempt to present a model of conversion to Islam.

The initial recipients of this revelation were the inhabitants of seventh century Arabia. When they heard it recited in their own tongue, its style was so sublime and its language so powerful that, as the Qur'an points out, even the disbelievers called its effect "spell-binding magic" (10:2; 38:4).

The Arab of that era did not have to struggle to translate the images he was hearing into categories of thought to which he could relate, for he already had an intimate and direct association with them.[7] When the Qur'an teaches us to ask God to "show us the straight path" (1:6), the Western reader may understand this to refer to the delicate and subtle distinction between truly serving God and someone or something else. Or perhaps he may be asking to be guided to that fragile equilibrium between materialism and spiritualism. The desert traveler of the seventh century may have had a similar understanding, but it also must have provoked something of a psychological reflex, because, in his travels, knowledge of the sometimes illusive "straight path" was also a matter of life and death. The

[5]Muhammad Asad, *The Road to Mecca* (Gibraltar: Dar al Andalus, 1980); Hamid Algar, *The Roots of the Islamic Revolution* (Ontario: Open Press, 1983); Irving *The Qur'an*; Maryam Jameelah, *Western Civilization Condemned by Itself* (Lahore: Kazi Productions, n.d.); Martin Lings, *What is Sufism?* (London: George Allen & Unwin, 1983); Pickthall, *Meaning of the Glorious Qur'an*.

[6]Maxime Rodinson, *Islam and Capitalism* (London: Penguin Books, 1974); Frithjof Schuon, *Understanding Islam* (London: George Allen & Unwin Ltd., 1963), trans. D. M. Matheson, 1963; Fredrick Denny, *An Introduction to Islam* (New York: Macmillan, 1985); John L. Esposito, *Islam: the Straight Path* (New York: Oxford Press, 1988).

[7]Toshihiko Izutsu has an excellent analysis of the Qur'an's semantic structures in his *God and Man in the Koran* (Salem, MA: Ayers Publishers, 1964). Also see Kenneth Cragg's very insightful *The Event of the Qur'an* (London: George Allen & Unwin, 1973).

Qur'an's references to books, balances, debts, and rewards on the Day of Judgment, the making of a loan to God that will be repaid with manifold increase, and to the bargain that God has struck with the believers have obvious links to the commercial lifestyle of Makkah, the center for trade in Arabia during the lifetime of Muhammad. When the Qur'an compares the state of disbelief with that of dying of thirst in the desert, or when it draws a parallel between resurrection and the restoring of life to dead earth after rain, or when it describes Paradise in vivid sensual terms, we can imagine how immediate and alive these images must have been for those who first heard them from the lips of the Prophet.

The Arabs of Muhammad's time were not atheists or agnostics, but neither were they deeply religious. Their attitude toward religion was a little like that of many people today: religious faith was one part of a larger tradition, a cultural appendage that had its limited time and place and could be called upon when needed. In technical terms, they were idol worshippers, for they believed in a plurality of more or less superhuman deities who had a limited ability to affect an individual's life. The Qur'an's problem with the Arabs was not their lack of belief in God, but that their false beliefs about God permitted and fostered depravity.

The Qur'an sought to reform, not to destroy and start from scratch, to salvage what was useful and then to modify and build on it. The task was to get the Arabs to think about religion in a novel way, to inculcate in them a new conceptual frame of reference, to transfer them from one worldview to another, and higher, one. This process of transformation took them from traditionalism to individualism, from impulsiveness to discipline, from supernaturalism to science, from intuition to conscious reasoning and, in the end, ideally, harmonized the whole.

In contemporary Western society, the situation is almost the exact opposite. With theories of natural selection or evolution by chance, religion is no longer needed to explain existence. The belief that modern psychology has succeeded in showing that values, spiritual inclinations, virtues, and morality are the result of social and evolutionary dynamics, and therefore not "real" or "absolute" but only "relative" and mainly a product of our imagination, is widespread. God is no longer necessary as an answer, for science and logic can now fulfill this function. As a result, the Western convert finds himself or herself traveling a path that is in many ways the opposite to that followed by the initial Muslims fourteen hundred years ago.

Many attitudes toward religion are similar, but their origins are different. Conversion to Islam today is often a journey from individualism to traditionalism, from learning to illumination, from the sensible to the unseen, from reason to intuition, in the end, ideally, harmonizing the whole.

INITIAL OBSERVATIONS

A Challenge to Reason

Dudley Woodbury of the Zwemmer Institute is a gifted and experienced communicator of the Christian perspective in interfaith dialogues. Recently, while lecturing to fellow Christian missionaries, he mentioned that one of the first images one gets of Muslims is that they love to debate. They will debate whether the Qur'an or the Bible is God's word, or if Jesus is God or man, or whether or not the coming of Muhammad is foretold in the Bible, and on many other topics. But, Woodbury pointed out, if you ask them to discuss their experience of faith, they are often taken aback. He relates how one popular Muslim lecturer had challenged him to a public debate. Woodbury responded that while debating did not appeal to him, he would be very interested in a public sharing and exchanging of faith experiences. The challenger had no interest in such an encounter, and so no progress was made.

To Americans, the experience of faith is the crux, the validation, and the purpose of religion. For myself, the most decisive moment in my search for God was when the Muslim student leader explained to me, after some deliberation, what it meant to him to be a Muslim. This book is my attempt to do the same.

Such a perspective should not be taken to mean that belief in God should be irrational, but rather that the emphasis is on feelings and spirituality. "What does your belief do to and for you?" is a legitimate question. However, it is also not the only question, for faith must be more than an exercise in rational thinking or a spiritual encounter. To concentrate on only one of these elements is to disregard a vital part of our humanity.

The Muslim inclination and preference for polemics in interfaith discourse is better understood in light of two considerations. First, a Muslim has no experience in dividing his or her life into "sacred" and "secular" aspects. All of life is a sacred experience, as can be seen in the fact that even the most mundane acts are consecrated by the almost ceaseless invocation of the divine names. If this seems too formalistic to non-Muslims, Muslims see it as appropriate and natural, for if God's influence in our lives is continuous and pervasive, how could it be otherwise? So when a Muslim is asked to relate his or her experience of belief, he or she is being asked to do something unfamiliar, to dissect and think about faith in a way that is outside of the Islamic perspective. Second, Muslims believe that religion must make sense, that there must be a wisdom and a rationale behind every one of its elements. While admitting the limitations of human thought, they nonetheless see reason as playing a vital role. The source of this insistence is undoubtedly the Qur'an, which leads us to discuss one of the most common first impressions readers have of the Muslim scripture. A central Qur'anic concept is the extreme importance of reason and contemplative thought in the attainment of faith. Almost every modern-day Western orientalist has noted this. For example, Rodinson writes:

> The Koran continually expounds the rational proofs of Allah's omnipotence: the wonders of creation, such as the gestation of animals, the movements of the heavenly bodies, atmospheric phenomena, the variety of animal and vegetable life so marvelously well adapted to man's needs. All those things "are signs (*ayat*) for those of insight." (3:190)

And a little further on he adds:

> Repeated about fifty times in the Koran is the verb aqala which means "connect ideas together, reason, understand an intellectual argument." Thirteen times we come upon the refrain, after a piece of reasoning: *a fa-la taqilun*—"have ye then no sense?" (2:41-44, etc.) The infidels, those who remain insensible to Muhammad's preaching, are stigmatized as "a people of no intelligence," persons incapable of the intellectual effort needed to cast off routine thinking (5:53-58, 102-103; 10:42-43; 22:45-46; 59:14). In this respect they are like cattle (2:166-171; 25:44-46).[8]

H. Lammens wrote that the Qur'an "is not far from considering unbelief as an infirmity of the human mind."[9]

The Qur'anic term *kafir*, which interpreters most often render as "disbeliever," comes from the root *kafara*, which means "to cover or conceal." In Qur'anic usage, it has the general sense of one who conceals or rejects, consciously or unconsciously, a divine gift, a divine favor, or truth. When talking of such people, the Qur'an asks, almost incredulously, "Do they not travel through the land, so that their hearts may thus learn wisdom?" (22:44); "Do they not examine the earth?" (26:7); "Do they not travel through the earth and see what was the end of those before them?" (30:9); "Do they not look at the sky above them?" (50:6); "Do they not look at the camels, how they are made?" (88:17); and "Have you not seen the seeds

---

[8]Rodinson, *Islam and Capitalism*, 79-80.
[9]H. Lammens, "Caracteristique de Mohomet d'apres le Qoran," *Recherches de science religieuse* 20 (1930), pp. 416-38, 430.

which you sow?" (56:63). The implication behind all these questions is that evidence of the truth of this message is to be found in the study of history, cultures, the earth, the cosmos, and nature, among others. The Qur'an insists that it contains signs for those who "are wise" (2:269), "are knowledgeable" (29:42-43), "are endowed with insight" (39:9), and who "reflect" (45:13).

The very first revelation to Muhammad, consisting of the first five verses of the ninety-sixth surah, stresses the acquisition and transmission of knowledge in the human quest for advancement:

> Read, in the name of your Lord, who created—created man from a tiny thing that clings. Read, for your Lord is the Most Bountiful, who taught [man] the use of the pen, taught man what he did not know. (96:1-5)

Thus the first command revealed to mankind through the Prophet was, quite literally, "Read!" And the ability to do so is proclaimed as one of the great divine gifts. Asad comments:

> "The pen" is used here as a symbol for the art of writing or, more specifically, for all knowledge recorded by means of writing: and this explains the symbolic summons "Read!" at the beginning of verses 1 and 3. Man's unique ability to transmit, by means of written records, his thoughts, experiences and insights from individual to individual, from generation to generation, and from one cultural environment to another endows all human knowledge with a cumulative character; and since, thanks to this God-given ability, every human being partakes, in one way or another, in mankind's continuous accumulation of knowledge, man is spoken of as being "taught by God" things which the individual does not—and, indeed, cannot—know by himself. (This double stress on man's utter dependence on God, who creates man as a biological entity and implants in him the will and ability to acquire knowledge, receives its final accent, as it were in the next three verses) [which read: No, truly, man is rebellious, seeing himself as independent. Surely unto your Lord is the return. (96:6-8)][10]

These last three verses characterize the attitude of modern man, who, because of the achievements of science, has come to believe that he is independent of the need for God. From the Qur'anic perspective, he

---

[10]Asad, *The Message*, 963-64.

"transgresses all bounds" in his abuse of the divine gift of intelligence. The Qur'an's dual challenge to test one's own positions against those of the Qur'an according to the standards of reason, coherence, and accepted truths is well-suited to this attitude and, moreover, its acceptance has been the first step for many who eventually converted to Islam. However, before proceeding further, a note must be made concerning the style and the translations of the Qur'an.

Interpretations and Distinctive Features of the Qur'an

When a Muslim reads the Qur'an in Arabic, he discovers transcendent beauty, coherence, and wisdom. Many non-Muslim readers, relying on translations, describe the Qur'an as incoherent, uninspiring, and profane. One source of such radically different perceptions is that most of the previous and present translators are either Western orientalists or scholars of Arabic who have mastered Arabic grammar. For many of these translators, Arabic never became a living language. And here is the source of the entire problem, for mastery of grammar and acquaintance with Arabic literature "cannot render the translator independent of that intangible communion with the spirit of the language which can be achieved only by living with and in it."[11]

The Arabic of the Qur'an, with its frequent use of ellipticism (called *i'jaz* by Arab philologists), was preserved and understood most accurately by the bedouins of the Arabian peninsula, both in the days of the Prophet and in the centuries thereafter.[12] As even Arab Muslims born outside of that tradition struggle with many verses of their sacred scripture, the obstacles encountered when trying to render the Qur'an in a foreign language are compounded all the more. Asad's interpretation of the Qur'an makes significant progress in overcoming some of these difficulties, and Yusuf Ali's translation and commentary is perhaps the most widely read among English-speaking Muslims. Many prefer Marmaduke Pickthall's rendition, since it stays very close to the literal Arabic. But for all Muslims, the Qur'an represents the revealed word of God. Therefore, any translation of it into another language is *a priori* imperfect and, in the final analysis, is **neither the Qur'an or a translation of it, but merely an interpretation.**

A reader who comes from a Jewish or Christian background, as most Western converts do, initially is faced with three significant features of the Qur'an that contrast sharply with what he has come to regard as scripture.

---

[11]Ibid., iii.
[12]Muhammad H. Haykal, *The Life of Muhammad*, trans. Isma'il al Faruqi (Indianapolis: North American Trust Publications, 1976), 52.

The first is that the Qur'an is a personal revelation, in the sense that, outside of the first seven verses that form a petition for divine guidance, the perspective of the Qur'an is always that of God addressing humanity. For example: "O my servants who have sinned against yourselves, never despair of the mercy of God" (39:53), and "By the bright morning light and by the night when it is still, your Lord has not forsaken you nor is he displeased" (93:1-3). Even when the Qur'an teaches the reader a supplication, it most often begins by instructing him to literally "say" it, as in, "Say: I seek refuge with the Lord of mankind" (114:1).

Another feature is that the Qur'an, unlike the Bible, has no specific chronology. While the Bible contains history and biography, it is virtually impossible to date or place Qur'anic passages without referring to outside sources. One can read the Qur'an in nearly any order and, as long as all of its contents are covered, a thorough understanding of its major precepts can be obtained without additional references. Thus, in a practical sense, the Qur'an has no real beginning or end. For Muslims, this is a very relevant symbol demonstrating that the message contained in the Qur'an transcends the limitations of space and time, and that it has existed in the knowledge and wisdom of God beyond the confines of creation.

As Islam does not divide reality into "sacred" and "secular" compartments, the Qur'an interweaves diverse facets of the human experience throughout its discourse—the rise and fall of nations and individuals, observation of the natural world, the making of society and laws, and human psychology—both to guide the reader in this earthly life and to enlighten him or her concerning the existence and the oneness of God. As these elements merge together in life, so it is in the Qur'an. It is as if all history, life, and creation is a witness to and convergence toward a single supreme reality: that God is the Sustainer, Regulator, and Master of it all. This is a major departure from the scriptures of all other major religions.

Parallels with the Old and New Testament

The Qur'an asserts that, in the course of history, each nation has received the same essential message through divinely inspired human beings: that man must submit his will to God's (42:13; 2:136; 7:69-78; 35:24). While differences existed in terms of ritual and law, according to the exigencies of the individual communities, mankind would continue to develop and progress until it was prepared to receive and preserve without alteration a universal guidance—the Qur'an—that would be revealed through Muhammad, the final prophet. This descendent of the patriarch

26

Abraham (the Makkan tribe of Quraysh, to which Muhammad belonged, having long prided itself on its descent from the prophet Ishmael) is, according to the Qur'an, the fulfillment of the divine promise and the long-awaited prophet "like unto Moses" from the "brethren" of the Hebrews (2:129; 3:81; 7:157; Genesis 12:2-3; 17:20 and Deuteronomy 18:18).[13]

The Qur'an presents the mission of Muhammad as the restoration and culmination of the missions of each prior prophet, and in so doing, narrates various episodes from their lives. While it mentions prophets who were indigenous to the Arabian peninsula and others who are of untraceable identity and origin, the great majority are also found in the Bible.

One obvious reason for this is that most of the prophets, including Muhammad, have a common ancestry through Abraham. More importantly, because the Qur'an assumes at least a limited familiarity with many of the Biblical prophets, we may surmise that some of their histories were known to the Arabs, and consequently to many of those who would embrace Islam in the years immediately following Muhammad's death, many of whom were originally Christians and Jews. Thus, these familiar accounts were an effective means of catching and holding their attention.

In recent years, Muslim student groups at American universities have sponsored many debates between Christian and Muslim speakers on the topic of whether the Bible or the Qur'an is the word of God. The usual Muslim position is that since the Old and New Testaments contain statements (mostly numerical in nature) that contradict each other or that are inconsistent with established facts, the Bible cannot be a divinely revealed scripture. The evidence resorted to is almost entirely the product of centuries of Western Biblical scholarship.

Most Christian participants have been willing to accept the premise but not the conclusion, for each side has in mind a different conception of revelation. When the Muslim speaks of revelation, he is usually referring to the most direct kind: the Prophet is the human instrument through whom God literally "speaks" or reveals His Will, as in the Biblical descriptions: "I will raise them up a Prophet from among their brethren, like unto thee, and I will put my words in his mouth; and he shall speak unto them all that I shall command them" (Deuteronomy 18:18), and "Howbeit when he, the Spirit of Truth, is come, he will guide you unto all truth: for he shall not speak of himself: but whatever he shall hear, that shall he speak: and he shall show you things to come" (John 16:13). The Muslim does acknowledge, however, that this is not the only type of divine communication. It is stated in the Qur'an:

---

[13]*The Holy Bible, King James Version* (Thomas Nelson, Inc. 1977).

And it is not given to any mortal that God should speak to him except by inspiration, or from behind a veil, or by sending a messenger to reveal, by His leave, whatever He wills: for, verily, He is Exalted, Wise. (42:51)

The majority opinion of Christian scholars today is that the Bible is a synthesis of different levels of holy inspiration. Bucaille notes:

The idea of a text of revelation—to be accepted without questioning a single sentence—gave way to the notion of a text inspired by God. The text of inspiration was written by mortal men at different points in time, it took its cue from ideas of the day, and included the traditions, myths and superstitions prevalent at the time it was written.[14]

Concerning the New Testament, Cragg writes:

Though the Gospels undoubtedly contain verbatim accounts of what Jesus said, there are many places, not the least in St. John, where the evangelist merges imperceptibly into his material. There is condensation and editing; there is choice, reproduction, and witness. The Gospels have come through the minds of their authors. They are history told out of the experience to which it gave rise. This may be seen as eminently suitable, distinctly appropriate.[15]

And concerning the Old Testament, in particular the Psalms, Cragg emphasizes that

in their accumulative witness to the meaning of God in human life they communicate the "felt" significance of the truth that God willed humans to understand. As they wrestle with their situation in the context of what they know of God, that knowledge is enlarged and deepened by God and brought to light and life for all who read. The revealing process, so to speak, enlists and allows the mental and spiritual capacities of particular persons through whom it addresses the minds and spirits of all persons.[16]

---

[14]Maurice Bucaille, *What is the Origin of Man?* (Paris: Seghers, 1983), 10.
[15]Kenneth Cragg, *The Call of the Minaret* (Nigeria: Daystar Press, 1985), 249.
[16]Ibid., 252.

From the Christian perspective then, the types of inconsistencies mentioned above are to be expected, since they are a natural consequence of a sometimes indirect revelatory experience. This position is difficult to test, as it is meant to be, but both parties should agree that the truest measure of the sacredness of a scripture is its efficacy in directing men's hearts to the one God and to save, reform, and guide them.

The usual Christian approach at these debates is to suggest that Muhammad was, for the most part, a plagiarist who concocted Islam from the various religious and ideological currents that existed in Arabia during his time. While this concept has lost its currency among contemporary orientalists,[17] the interesting thing is that virtually every argument used against Islam by Christians could be used with much greater force and effect against Christianity.

One positive impression that does emerge from such confrontations is that the Qur'an appears virtually devoid of factual inconsistencies. This is not to say that the Qur'an avoids metaphors, legends, and allegories, for this is not the case, as is explicitly stated (3:7), but that the kinds of contradictions that led Christian scholars to reformulate their position on the revelation of the Bible are extremely difficult—the Muslim would say impossible—to find in the Qur'an.[18] While the Muslim stance on the in-

---

[17]Many modern Western writers on Islam agree that Prophet Muhammad was completely sincere in his conviction that the Qur'an was revealed to him by God Himself. See, for example, H. A. R. Gibb, *Muhammadanism* (London: Oxford University Press, 1962), 25, where he states: "It is clear from Mohammed's fervent denunciations of social injustice and fraud that this was one of the deep inner causes of his unsettlement. But the ferment within him did not break out in the preaching of social revolution; it was thrust instead into a religious channel and issued in a deep and unshakable conviction that he was called by God to proclaim to his fellow citizens the old warning of Semitic prophets: 'Repent, for the judgement of God is at hand.'"Also see E. Montgomery Watt's *Muhammad at Mecca* (London: Oxford University Press, 1953), 80-85, where he describes the Qur'an as a "creative irruption."

[18]Christian opponents have discovered what they considered to be inconsistencies, but the paucity (and frequently the frivolity) of such criticism is striking. Almost every Christian speaker or writer resorts to the same scant evidence. The verse in the Qur'an where Mary, the mother of Jesus, is addressed by her kinsmen as "sister of Aaron" (19:28) is cited universally as a Qur'anic anachronism. The duplicity of this criticism is apparent to anyone familiar with the New Testament, where Mary calls Elisabeth, her cousin, a "daughter of Aaron." In Semitic cultures and among Arabs and Muslims to this day, such expressions as "daughter," "brother," "uncle," "aunt," and "son" are used with much greater liberality than in the West. For example, the designations "Children of Israel," "son of David," and "my Muslim brother" are seldom to be taken literally. If one accepts that Mary was a cousin of a direct descendant of Aaron—Elisabeth—but she herself was not a direct paternal descendent of Aaron, then the title "sister of Aaron" would be all the more appropriate. A frequently used tactic is to assign an interpretation to a Qur'anic verse that is not implied in the =

29

errancy and infallibility of the Qur'an might seem extreme and perilous, and a more moderate position less susceptible to attack, the Muslim is constrained from changing his stance by the Qur'an itself:

Have they not considered this Qur'an? If it were not from God, surely they would find in it many a contradiction. (4:82)

A colleague in the religious studies department viewed the Qur'an's coherence as testimony to the genius of Muhammad, who, in his opinion, indeed "perfected" the Bible. By this he meant that as Muhammad drew from Jewish and Christian sources, he was insightful enough to omit qualifying and quantitative details, such as references to time, place, number, that might reveal contradictions at some point in the future.

First, it must be admitted that the Qur'an does not merely retell Biblical narratives after deleting certain details. In almost every parallel account there are important, sometimes subtle, variations. For example, the Qur'anic version of the story of Solomon rejects explicitly the charge that this prophet, who was divinely chosen and guided throughout his life, should have been a worshiper of idols (2:102; I Kings 11:4). In the Biblical account of Abraham's sacrificial offering of his son (Genesis 22:1-19), God speaks directly to Abraham, commanding him to sacrifice his son Isaac, who has no knowledge of his father's plans. In the Qur'an, it is Abraham's interpretation of a dream that initiates this drama, and his son, who is not identified, offers himself willingly and is saved by God's direct intervention (37:99-111).[19] And one of the most critical differences between corresponding Qur'anic and Biblical narratives is that the Qur'an insists that the crucifixion of Jesus never took place.

But a more important observation is that the Qur'an will often correct elements of Biblical accounts that were found to be problematic by

---

= original Arabic. I recall one speaker, who, in a desperate attempt to produce evidence of a scientific incompatibility, stated that the annual flood of the Nile brought life to the Egyptians, rather than rain, as the Qur'an states, as if the Qur'an excluded the benefits of the yearly floods or as if rain were not important to Egyptian farmers. I should also mention that some

critics who seek to disparage the Qur'an have exploited certain early Qur'anic commentaries, such as that of Abu 'Ubaydah, where grammatical irregularities in the Qur'an are listed and explained. These irregularities include ellipses due to omission, plural verbs with singular subjects, and variation in the treatment of the gender of nouns. The early Muslim commentators **explained** that these were well-known rhetorical devices employed by early Arab poets. Many of these remain in use to this day, although they are unknown to many Western students of Arabic, who do not study the language in such depth.

[19]The sequence of the Qur'anic version indicates that Ishmael (Isma'il) was the intended sacrifice, but this was a much debated topic among early Muslim exegetes. See Firestone's discussion in *Journeys in the Holy Land* (New York: State University of New York, 1990).

Western scholars centuries after the time of Muhammad.[20] In the Biblical story of Joseph, for example, Jacob's sons travel the vast expanse of the Sinai desert on donkeys (Genesis 42:26). However, donkeys are both unsuitable for extended desert travel and also anomalous to the lifestyle of nomads, which is what the descendants of Abraham were until they settled in Egypt. In the Qur'anic account, they make this journey in camel caravans (12:65, 70, 72, 82). In the same narrative, the Biblical version anticipates an antagonism between Egyptians and Hebrews that did not develop until much later. It has, for example, Joseph not dining with his brothers "because the Egyptians might not eat bread with the Hebrews; for that is an abomination unto the Egyptians" (Genesis 43:32). No such anachronism appears in the Qur'anic version, where there is no indication of any Egyptian prejudice toward Jacob's family (12:58-93).

In Genesis 7:23, we read that in the Great Flood,

> every living substance was destroyed which was upon the face of the ground, both man, and cattle, and the creeping things, and the fowl of the heaven; and they were destroyed from the earth: and Noah only remained alive, and they that were with him in the ark.

Based on the chronological data contained in old editions of the Bible, this cataclysm would have had to have taken place no earlier than the twenty-second century BC.[21] But scientific evidence has proved that from this period down to the present, there have always existed flourishing civilizations in several parts of the globe, thus contradicting the Flood narrative in the Bible. Concerning the extent of the Flood, the Qur'an mentions only that the people of Noah were destroyed, which is not in conflict with what we know now (25:37).

A most startling contrast exists between the two scriptures' accounts of the Days of Creation. Genesis gives the impression that these various stages or periods in the creation of the earth consisted of twenty-four hour periods or "days," as we commonly understand them, by adding after the completion of each successive stage, "And the evening and the morning of the first (second, third, etc. . . .) day" (Genesis 1:5, 8, 13, 19, 23, 31). Of course, this is exactly what was believed for many centuries until the discovery that the periods of the earth's development actually involved much greater expanses of time. In the Qur'anic discussion of these same "days" of creation, we find the following qualifying note: "in a day, where of the

---

[20]See Malik Bennabi, *The Qur'anic Phenomena*, trans. A. B. Kirkary (Indianapolis: American Trust Publications, 1983) for a more detailed discussion.
[21]Bucaille, *The Bible, the Qur'an and Science*, 32-35.

31

measure is as a thousand years according to your reckoning" (32:5). This indicates two facts: a) that these "days" are not to be understood in a literal earthly sense, but that they involve much longer intervals of time; and b) that when the Qur'an uses the word "day" in relation to God's activity, it is not necessarily to be understood as a fixed interval of time, as in the verse, "in a day whereof the measure is as 50,000 years" (70:4).

Sometimes, when relating a story of a prophet, the Qur'an will include a detail that is not found in the Bible and then call it to your attention by stating that God made this person, people, or event a "sign" for later times. This occurs in the brief account of the Flood mentioned above. One of the most interesting cases of this occurs in the Qur'an's narrative of the Exodus:

> And We brought the Children of Israel across the sea. Then Pharaoh with his hosts pursued them in rebellion and hostility until, when the fact of his drowning overtook him, he said: "I believe there is no god except the one in whom the Children of Israel believe, and I am of those who surrender to him." God said: "What—now, after you have rebelled and caused corruption? This day We shall save you in your body so that you may be a sign for those who come after you. But truly, many among mankind are heedless of Our signs." (10:90-92)

This is a curious reference in verse 92 to the saving of Pharaoh's body as a "sign" or evidence for people of later times. The identity of the pharaoh of the Exodus has been the subject of much speculation. Bucaille, after extensive study, argues convincingly in favor of the once held view that Merneptah, the successor to Ramses II, was pharaoh at the time of the Exodus. His mummified body, on which Bucaille performed a medical examination in 1975, was discovered in 1898 in the King's Valley at Thebes.[22] Bucaille speculates that verse 10:92 may be an allusion to this discovery, almost thirteen centuries after the revelation of this verse. Since the actual identity of this pharaoh is never divulged in the Qur'an, the designation "pharaoh" may be a generic one, in which case 10:92 may be a reference to the general practice by the Egyptians of mummifying, and thus "saving," their dead monarchs. Whatever the actual case may be, for those who believe in the Qur'an, the finding of the preserved bodies of the pharaohs is seen as another possible confirmation or "sign" of the truth of its claims.

---

[22]Ibid., 219-41.

The Qur'an and Science

A topic that has received more attention from Muslim lecturers in the West during the last two decades is the comparison of modern scientific findings with Qur'anic references to natural phenomena. The work of two non-Muslim scientists, Bucaille[23] and (to a lesser extent) Moore,[24] are most often cited. However, this subject has been in vogue among Muslim writers since the turn of the twentieth century.

Muslim **religious** scholars are somewhat wary of this topic, however. This may in part be due to the fact that some have little education in modern science. It may also be because they have a more critical and justifiable concern: that although the Qur'an frequently invites us to consider various facets of nature as an indication of God's beneficence and wisdom, it is far from being a textbook on science. I believe that many Muslim scholars would agree with Schuon's statement that God's principal aim "is to save, not to instruct, and His concern is with wisdom and immortality, not with external knowledge, still less with satisfying human curiosity."[25] Accepting this caution, we cannot deny that these references to the workings of nature are there and that they deserve consideration as "signs" or evidences of the Qur'an's divine origin.

There is also another reason for caution: the tendency to view the Qur'an as anticipating almost every discovery and theory of modern science, such as the splitting of the atom, Darwinian evolution, the discovery of "black holes," and the uniqueness of fingerprints. Often these arguments involve assigning to certain Arabic words meanings that did not exist at the time of the revelation. For example, the Arabic word *dharrah,* occurring in 99:8, which originally meant "a tiny speck" or "a particle of dust," is frequently interpreted as "atom," because it conveys the sense in this verse of being the smallest particle of matter known to man. It is assigned this meaning by interpreters for the benefit of the modern reader, which is fine. Problems arise, however, when one employs this meaning in the context of other passages to argue, for instance, based on 10:61, that the Qur'an predicts the discovery of subatomic particles.[26] These pitfalls

---

[23]Ibid.

[24]Keith L. Moore, *The Developing Human*, 3d ed. (Philadelphia: W. B. Saunders, 1982).

[25]Schuon,*Understanding Islam*, 45.

[26]This trend exists in other religious communities as well. A speaker once informed his audience that the New Testament contains the Big Bang Theory of creation, for in the Gospel of John it states that "in the beginning was the 'word.'" Since a word is a single entity in the universe of language that when voiced produces a vibration of sound, we obtain, by some isomorphism to the physical universe, the theory of a single original point mass of infinite density that explodes.

could be avoided by referring to such philological studies as those of al Raghib al Isfahani[27] and Lane[28] in order to arrive at the original sense of the terms in the Qur'an, and only to those discoveries of modern science that we accept as facts. Even then, we should not insist on a particular understanding of a Qur'anic passage because truly "none but God knows its final meaning" (3:7).

As mentioned above, the first words revealed through Muhammad were: "Read, in the name of your Lord, who created—created man from a tiny thing that clings" (96:1-2). The Arabic word which I have translated as "a tiny thing that clings" is 'alaq. In many translations it is rendered as "blood clot," which a human being never is at any stage in his development and which is not the original meaning of the term, although it has a nice ring to it in English. Originally 'alaq denoted a tiny leech-like creature with the ability to attach itself by one of its ends to a surface. This is an apt description of the fertilized egg during the initial stages of development, a time when it literally implants itself in the womb:

The implantation of the egg in the uterus (womb) is the result of the development of villosities, veritable elongations of the egg, which, like roots in the soil, draw nourishment from the thickness of the uterus necessary to the egg's growth. These formations make the egg literally cling to the uterus. This is a discovery of modern times.[29]

After implantation, the embryo continues to grow until it looks to the naked eye like a piece of chewed flesh. The bone structure then develops inside this mass, followed by the development of muscle tissue that covers the bones. This is well known to us today. We find this description in the Qur'an:

We fashioned the thing which clings into a chewed lump of flesh (mudghah) and We fashioned the chewed flesh into bones and We enclothed the bones with intact flesh (lahm). (23:1)

One has to acknowledge a fascinating parallelism between the Qur'anic description of a human being's development and the recent discoveries of embryology, especially when we consider the preponderance

---

[27]Abu al Qasim Husayn al Raghib al Isfahani (d. 503H.), al Mufradat fi Gharib al Qur'an.
[28]William E. Lane, Arabic-English Lexicon (London: 1863-93).
[29]Bucaille, The Bible, the Qur'an and Science, 204.

of mistaken notions concerning human development that persisted for over a thousand years after its revelation.

In several places (7:54; 35:37; 31:29), the Qur'an directs us to consider the alternation of night and day as another sign from the Almighty. An interesting case is the following: "He wraps the night around the day and He wraps the day around the night" (39:5). The Arabic verb *kawwara*, translated above as "to wrap around," has a more precise meaning. It comes from the same root as the Arabic word for ball (*kurah*) and has the definite connotation of wrapping or winding something around a spherical object, such as winding a strand of yarn around its ball. From the perspective of the planet earth, this is exactly what takes place in that a half sphere of night followed by a half sphere of day is perpetually being wrapped around its surface. This is due to the earth's rotation and the sun's relatively stationary position in relation to the earth. The Qur'an's phrasing in this description is remarkable, unless one accepts its claim to being a revelation from God.

Another example of subtle yet extraordinary precision in describing a natural phenomenon occurs in 16:68: "And your Lord inspired the bee, (saying,) "Take for yourself dwellings in hills, on trees, and in what they (mankind) build." The imperative "take" above is the translation of the Arabic word *attakhithi*, which is a feminine form (for Arabic, unlike English, differentiates between the sexes). The feminine form is used when all of those it refers to are female, whereas the masculine is used when a group consists of at least one male. Therefore the Qur'an is in fact saying: "Take for yourself, you female bees, dwellings. . . ." A swarm of bees is comprised of three types: a queen, the worker bees who collect honey and build the hive, and the male drones, whose sole purpose is to impregnate the queen and who are then killed off by the worker bees. The latter type are females with underdeveloped sex organs. Thus, the phrasing of this command is in agreement with the fact that male bees do not participate in the construction of the hive or "dwelling," which is the sole work of the females.

Some verses seem to parallel the most modern discoveries. For example, by studying the galactic spectrum, scientists have recently established that the universe is expanding. In the Qur'an, we read: "The firmament, We have built it with power. Verily, We are expanding it." (51:47). Arberry's interpretation comes very close to this, for the word *sama'* means firmament or heaven in the sense of the extra-terrestrial world, and the word *musi'un* is the present plural participle of the verb *awsa'a*, which means "to widen, to extend, to expand."

In a similar example, we read:

Have not those who disbelieve seen that the heavens and the earth were fused (*ratq*) and then We broke them apart (*fataqa*), and we made every living thing out of water. Will they then not believe? (21:30)

With the above verse in mind, another tenet of modern science becomes quite intriguing. Scientists have postulated for some time that the universe was originally a single primary mass of nearly infinite density that subsequently split into multiple fragments after a tremendous explosion, the "Big Bang." It has also been established that all living cells are made up mostly of water, which is the essential element for the existence of life as we know it. This verse accords with these conceptions. But the more interesting observation is that this challenge to unbelievers was proclaimed in the seventh century. We may ask ourselves: Which unbelievers are being addressed here? For the contemporaries of Muhammad, this revelation had many compelling aspects, but this question could not have made much sense to them unless there was some ancient, and presently unknown, Arabian mythology to which they could relate it. Was it then meant to be understood by people of a much later era who would be familiar with modern scientific findings?

The last remark leads us to inquire how those Qur'an exegetes who lived before the modern era understood these passages. First of all, with perhaps a few exceptions, all of these verses could be comprehended on some level by anyone according to his level of knowledge, for all languages, especially those that are scriptural, contain words that have several shades of meaning. Even if one does not know that the earth is spherical, he is still aware of the alternation of night and day, and hence may only consider the choice of words in 39:5 above peculiar. Also, commentators often understood such words in a symbolic or esoteric sense, which is a reflection of the fact that these verses have meanings and purposes on several simultaneous levels, a subject that we will look into shortly. Sometimes commentators would hazard scientific explanations that were, more often than not, completely wrong; in other instances, their understandings were quite close to what was discovered later. Most importantly, the "signs" (*ayat*) appear as parts of larger passages whose primary emphasis is on the guiding and saving of mankind, and therefore such technical significances are likely to be missed by those not familiar with modern scientific thought.

It should be mentioned that there are expressions in the Qur'an that seem to denote the possibility of future scientific explication. The mysterious symbolic letters (*al muqatta'at*) that appear at the beginning of many surahs is one such example.[30] Bucaille puts forth a conjecture concerning the repeated reference in the Qur'an to "the heavens, and earth and everything between them" in his book, The Bible, the Qur'an and Science.[31]

The Qur'an contains an intriguing description of the Day of Judgment:

> The Day when We will roll up the heavens as written scrolls are rolled up. As We brought into being the first creation, so shall We bring it forth anew—a promise [which We have made binding] upon Ourselves. Behold, We are able to do [all things]! (21:104)

From this reference to rolling up the heavens like scrolls as in the first creation and our notions of the Big Bang spoken of above, is it possible to infer that the universe continued to fragment and expand in an unscrolling fashion after the Big Bang, revolving outwardly from some linear axis? Will the end of this cosmos involve a reversal of that process? Of course, this is only speculation, based on widely held conjectures, but it serves to demonstrate the existence of verses having implications that might one day be found to have a scientific basis. Here is still another example:

> He Who created the seven heavens one above another. No fault will you see in the creation of the Most Merciful. So turn your vision again. Do you see any flaw? Again turn your vision, and again your vision will come back to you, dazzled, defeated. (67:3-4)

Although the inability of man to encompass the mysteries and complexity of creation is expressed in this passage, it seems to point to various natural phenomenon as well.

We are not taking this opportunity to assert that there are specific Qur'anic verses that refer to specific scientific discoveries. We are merely comparing Qur'anic statements that deal with the physical universe and certain scientific notions. Often there appears to be profound similarities. But, more notably, as Bucaille observes, the Qur'an is distinguished from all other works of antiquity that describe or attempt to explain the workings of nature in that it avoids mistaken concepts. For in the Qur'an, "many subjects are referred to that have a bearing on modern knowledge,

---

[30]Rashad Khalifa claimed to have unveiled the mystery behind these symbolic letters. He makes a connection between these letters and the number nineteen (19) mentioned in 74:30. Muslim scholars are rightly skeptical about his findings. See Rashad Khalifa, Qur'an: The Final Testament (Tucson, AZ: Islamic Prod., 1989).

[31]Bucaille, The Bible, the Qur'an and Science, 148.

without one of them containing a statement that contradicts what has been established by present-day science."[32]

The "signs" accomplish exactly what their designation suggest: they act as guideposts, capture one's attention, assist in guiding one to deeper reflection, and, sometimes, to belief. Their power lies not in giving explicit and precise descriptions of natural phenomena, but in their ability to inspire man's curiosity and awe throughout the ages. Although we may argue about the true meaning of any of these passages, the topics discussed thus far in this chapter lead to the definite impression that the author of the Qur'an anticipated an evolution in the mentality of man, culminating in an age when reason and science would be viewed as the final criterion of truth.

CENTRAL CONSIDERATIONS

The above observations, to the dismay of many Muslims, are unlikely to convince non-Muslims that the Qur'an is the word of God. Genius, however great, is always mysterious but not necessarily divine. They may, however, stimulate further investigation. At some stage the Qur'an must arouse in the reader the eternal questions: "Is there a God, and if so, then what is our relationship to Him and the purpose and meaning of life?"

Qur'anic Imagery

There is an undeniable loss of meaning when a sacred scripture is translated. But if the translator is motivated by commitment and devotion, there may survive something of divine effulgence that cannot be restrained by human limitations. Though surely more powerful in the original, something of the wonder and horror, the beauty and brilliance of the Qur'an's imagery and description may survive to provoke deeper reflection. The graphic and terrifying visions of Hell, for example, that seem to outweigh the descriptions of the glory and splendor of Paradise impel us to consider its possibility. Due to this emphasis, some have seen the God portrayed in the Qur'an as more vindictive than forgiving. However, within the total context of the Qur'an, He emerges as more intent on saving than on reas-

---

[32]Bucaille, *The Bible, the Qur'an and Science*, 163. The author goes so far as to conclude his study with the following remark: "In view of the level of knowledge in Muhammad's day, it is inconceivable that many statements in the Qur'an which are connected with science could have been the work of a man. It is, moreover, perfectly legitimate, not only to regard the Qur'an as an expression of Revelation, but also to award it a very special place, on account of the guarantee of authenticity it provides and the presence in it of scientific statements which, when studied today, appear as a challenge to explanation in human terms."

suring. Certainly this matter requires further investigation, which we will take up later.

Although they are forced to depend on interpretations, I feel sure that nearly all Western converts would characterize the literary style of the Qur'an as its most compelling feature, for it infuses in the reader that intangible sense that he/she is an active participant in divine revelation. Denny's testimony puts it best:

> There comes a moment in the reading of the Qur'an, as for example in personal study focused on understanding the meaning, whether reciting out loud or reading it silently, when readers start feeling an uncanny, sometimes frightening presence. Instead of reading the Qur'an, the reader begins feeling the Qur'an is "reading" the reader! This is a wonderfully disturbing experience, by no means requiring a person to be a Muslim before it can be felt. This expression of the Qur'an's inherent power has been a major factor in the spread of Islam, as well as Muslims' continuing loyalty to the Straight Path, as the Qur'an itself characterizes the religion.[33]

Back to the "Signs"

> We will show them Our signs (*ayat*) in the farthest reaches and within themselves until it is clear to them that it is the truth. (41:53)

Signs do not only guide; they also confirm and validate our steps and decisions. So it is with the ayat of the Qur'an in our journey from "the farthest reaches" and within our own selves. Virtually all of the Qur'an's "signs" from nature appear amid reminders of man's duty and accountability to God, and the impending judgment. Each of those verses that have already been cited can serve to illustrate this point. The following have been selected primarily for their beauty.

> A surah which We have sent down and which We have ordained.
> In it, We sent down clear signs, in order that you may remember. (24:1).

This begins *Surat al Nur*, one of the best-known surahs of the Qur'an for both Muslim and non-Muslim writers. Ingeniously, Malik Bennabi discovered what for him were "clear signs" in two magnificent passages:[34]

---

[33]Fredrick Denny, *Islam* (New York: Harper & Row, 1987), 88.
[34]Bennabi, *The Qur'anic Phenomenon*, 165-84.

God is the Light of the heavens and the earth. The likeness of His Light is that of a niche wherein is a lamp. The lamp is enclosed in glass. The glass is as it were a brilliant star, lit from a blessed tree, an olive that is neither of the East nor of the West, whose oil well-nigh would shine, even though no fire touched it. Light upon Light. God guides to His Light whomever He wills. And God propounds similitudes for men, and God has knowledge of all things. In houses God has allowed to be raised up and His Name to be commemorated therein, glorifying Him in the mornings and the evenings, are men whom neither trade nor sale diverts from the remembrance of God and the establishment of prayer, and paying the zakah, fearing a day when the hearts and the eyes shall be turned upside-down, in order that God may recompense them for their best deeds and give them increase out of His bounty; and God provides for whomsoever He wills without count. (24:35-38)

In the resplendent "Verse of Light," Bennabi sees an intriguing presage. The allegory invokes the image of a brightly shining light within a container enclosed in glass, lit from a source unknown at the time of this revelation, "neither of the East nor of the West," that shines although no flame touches it. This parable may indeed serve, as Bennabi suggests, as the description of an electric light, at which, when brought to our attention, we can only wonder. At first such speculation may seem to violate the beauty of the passage, but it is not uncharacteristic of the Qur'an, in its theme of harmony, to simultaneously relate mystical and temporal information, with the former appropriately almost blinding us to the latter.

Two parables concerning disbelief and its destructive consequences immediately follow this verse:

And those who disbelieve, their deeds are like a mirage in a desert, which the thirsting one deems to be water, until, when he comes to it, he finds it is nothing, and there indeed he finds God, and He pays him his account in full; and God is swift in the reckoning. Or like darkness in a deep sea; there covers him a wave, above which is a wave, above which is a cloud—darknesses, one above another; when he holds out his hand, he is barely able to see it. And the one to whom God does not give light, he has no light. (24:39-40)

Bennabi points out that the first simile would be expected from a resident of seventh century Makkah, but he sees the second, with its images of dark clouds and billowing waves, as better suited to someone from the northern coastal regions. He links the reference to the existence of layers of waves upon waves in the ocean to what is now known in oceanography as the phenomenon of superimposition of waves and the increasing darkness one encounters at greater depths of the ocean to the discovery in the field of optics of the absorption of light in water.

The obvious theme here is that a life dedicated mainly to worldly pursuits ends in utter disillusionment and spiritual suffocation. We are more likely to discern this from the verse than what Bennabi has derived. However, the phraseology is notable. If I were to compare the state of disbelief to drowning in the sea—and having grown up on the New England coastline, I might—I would use "wave after wave" instead of "wave above wave," for one often thinks of waves existing only on the ocean's surface and as occurring sequentially, one after another. This is how it appears to us, but the Qur'anic description is, in fact, more accurate. Also, unless I had experienced deep-sea diving, it is unlikely that I would think of graduated levels of darkness in the ocean depths, since in relatively shallow water—a pool or lake—the degree of light is more or less constant.

Bennabi's findings, if we accept them as valid, are obscured by the more obvious messages of the passages into which they are woven, while the majority of *ayat* are presented independently as evidences from human experience or nature. They serve to illustrate one of the many ways by which the Qur'an invites its own investigation and merges worldly into spiritual considerations.

The Role of Reason

Will you not then use your reason? (2:44)

The Qur'an enjoins us to study critically our behavior and beliefs. Salvation is obtained through searching out and surrendering to the truth. One of the aims of the Qur'an is to teach us to approach religious questions with discipline, to reason accurately, in order to uncover contradictions and inconsistencies within ourselves. Embedded in many of the Qur'an's parables, stories, and admonitions are lessons that deal with correct and incorrect reasoning. Characteristically, the Qur'an accentuates the importance of proof and evidence in argument:

And they say: "No one will enter Paradise unless he is a Jew or a Christian." Those are their desires. Say: "Produce your proof if you are truthful." (2:111)

The idolaters will say: "If God had wished, we would not have ascribed partners to Him, nor would our fathers, nor would we have prohibited anything." Thus did their ancestors argue falsely, until they tasted Our might. Say: "Have you any (certain) knowledge? If so, produce it for us. You follow nothing but conjecture." (6:148)

Or do they say: "He has invented it?" No, but they do not believe. Then let them bring a discourse like it, if they speak truly. (52:33-34)

Why did they not bring four witnesses to prove it? But since they did not bring the witnesses, in God's sight they are liars. (24:13)

In several places, the Qur'an exposes the logical flaws of some common approaches to religious questions:

The Jews say the Christians have nothing to stand on, and the Christians say the Jews have nothing to stand on, while both recite the (same) Book! Thus, like what they say, say those who do not know. (2:113)

When they are told, "Spend of that which God has provided you," the ungrateful say to those who believe, "Shall we feed those whom, if God had willed, He would have fed (Himself)? You are in nothing but manifest error." (36:47)

The first of the above verses illustrates the "glass house syndrome," whereby arguments used against another religion apply equally to one's own. The implication in the second is that a response such as that quoted not only denies man's charitable impulse, but, if this reasoning is adopted, there is no need to pursue any human endeavor, including self-preservation.

Surat al A'raf presents a parable of how people stray from the truth based on circumstantial evidence:

The similitude is that of a dog: if you attack it, it lolls out its tongue, or if you leave it alone, it lolls out its tongue. That is an example of [how] people reject the truth.[35] (7:176)

---

[35]Gary Miller brought this example to my attention.

The tendency to lose oneself in senseless arguments over insignificant details is criticized in *Surat al Kahf*:

Some say they were three, the dog being the fourth among them. Others say they were five, the dog being the sixth, guessing at the unseen. Yet others say seven, the dog being the eighth. Say: "My Lord knows best their number, and none knows them but a few. Therefore, do not enter into controversies concerning them, except on a matter that is clear, and do not ask of anyone to make a pronouncement concerning them." (18:22)

There are marvelous lessons in wisdom in the Qur'anic narratives. As the tale of Moses and the sage unfolds (18:60-82), the reader finds himself attempting to anticipate the solution of a timeless riddle: how can ostensibly evil things serve a greater good? As he tries in his own mind to resolve it, he is in fact teaching himself about divine justice and the nature of good and evil. Similarly, in *Surat Yusuf,* we learn about the subtle workings of God's will and the meaning and purpose behind life's adversities. In the story of David and Solomon (21:78-79), we are given a lesson in sound judgment. With the Qur'an's persistent attack on errors of disbelief, either directly or in its many accounts of believers—disbeliever showdowns, the reader, regardless of his position, becomes engaged in an ongoing debate. He is in fact receiving instruction by almost reliving critical episodes in other people's lives.

Another important device to make us ponder more deeply on fundamental issues is the intentional contradiction. On the question of good and evil, we are told:

Say: "All things are from God." But what is amiss with these people that they fail to understand a single fact? Whatever happens to you of good is from God, but whatever happens to you of evil is from yourself. (4:78-79)

Here we are learning the distinction between acts that belong "to God" and those that come "from God."[36] While we are the authors of our own actions, our potential for and our ability to do evil comes "from God." Thus the evil act itself is attributable "to us" and not "to God." But with a little deeper reflection, we come to understand the relativity of evil, for the evil that exists in this world is not absolute but serves a greater good.

---

[36]Murtaza Mutahhari, *Fundamentals of Islamic Thought*, trans. R. Campbell (Berkeley: Mizan Press, 1985), 106-12.

Unavoidably, this brings us to a discussion of one of the great barriers between faith and unfaith, and it looms as large today as ever—the age-old conflict of "faith and reason."

Faith and Reason

If God is all-merciful and all-compassionate, why does He expose us to suffering? If all-knowing, why does He test us? If self-sufficient, why does He require us to worship Him? What value is prayer if all is predetermined? How does one reconcile divine justice and predestination, or divine love with punishment?

These questions of course are not new. They have plagued religion since man first became conscious of the divine; they have led to schism, violence, and disbelief. Although every orthodox belief system provides an answer, the laity has been discouraged, and often forbidden, to delve into such matters. There have been brilliant attempts in the past—among Muslim philosophers, most notably that of Ibn Sina.[37] In today's world, in particular in academia, such questions remain for many the biggest obstacle to belief in God. We preface our investigation of these issues with a discussion of two important aspects of the Qur'an.

Allegory

Asad submits that "the key-phrase of all its [the Qur'an's] key-phrases" is the statement in verse 7 of *Al 'Imran*:[38]

> He it is who has bestowed upon you from on high this divine writ, containing messages clear in and of themselves (*ayat muhka-mat*)—and these are the essence of the divine writ—as well as others that are allegorical (*mutashabihat*). Now, those whose hearts are given to swerving from the truth go after that part of it which has been expressed in allegory, seeking out confusion, and seeking its final meaning, but none save God knows its final meaning.

Exactly which verses are symbolic and which are to be taken literally has been the subject of differing opinions. In his *The Message of the Qur'an*, Asad offers the extremely plausible explanation that the verses that are to be understood in a symbolic sense correspond to those aspects

---

[37] Arthur J. Arberry, *Avicenna on Theology* (London: J. Murray, 1951).
[38] Asad, *The Message*, 989-91.

44

of reality that are beyond the reach of human experience and perception, which the Qur'an designates as *al ghayb* (the hidden, unseen, or imperceptible). He argues that the human mind can operate only on the basis of previously realized experiences and, once this is admitted,

> we are faced by a weighty question: Since the metaphysical ideas of religion relate, by virtue of their nature, to a realm beyond the reach of human perception or experience—how can they be successfully conveyed to us? How can we be expected to grasp ideas that have no counterpart, not even a fractional one in any of the apperceptions which we have arrived at empirically?[39]

A poor analogy might be seen in an attempt at describing a cloud to someone who is blind, or, as in Abbott's book *Flatland*, three dimensional space to a being who exists entirely in two dimensions.[40] Asad maintains that from this consideration, the answer is self-evident. We can come to an intuitive appreciation of realities beyond the reach of our perception

> By means of loan images derived from our actual—physical or mental—experiences; or as Zamakhshari phrases it in his commentary on 13:35, "through a parabolic illustration, by means of something which we know from our experience, of something that is beyond the reach of our perception. . . ." Thus, the Qur'an tells us clearly that many of its passages and expressions **must** be understood in an allegorical sense for the simple reason that, being intended for human understanding, they could not have been conveyed in any other way. It follows, therefore, that if we were to take every Qur'anic passage, statement or expression in its outward, literal sense and disregard the possibility of allegory, a metaphor or a parable, we would be offending against the very spirit of the divine writ.[41]

Thus we find in the Qur'an very carnal descriptions of Paradise that are particularly suited to the seventh-century Arabs, while at the same time 32:17 informs us that "no soul knows what delights of the eye are kept hidden for them [the believers] as a reward for their deeds." Similarly, although God is "glorified and exalted above whatever they ascribe to Him" (6:100), and "there is nothing like Him" (42:11) and "nothing that can be

---

[39]Ibid., pp. 989-90.
[40]Edwin A. Abbott, *Flatland* (New York: Dover, 1952).
[41]Asad, *The Message*, 989-91.

compared to Him" (112:4), we still have the need to relate to Him and His activity. This human need is realized by the employment of allegory and symbolism, so that in describing God's attributes, the Day of Judgment, Paradise and Hell, and other subjects of this kind, the *ayat mutashabihat* do not define nor fully explicate these realities, but suggest to us, due to the limitations of human thought and language, something similar from within the realm of our experience. This explains

> the use of expressions which at first sight have an almost anthropomorphic hue, for instance, God's "wrath" (*ghadab*) or "condemnation"; His "pleasure" at good deeds or "love" for His creatures; or His being "oblivious" of a sinner who was oblivious of Him; or "asking" a wrongdoer on Resurrection Day about his wrongdoing; and so forth. All such verbal "translations" of God's activity into human terminology are unavoidable as long as we are expected to conform to ethical principals revealed to us by means of a human language; but there can be no greater mistake than to think that these "translations" could ever enable us to define the Undefinable.[42]

Satans and Jinn

The Qur'anic terms *shaytan* and *jinn* are often translated as "satan" and "genie," respectively. In the Western mind, the word "satan" conjures up the image of a supernatural being, half-man, half-animal, with horns on his head and a tail and pitchfork. A genie is a similar demon who lives in a bottle. Our understanding is largely influenced by the folklore that grew around these words in the Middle East and the Far East, where in time "they became personified into fantastic forms."[43] Due to such misconceptions, we will need to discuss their original connotation.

The word *jinn* is derived from the root *janna*, which means "to cover, conceal, hide, or protect." Hence, originally, the word *jinn* denoted "a being that cannot be perceived with the senses."[44] Thus, Yusuf Ali opines that it designates "a spirit or an invisible or hidden force."[45] The Arabs, as pointed out by Muhammad Ali, would commonly use the term jinn to refer to humans. He quotes Arabic lexicologists who explain that it could be

---

[42]Ibid., 989-91.
[43]Ali, *The Meaning of the Holy Qur'an*, footnote 929.
[44]Muhammad Ali, *The Religion of Islam* (New Delhi: S. Chand & Co., n.d.), 188.
[45]Ali, *The Meaning of the Holy Qur'an*, footnote 929.

used to designate *mu'zam al nas*, i.e., "the main body of men or the bulk of mankind."[46]

In the mouth of an Arab, the main body of men would mean the non-Arab world. They called all foreigners *jinn* because they were concealed from their eyes.[47]

Therefore *jinn*, in its most general connotation, is an imperceptible being or force.

Concerning the word "Shaytan," in his commentary on the Qur'an, al-Tabari asserts that

Shaytan in the speech of the Arabs is every rebel among the jinn, mankind, beasts, and everything. . . .The rebel among every kind of thing is called a shaytan, because its behavior and actions differ from those of the rest of its kind, and it is far from good.[48]

The word "Shaytan" derives its meaning from an Arabic root which means "to be remote or banished."

It is said that the word is derived from [the use of the 1st form verb *shatana*] in the expression *shatana dari min darik* (my home was far from yours).[49]

Once again, this term can be used to refer to humans. Commenting on 2:14, al Tabari quotes Ibn 'Abbas:

There were some Jewish men who, when they met one or several of the Companions of the Prophet, may God bless him and grant him peace, would say; "We follow your religion," but when they went in seclusion to their own companions, who were their satans, they would say: "We are with you, we were only mocking."[50]

He also quotes Qatadah and Mujahid, who claimed that these satans were "their leaders in evil" and "their companions among the hypocrites and polytheists."

---

[46]Ali, *Religion of Islam*,191.
[47]Ibid., 191.
[48]*Al-Tabari: The Commentary on the Qur'an*, vol. I, trans. J. Cooper (London: Oxford University Press, 1987), 47.
[49]Ibid., 47.
[49]Ibid., 131.

47

The Qur'an, as well as certain sayings of Muhammad, certainly suggests the existence of beings and even worlds beyond our perception. But the words shaytan and jinn should not be construed only in this sense, both because of the folklore attached to the terms "satan" and "genie," and because they do not express the more general meaning of the original Arabic. To avoid confusion, I will sometimes employ phrases such as "spiritual beings/forces" or "unseen beings" when discussing them below.

Time and Eternity

The concepts of time and eternity and their relationship to God have been subjected to diverse philosophical speculations throughout the history of religion. This is demonstrated amply in Muhammad Iqbal's *Reconstruction of Religious Thought in Islam*,[51] in which he attempts a new interpretation in conformity with modern thought and the doctrinal sources of Islam. The attempt itself has received considerable praise from Muslim and non-Muslim scholars, despite considerable disagreement on both sides about the validity of his ideas.[52] In the words of Iqbal, we should not underestimate the importance of such efforts, since many theological paradoxes arise from our understanding of these concepts. On the one hand, we cannot resist, as the scriptures themselves cannot, relating time to God. On the other hand—and this is more important—we must alert ourselves to the deficiencies in our understanding.

The greatest perplexities arise from attributing human limitations to God when dealing with time. As God transcends space, we naturally do not associate with Him any spatial limitations. For instance, we would not say that God literally descends to earth or walks in the garden; equally, we would not insist that God is a three-dimensional being or that He travels from one point to another in space. In the same way, we should not demand that God have a past, a present, and a future, for this assumes that His existence is, like ours, in time. Again, this conflicts with His infinite transcendence.

We have little difficulty accepting the idea that God's knowledge can encompass two different points in space simultaneously. This is perhaps because we assume that the attribute of transcending space implies a unique vantage point. We could compare it, however imperfectly, to the experience of being high above the ground and hence having simultaneous

[51]Muhammad Iqbal, *The Reconstruction of Religious Thought in Islam* (Lahore: S. H. Muhammad Ashraf Publ., 1982).
[52]Hafeez Malik, *Iqbal: Poet Philosopher of Pakistan* (New York: Columbia University Press, 1971).

knowledge of very distant events. But unlike space, with respect to time, we are immobile: we cannot travel forward or backward in time. An hour from now, we will be at an hour from now, a fact that cannot be changed. Therefore, it is more difficult to comprehend that God's existence is independent of or beyond time, as indeed it must be, for it is impossible to believe that His existence is contained within or constrained by any of the dimensions of the space-time environment which He created for us to live and grow in. Once again, because of His unique vantage point, His knowledge encompasses all events, regardless of their distance in space or time.

Another key point, one that is well-established in the Qur'an, is that our perception of time is not objectively real. The Day of Judgment, for example, is portrayed as belonging to a different ordering of time, one in which we will comprehend suddenly that our former perceptions of time are no longer valid and were not absolute.

> The Day they see it, (it will be) as if they had stayed only a single evening, or the morning following it (79:46)

> And the Day He will gather them all together, it will be as if they had stayed only an hour of a day. (10:45)

> It will be on a Day when He will call you, and you will answer with His praise, and you will think that you stayed only a little while. (17:52)

> In whispers they will consult each other: "You stayed not longer than ten (days)." (20:103)

> "You stayed not longer than a day." (20:104)

> He will say: "What number of years did you stay on earth?" They will say, "We stayed a day or part of a day: ask those who keep account." He will say: "You stayed only a little, if you had but known!" (23:112-114)

> On the Day that the Hour will be established, the transgressors will swear that they stayed only an hour: thus were they used to being deluded. (30:55)

Interpreters will always render all references to the Day of Judgment in the future tense, because, from our perspective, that is when it will take place. However, several of the passages actually use the past tense. Commentators assume, quite correctly, that this is a literary device that stresses the inevitability of these happenings. The use of the present and past tenses in referring to the Day of Judgment also reinforces the idea that it will take place in a very different environment, one in which our current conceptions of time and space will no longer apply. The illusory character of time is further supported by the comparisons of the "days of God" with earthly days, in which a "day" of God's is said to be "as a thousand years of your reckoning" (32:5) and like "50,000 years" (70:4).

No attempt has been made here to provide a model or to interpret the precise relationship between God and time. Rather, I want to suggest the futility of such an endeavor. It cannot be otherwise, since our perceptions of time are not objectively real. Conflicts arise precisely **because** a given interpretation is assumed.

The question, "What is the value of prayer if God has already predestined the future?" assumes that in some way God has a future. That is, it assumes that God is situated in time and peering into a preordained future as we pray. But in order to have a future, one's existence must be contained within time and, as a result, finite. The reason this question leads to contradictions is that it assumes a contradiction in the first place—that God both transcends and is finite in time. Any question that assumes two mutually incompatible premises will always result in conflicting conclusions. Assume, for example, that a circle is a square. With this assumption in mind, we can ask if a circle has corners. If we emphasize the circle's roundness, then the answer is no. If we concentrate on the properties of a square, the answer is yes. When the consideration of a question inevitably ends in contradiction, it should be asked if the question itself makes sense.

The word "predestination" alone is problematic. If it is used to mean that at some time in the past God programmed all events for the future, the underlying assumption is that God exists in time. If we mean that God's wisdom and knowledge encompass all and that nothing in creation can conflict with that, then it has to be admitted. But that is not the primary sense of the word "predestine," which means "to determine in advance." It also does not conflict with the idea that God responds to our prayers.

For many Muslim and orientalist scholars, the Qur'anic words *qadar* and *taqdir* have come to mean the "absolute decree of good and evil by God"—in other words, that God has preordained all of our acts, even our moral choices. But as Muhammad Ali argues, this doctrine is "neither known to the Holy Qur'an nor even to Arabic lexicology. The doctrine of predestination is of later growth, and seems to have been the result of the clash of Islam with Persian religious thought."[53]

---

[53]Ali, *Religion of Islam*, 317-18.

According to al Raghib al Isfahani, the words *qadar* and *taqdir* mean "the making manifest of the measure of a thing," or simply "measure." In the Qur'an, they signify the divine laws regulating and balancing creation:

Glorify the name of your Lord, the Most High, Who creates, then makes complete, and Who makes things according to a measure (*qaddara*, from *taqdir*), then guides them to their goal. (87:1-3)

Who created everything, then ordained for it a measure (*qadar*). (54:49)

And the sun runs on to a term appointed for it; that is the ordaining (taqdir) of the Mighty, the Knowing. And as for the moon, We ordained (*qaddarnahu*, from *taqdir*) for it stages. (36:38-39)

Of what thing did He create him [man]? Of a small life-germ He created him, then He made him according to a measure (*qaddarahu*). (80:18-9)

This is not to claim that God subjected the universe to certain natural laws and then abandoned it to let it run its course. No reader of the Qur'an receives this impression. In the Qur'an, God is *al Rabb*: the Sustainer, Cherisher, Regulator, and Governor of all. He is the omnipresent source of the harmony and balance of nature.

Man's Purpose in Life

We may admit that there are existents beyond our perception or that time is illusory, but to accept that our virtues and ethics are delusive and tell us nothing about God is either to deny His existence or to say that our surrender to Him has no real purpose. If we are to believe in God, then we must assume that our perceptions of justice, love, compassion, forgiveness, truth, and mercy are perhaps imperfect but are nevertheless composed of something real that emanates from God. This is why life, with all of its suffering and adversity, trial and error, is so antilogical. What possible purpose can such difficulties serve? Why did life not begin in Paradise? And yet the Qur'an insists that, in the design of God, our earthly life is a necessary stage in human existence:

Those [are believers] who remember God standing and sitting and lying down, and reflect upon the creation of the heavens and the earth, [saying]: "Our Lord, you did not create all this in vain." (3:191)

We did not create the heavens and the earth and all that is between them in vain. (44:38)

And We did not create the heaven and the earth and whatever is between them as a game. If We wished to take a pastime, We would have taken it by Ourselves, if We were to do that at all! (21:16-17)

Do you think that We created you for nothing and that you will not be returned to Us? The true Sovereign is too exalted above that. (23:115-116)

It is reported that Prophet Muhammad said, "Your deeds will be judged according to your intentions."[54] We have our first intimation concerning the purpose of life when this understanding is combined with the Qur'anic affirmation of the inextricable interdependence of true belief and good works, and happiness in this life and hereafter (19:59-63; 92:17-21; 95:6; 99:7-8). Faith should produce good works and abiding happiness; righteous deeds, when performed with pure intentions, should nurture deeper faith, peace, and well-being. God does not need our works, and salvation is not obtained by mere adherence to rituals and formalism. In human relations, true faith translates into deep concern for fellow man and social activism:

It is not righteousness that you turn your faces toward the East or the West; but it is righteousness to believe in God and the Last Day, and the angels, and the Book and the messengers; to spend of your sustenance, out of love for Him, for your kin, for orphans, for the needy, for the wayfarer, for those who ask, and the ransom of slaves; to be steadfast in prayer, and to give the zakah; to fulfill the covenants you have made; and to be firm and patient in pain and adversity and peril. These are they who are true, those are the God-conscious. (2:177)

The sacrificial camels We have made for you as among the rites of God; in them is good for you. Then pronounce the name of God over them as they line up (for sacrifice). When they are down on their sides (after slaughter), eat thereof and feed the beggar and

---

[54] *Sahih al Bukhari*, trans. Muhammad Muhsin Khan (Beirut: Islamic University, al Dar al Arabia Publishers, n.d.), vol. 5.

the needy one who does not beg. Thus have We made them [domestic animals] subject to you, in order that you may be grateful. Their meat and their flesh do not reach God, but rather God-consciousness from you reaches Him. (22:36-37)

You are the best community brought forth for mankind: you enjoin what is right and forbid that which is wrong, and you believe in God. (3:110)

And if anyone strives, he strives only for himself. Indeed, God is free of need from all creation. (29:6)

Truly, those who believe and do righteous deeds, will the Most Merciful endow with love; and only to this end have We made this easy to understand, in your own tongue, so that you might convey thereby a glad tiding to the God-conscious and warn thereby those given to contention. (19:96-97)

The Qur'an ties our happiness or suffering, both in the present and in the hereafter, to our beliefs and to their actualization in our human relationships. Thus, we find trials and tests in every aspect of our lives: in our spouses, children, parents, kindred, the indigent, the orphan, the wayfarer, our wealth, and our conflicts. We know that it is better to give than receive, to forgive than to seek vengeance, to love than to hate, to have compassion, to be just, for these are the things that bring us real happiness and serenity. The Qur'an maintains that, although our attachment to material things is necessary, we should not lose sight of the fact that "the most beautiful of all goals is with God."

Attractive to man is the love of things they covet—spouses and sons, and heaped up piles of gold and silver, and horses of mark and cattle and cultivated lands. That is stuff of the life of this world—but the most beautiful of all goals is with God. Say: "Shall I tell you of better things than those?" (3:14-15)

The Qur'an then goes on to describe the bliss of the next life for

the patient and the truthful and the devout and those who are generous and those who pray for forgiveness from their innermost hearts. (3:17)

When I was a child, I asked my father if he thought heaven were possible. He replied that he could not conceive of it, because man could never overcome the jealousy, hate, greed, and anger that is in his heart. To some extent I believe he was right, for one can neither experience nor even exist in a heaven or paradise unless he or she progresses to a high level of goodness. This does not mean that one must become perfect, but at least perfect enough so that when the actuality and purpose of earthly life is revealed to him or her, all remaining imperfections will be overcome and effaced:

And We shall remove whatever of enmity is in their breasts. (7:43)

Those who believe and work righteous deeds, We shall surely efface their sins and shall reward them according to the best of what they were doing. (29:7)

And so the purpose of life begins to emerge. We are to grow in virtue, wisdom, justice, mercy, forgiveness, righteousness, concern and love of our fellow man, compassion, patience, and generosity through our personal striving, and struggling. In the Qur'an, these qualities are mentioned as being among the attributes of true faith. We are to pursue them not only to make the world a better place, but out of the conviction that they exist as transcendent realities that emanate from the One and Only Eternal Absolute—God. By developing such attributes, we simultaneously grow in our ability to receive and experience God's mercy, forgiveness, compassion, justice, and love. In this way, we are increasing in nearness to God.

Take love as an example. The more we taste of human love, the more we can experience the love of God. I understand that my child's experience of my love is greater than my dog's experience of my love, which is greater than that of my fish, because a child comes to know love at a higher level than a dog and a dog at a higher level than a fish. And I believe that my love for my parents today is greater than the love I had for them when I was a child, for by having my own children I have come to better know and feel the power of the love given to me by my mother and father. Thus, the more we increase in the above attributes, the greater will be our experience of the majesty and beauty of God, both here and infinitely more hereafter.

The Day of Judgment is depicted in the Qur'an as a moment of immeasurable intensity, when the reality of our earthly striving becomes clear. On that day we will face the truth of what we have become, as all temporal distractions and illusions are stripped away and we are left alone with only our core beliefs and moral-spiritual achievements:

Then anyone who has done an atom's weight of good will see it. And anyone who has done an atom's weight of evil will see it. (99:7-8)

If, to use Qur'anic terminology, in the "balance" we are good, we will experience extreme joy and well-being. If we are essentially evil, then ours will be terrible loss and suffering. This joy or suffering is not arbitrary, but is intimately connected to our spiritual-moral growth. Just as there are differing levels of piety and goodness, wrong-doing and evil, so do the Qur'an and the Prophet's sayings assert that there are varied levels of Heaven and Hell. As the growth of the fetus in the womb decidedly effects the next stage of its existence, our moral-spiritual evolution in this life is bound inseparably to our condition in the next. Then, obviously, "no one will be able to bear another's burden" (17:15).

Life contains experiences that give a fraction of a hint of the bliss of Paradise. Unselfish, self-sacrificing love has its highest human manifestation in the love of a parent for his or her child. When I look at my three little girls sleeping at night, I find myself overwhelmed by such tender feelings of affection that tears fill my eyes. My wife and I will stand there embracing, flooded with feelings of warmth and love that are, as Muslims would say, "worth more than the world and all it contains."

With this great potential for growth and happiness comes the parallel danger of moral decay and suffering. But why? One may admit that love, compassion, truth, and other qualities bring the greatest joy—so why were we not created with these qualities from the start? It seems that we have arrived at where we began. Why were we not put into Paradise from the start? Why were these virtues not simply programmed into us?

The answer is almost obvious: virtue, if programmed, is not true virtue; it is always something less. You can program a computer to never make an incorrect statement but it does not thereby become a **truthful** computer; nor does a CAT scanner possess compassion, although it is made to help the sick. The Qur'an presents angels as non-discriminating beings (66:6), while man is a potentially much greater and alternatively much worse creature (2:30-34). It emphasizes three essential components of this stage of man's moral-spiritual evolution: **Free will**, or the ability to choose; **intellect**, the tool for weighing the consequences of one's choices and learning from them; and third and equally important, an environment of **adversity**.

Returning to the previous two examples, to learn to be truthful requires the option to lie, and hence the ability to choose and discern. A higher level of honesty is attained if we insist on speaking the truth in adversity, say at the threat of physical or material loss. To grow in compassion, there must be suffering and the choice to ignore it. And so it is with all the virtues: love, charity, justice, forgiveness, and the like. To grow in each of them, we must have the alternative to do otherwise and the possibility for the existence of hate, indifference, greed, vengeance, and, obviously, suffering.

Of course, we must have at least an inclination toward goodness from the start, at least the seed of virtue and piety when we come into this world. This is precisely how Muslim exegetes understood the statement of the Qur'an that God "breathed into him (man) something of His spirit" (15:29) and the saying of Muhammad that every human being is born with a natural inclination (fitrah) toward self-surrender to God.[55]

This idea of the necessity of suffering, adversity, and struggle to prompt our quest for moral-spiritual evolution, as well as our need to remember life's ultimate purpose in difficult times, recurs throughout the Qur'an.

Assuredly We will try you with something of danger and hunger and the loss of worldly goods, and of lives and the fruits of your labor. But give glad tidings to those who are patient in adversity— those who, when calamity befalls them, say, "Truly, to God we belong and, truly, to Him we shall return." (2:155-156)

Do you think that you can enter Paradise without having suffered like those who passed away before you? Misfortune and hardship befell them, and they were so shaken that the messenger and the believers with him said, "When will God's help come?" Oh, truly, God's help is always near. (2:214)

You will certainly be tried in your possessions and yourselves. (3:186)

O man, truly you have been toiling toward your Lord in painful toil; but you will meet Him! (84:6)

Oh you who believe! Be patient in adversity, and vie with one another in perseverance, and be ever ready, and remain conscious of God, so that you may attain success.(3:200)

Thus, life is a continuous process of growth and decay. Although God presents us with innumerable opportunities to receive guidance, He also

---

[55]Ibid., (23:80, 93).

allows us to err and stray (16:9). It is by trial and error, and by realizing and rising above our mistakes, that we learn and progress to higher levels of goodness. In this way, error, if realized and repented of sincerely, can lead ultimately to a higher state: "Excepting the one who repents and believes and does righteous deeds—then for those, God will change their evil deeds into good deeds, for God is Most Forgiving, Most Merciful." (25:70).

Denial of God, for example, is no doubt one of the gravest sins, but to have done that and known the terrible loss and emptiness, to have been crippled by that error and then to have found faith, is an extremely valuable albeit painful experience, for the consequence of rejecting belief has now become more than warnings—it has become internalized lessons. Our spirituality would stagnate without the potential for error, realization, and reform. So vital are these to our development in this earthly stage, that the Prophet reported that if mankind ceased sinning, God would replace it by another creation that would continue to sin and repent and gain His forgiveness. (Muslim)[56]

In the Qur'an we read that "God guides whomsoever He will and leads astray whomsoever He will" (18:17; 35:8; 39:23). Goldziher argues that such statements

> do not mean that God directly leads the latter into error. The decisive verb (adalla) is not, in this context, to be understood as "lead astray," but rather as "allow to go astray," that is, not to care about someone, not to show him the way out of his predicament. "We let them (nadharuhum) stray in disobedience" (6:110). We must imagine a solitary traveler in the desert: that image stands behind the Qur'an's manner of speaking about guidance and error. The traveler wanders, drifts in limitless space, on the watch for his true destination and goal. Such a traveler is man on the journey of life.[57]

The notion of straying and receiving guidance is understood better in light of the more numerous assertions that God guides us according to our choices and predisposition. We find that "God does not guide the unjust ones," "God does not guide the transgressors," and God guides aright those who "listen," are "sincere," and "fear God" (2:26, 258, 264; 3:86;

[56]*Gardens of the Righteous: Translation of Riyad al Salihin of Imam Nawawi,* trans. Muhammad Zafrullah Khan (London: Curzon Press Ltd., 1975), 95.

[57]Ignaz Goldziher, *Introduction to Islamic Theology and Law* (Princeton, NJ: Princeton University Press, 1981), 79-80.

5:16, 51, 67, 108; 6:88, 144; 9:19, 21, 37, 80, 109; 12:52; 13:27, 16:37, 107; 28:50; 39:3; 40:28; 42:13; 46:10; 47:8; 61:5, 7; 62:5; 63:6). Also, "when they went crooked, God bent their hearts crooked" (61:5).[58] This shows that one's being guided by God is affected by sincerity, disposition, and willingness. And surely God is responsive to those who seek Him: "And If my servants call on Me, surely I am near. I heed the call of every caller. So let them with a will call unto Me and let them believe in Me, in order that they may be guided aright" (2:186). For Muslims, one of the most cherished sayings of Muhammad is: "When you approach God by an arm's length, He approaches you by two, and if you come to Him walking, He comes to you running."[59]

According to the Qur'an, the principal beneficiary of our seeking guidance and of our good deeds, as well as the primary casualty of our evil acts, is no one but ourselves:

And the one who strives, he strives only for himself. Surely God is independent of all creation. (29:6)

Evidences have come to you from your Lord. Then the one who sees does so for his own soul, and the one who is blind, it is upon himself. (6:104)

We have revealed to you the Book for mankind with the truth. Then the one who is guided, it is for his own soul, and the one who strays, his straying is only upon himself. (39:41)

As we can see from the above, Islam views sin as an act of self-destruction, of rebellion against one's true nature. Finally, it is not God who wrongs us; it is we who destroy ourselves:

Taste the punishment of the burning. This is on account of what your own hands have sent on ahead, and God does not do the least wrong to His creatures. (3:181-182; 8:50-51)

They have lost their own souls, and whatever they invented has led them astray. (7:53)

And they did not do injustice to Us, but rather they wronged their own souls. (7:160)

---

[58]I am indebted to Fazlur Rahman's observations on this matter in his book, *Major Themes of the Quran* (Bibliotheca Islamica, 1980).

[59]*Gardens of the Righteous*, trans. Muhammad Zafrullah Khan, 28.

And so it was not God who wronged them, but rather it was they who wronged themselves. (9:70)

O My servants who have sinned against yourselves, never despair of God's mercy. Surely God forgives all sins. (39:53)

The Arabic word for "sin," which appears in the recurrent phrase "they sinned against themselves," is *zulm*. It comes from the verb *zalama*, which means "to do injustice, to oppress, to deprive one of what is rightfully his or hers," which accents further the idea of sin as self-destruction. When we, as the Qur'an so often says, commit *zulm* against ourselves, in reality we are doing injustice and violence to ourselves by oppressing and robbing ourselves of our spiritual ascent.

The Straight Path

Sigmund Freud identified three influences on the human psyche: the id, the ego, and the superego. In general terms, the id is that source of psychic energy that excites those animalistic tendencies that work for the individual's biological survival, such as greed, power, lust, envy, and pride. The superego is the source of our sense of virtue, morality, and guilt. It urges us to what we consider higher and nobler efforts. The ego is essentially the intellect, which regulates, controls, and balances the needs of the id with the demands of society and of the superego. Freud believed that a healthy personality is one in which the ego balances the other two forces effectively, for if one should dominate the other(s) completely, the individual may become either socially destructive or self-destructive. Freud's conception led to many attempts to identify the origin of these influences.

In Islamic thought, these three forces are very real and are embodied in the concepts of the **satanic,** the **self** (*al nafs*), and the **angelic.** The satans are those creations of God that whisper subtle suggestions into our hearts or minds (114:4-6) in an attempt to excite our base desires. The angels, among other things,[60] inspire magnanimity and self-sacrifice. The self is the human personality that must manage and balance these influences. Each of these has a fundamental purpose, which, if controlled effectively, could work to the individual's benefit. Thus, the Prophet stated that every human being is created with a companion satan, who excites his lower passions, and a companion angel, who inspires him with good and noble ideas. When Muhammad's audience asked if he had a companion

---

[60] Ali, *Religion of Islam*, 169-99.

satan, he responded: "Yes, but God helped me to overcome him, so that he has submitted and does not command me to anything but good."[61]

The spiritual as well as the physical world is composed of obverse forces, a reality that we find expressed in the Qur'an: "We have created everything in pairs" (13:3).[62] Together these forces make up a universe of complements, held in tension according to a "balance" (55:7) and a "law" willed by God Himself (qadar). The Muslim strives to find and keep to the "middle way" (2:143) between the extremes of creation—between the spiritual and material, the lofty and the base—through guidance, work, struggle, and trial and error. He attempts to grow in what the Qur'an calls taqwa, which is usually translated as "fear" but has the literal meaning of "vigilance" or "defensiveness" and, in terms of Islam, a state of self-critical awareness and readiness to submit to the demands of faith.[63]

In its many depictions of hypocrites, liars, cowards, and misers, the Qur'an warns the believer of his potential for ruin. The underlying intent of these admonitions is that the believer take an honest accounting of himself, checking his true intentions. It is also a "reminder" (21:84; 69:48; 74:31) that awakens the reader to his real self.

When Muhammad described his first experience of the Revelation, he said that an angel had appeared to him and overwhelmed him in an almost crushing embrace, commanding him, "Read!" He replied that he could not read or recite, for he was unlettered. Again the angel overwhelmed him in his embrace and repeated the same command. In desperation, Muhammad's response was the same. After the third time, the angel dictated to him what he was to read—the first four verses of the ninety-sixth surah.[64]

This episode in the life of the Prophet is much like the experience of reading the Qur'an: in some passages it illuminates, in others it threatens, and in others it embraces and assures.

The ritual prayers (salah), fasting, paying one's financial obligation (zakah), and pilgrimage support the individual throughout his life's journey. They remind him of his purpose and help him build the inner strength, resolve, and character needed to see it through. For when a person raised in the West first becomes a Muslim, he or she often feels like crawling into a corner somewhere. Suddenly one has to face the incredulity, the shock, even sometimes the rejection, of family, friends, and colleagues. While

[61] Ibn Hanbal, *Musnad* (Cairo: al Maimanah Press, n.d.), 1:385, 397, 401.

[62] See, Rahman, *Major Themes*, for a fuller discussion of this topic. Also see 31:10; 36:6; 42:ll; 43:12; 51:49; 53:45.

[63] Lane, *Arabic-English Lexicon*.

[64] *Sahih Al Bukhari*, trans. Muhammad Muhsin Khan, vol. 1, "The Book of How Divine Revelation Started (1)," Hadith no. 3.

this is no doubt due to centuries of Western misunderstanding and antagonism toward Islam and the generally negative image presented by the media, it is by far one of the most difficult challenges for a new convert.

For myself, I found the prayers to be a great help and comfort. The dawn prayer (*fajr*) is the most demanding, and I found it impossible to drag myself out of bed every morning at 5:00 a.m. until I finally discovered a scheme that worked.[65] I spaced three alarm clocks, set five minutes apart, between my bed and the bathroom. When the first rang by the side of my bed at 4:50 a.m., I would hit the shut-off button and, as usual, fall back to sleep. Five minutes later, the one midway between my bed and the bathroom would sound, and I would practically crawl over to it to turn it off and then fall asleep beside it. When the final one by the bathroom sounded five minutes later, I would struggle over to it, turn it off, and, since I was so close to the sink anyway, I would get up and wash for the prayer.

I found that conquering my desire to sleep morning after morning was a great source of strength; it made me feel better prepared to face my insecurities. I would tell friends that, regardless of your beliefs, if you can discipline yourself to get out of bed every morning at five o'clock, you begin to feel that no challenge is too great. As it turned out, after a few weeks I needed only two alarm clocks, and a short time later I had reduced it to only one. After that, even if I forgot to set it, I would still get up on time. And while all of the Islamic rituals have this element of character testing and building, there is much more to them than that.

After the first euphoria of conversion, there comes a stage where the rituals become routine and burdensome. As I said earlier, new believers will report that they find them to be a powerful test and strengthener of will. Later, they will say, the rituals become less of a discipline and more of an experience of peace, and this becomes their primary motivator in praying, fasting, and observing other aspects. At a further stage, and this is in conjunction with their persistent daily striving to better themselves, they will say that the rituals, especially the prayers, have become a very powerful emotional and spiritual encounter—a time during which they are acutely alert to God's presence, wherein the ritual is more an act of love, a divine embrace, and it is that love that comes to dominate their lives. For Muslims, the rituals are a door to a breath of life, a life more real and meaningful than anything on earth, and eventually this thirst for divine life and love conquers them.

---

[65] To me, praying the dawn prayer in the mosque is one of the most beautiful and moving rituals in Islam. There is something mystical in arising while everyone else sleeps to hear the music of the Qur'an filling the darkness. It is as if you temporarily leave this world and commune with the angels in extolling God's praises at dawn.

However, worship in Islam extends beyond the rituals. As with so many Islamic concepts, its essence is contained in its Arabic root form. The Islamic term for worship is *'abada*, which comes from the root *'abd* (lit. "slave"). The goal of worship is a total commitment to serving God. The vital implications of this are revealed in its negation. *Shirk*, the acceptance of anything other than God as an object of worship, is to enslave oneself to that which is other than the Creator, and its consequences are self-ruination. When the Qur'an says "Have you seen the one who takes his desires to be his god?" (25:43), it is describing a person who has become the slave of his passions. It presents many similar examples of individuals who have become enslaved to power, greed, tradition, pride, wealth, lusts of various types, as well as to human lords. To be enslaved to any of these false deities, to let the desire for these rival the worship due to God alone, is to turn away from growth and fulfillment, and begin moving toward self-oppression and destruction. Man's true peace and happiness lies in channeling his potential toward the service of God, and in never losing sight of this goal.

A Muslim does not view his or her surrender to God as a defeat or a humiliation; he or she sees it as the only way to real freedom and becoming a human being in the full sense of the word. Thus, for the Muslim, Islam is more than a religion. It is a system of guidance: inward toward his true self and outward toward his fellow creatures, with his return to his Lord as his ultimate goal. At least seventeen times a day in the course of the five daily prayers the Muslim asks God to "show us the straight path"—the middle way which leads to inner peace. If it is found, then a passage is unveiled to a powerful, beautiful, and serene felicity in this life and to an infinitely greater one in the next. Man's life is a struggle and a search for a wonderful, sublime, and most sweet surrender, and fortunate are those who attain that, for every human personality, whether it realizes it or not, yearns for submission—that is, Islam.

INNER CONSIDERATIONS

Scriptures have a discomfiting way of exposing us, of disclosing our secrets and weaknesses. They can be painful to read, imposing questions on us that we would prefer to ignore or postpone. Gradually and imperceptibly, the Qur'an begins to weaken our resistance. Unexpectedly, those verses that reveal our humanity begin to take their toll:

> And those who reject faith, their deeds are like a mirage in a desert, which the thirsting one deems to be water, until, when he

comes to it, he finds it is nothing, and there indeed he finds God, and He pays him his account in full; and God is swift in the reckoning. Or like darkness in a deep sea; there covers him a wave, above which is a wave, above which is a cloud—darknesses, one above another; when he holds out his hand, he is barely able to see it. And the one to whom God does not give light, he has no light. (24:39-40)

The atheist well recognizes this desperate searcher. His life is a futile quest for happiness in pursuit of one empty illusion after another, with each frustration only increasing his thirst as he grasps at darkness and drowns in temporality. He rationalizes and argues his case with conviction and challenges God in the process. Though he swears that he has the noblest of aims, he continues to hurt and be hurt. He is being enveloped slowly, encompassed by his own ruin.

And among people there are some whose speech concerning the life of this world pleases you, and he calls upon God to witness what is in his heart, while he is most adept at argument. And when he turns away, he hastens about the earth, to work corruption upon it. (2:204-205)

Should he enter the race to accumulate more than he can consume? To what end? Is there the perfect romance, family, or endeavor that will meet his needs? He longs for perfection, as if he contains an infinite void that no earthly pleasure can fill. The Qur'an assures him that he will come to realize the fruits of his striving at the moment of death, and then more keenly when he is resurrected. But if he could see now with the vision of reality, he would certainly see the hell he is already in:

The rivalry for worldly gain diverts you until you come to the graves. No, but you will soon know; thereafter you will soon know! No, but if you could only know with the knowledge of certainty, you will see Hell-fire; thereafter, you will see it with the eye of certainty! Then you will be questioned, upon that Day, concerning the favors (of God to you). (102:1-6)

When the Qur'an describes the coward, the hypocrite, the arrogant denier of truth, the tyrant and his cronies, the one who desires to be seen by men in his worship while he ignores the suffering of the needy, the reader knows that each of these, to some degree, lives within him. We read how the hypocrites, when it is time to pray, do so only grudgingly (4:142), and how there are those who pray but refuse acts of charity and ignore the needs of the poor (107:1-7), and we see a mirror of our own selfishness and lust for glory. When it comes to those who try to find excuses when asked to fight in a just cause, we have to admit to ourselves how often we have turned our back on the despair of others.

> What ails you that you do not fight in the cause of God and the helpless men, women, and children who say, "O our Lord, bring us out of this land whose people are oppressors, and appoint for us from Yourself a protector, and appoint for us from Yourself a helper." (4:75)

In these we discover our worst potentialities. They measure and reveal us to ourselves.

We are given examples of the best that man can be: the prophets Abraham, Moses, Jesus and Muhammad; such women as Mary, the mother of Jesus, Asiya, the wife of the oppressive Pharaoh, and the Queen of Sheba, who converted from paganism to belief in one God; the repentant magicians of Pharaoh, who announced publicly their belief in the God of Moses at the risk of crucifixion; the stranger among the Egyptians who emerged to defend the truth of the message of Moses; and the People of the Pit, who were thrown into the fire for their beliefs. They are young, like the People of the Cave, and old, like the aged Jacob in *Surat Yusuf*. We see men and women, parents and children, and husbands and wives, of both believers and disbelievers—practically every type of social perspective is seen in the unveiling of an unending conflict and the mandatory choice: "Will I surrender to what is right, or will I turn away?"

These narratives develop at a rapid pace. We are thrust into a confrontation between a denier and a defender of the truth. The tension builds to the point at which a decision must be reached quickly, for a life is in the balance. In almost all these showdowns, there looms the threat of persecution and violence to the believer. The Qur'an covers these conflicts from differing views: that of the prophet and those who believe in him, that of the tyrant and his followers, giving each other support and justification (7:109-110; 20:62), and that of the man in the street (40:28-44). Unavoidably, we begin to ask: "Where would I fit in? Which of these people am I?"

As one reads the Qur'an's descriptions of how people think and act, the state of spiritual loss of most of humanity, and the stories of so many different kinds of individuals, a remarkable transformation takes place.

From the Qur'an's images, verses, and surahs a more vivid picture starts to emerge. There begins to dawn, with increasing clarity, a sharp and penetrating view—of yourself. The Qur'an has somehow sneaked up on you and has become a mirror in which you see your flaws, weaknesses, pain and loss, potentials and failures. Peering deeply within yourself, you come to recognize something that you have always really known: that there is no god but God—*La ilaha illa Allah.*

However, recognition is not the same as commitment; there is still a barrier of fear and apprehension separating belief from submission. But there are verses in the Qur'an that come to the aid of one wrestling with this choice. Like a hand from Heaven reaching out to a stricken heart, they speak as much for the soul as to it. When you need most to know that God is with you, that He hears you, He confirms it:

> And if my servants call on Me, tell them that I am near. That I heed the call of every caller. So let them hear my call. And believe in Me, that they may walk in the right way.(2:186)

When you doubt, He assures you that there is always hope:

> O My servants who have sinned against yourselves, do not despair of the mercy of God. Surely God forgives all sins. Indeed, He is the Most Forgiving, the Most Merciful. (39:53)

And at that moment of surrender, as you call out to your Lord from the depths of your anguish, He embraces you:

> Our Lord, we have heard the call of one calling to faith, "Believe in your Lord," and we have believed. Our Lord, forgive us our sins, blot out from us our iniquities, and take to Yourself our souls in the company of the righteous. Our Lord, grant us what You did promise us through Your messengers, and save us from shame on the Day of Judgment: for you never break Your promise.

> And their Lord accepted of them their prayer, and answered: "Never will I suffer to be lost the work of any of you, be he male or female. You are members one of another. Those who have left their homes, Or were driven out there from, or suffered harm in My cause, or fought or were slain—Truly, I will blot out from them their iniquities, and admit them into gardens with rivers flowing underneath; A reward from the presence of God, and from His presence is the best of rewards.(3:195)

There are also verses that unblock the way to spiritual cleansing and repentance, such as:

> On no soul does God place a burden greater than it can bear. For it is every good that it earns and against it is every ill that it earns. Our Lord, do not take us to task if we forget or make a mistake. Our Lord, do not lay upon us a burden like that which You laid upon those before us. Our Lord, do not lay upon us what we do not have strength to bear. And pardon us and forgive us and have mercy on us. You are our Protector; then defend us against the people who disbelieve. (2:286)

And there are others that comfort and reassure one that God does not abandon those who seek Him. The first time I read the ninety-third surah of the Qur'an, I was so struck with its promise of God's nurturing love that I wept for what had to be at least a half hour. I felt like a lost child who had finally been rescued by his mother, for it tells us that through the brightest and darkest times, God does not forsake us, if we only turn to Him:

> By the glorious morning light, and the night when it is still and dark, your Guardian-Lord has not forsaken you, nor is He displeased. And the promise of the hereafter is greater than the promise of the present. And soon your Guardian Lord will give you (that with which) you will be well pleased. Did He not find you like an orphan and shelter you? And He found you lost and He guided you? And He found you in need and nurtured you?(93:1-8)

Earlier I had remarked that, in effect, the Qur'an has no beginning or end, that its fundamental concepts can be ascertained regardless of the order in which it is read. But for one who is about to respond to its call, the arrangement of the Qur'an is pivotal, for the further you progress through it, in the correct order, the more intense and emotive is its expression. As a result, the closer one comes to conversion, the more magnetic is the summons.

The short surahs at the end of the Qur'an recapitulate its major themes and intensify the exhortation. After one last reminder of the awful price of arrogance and a stubborn rejection of faith, one arrives at the last three surahs, which literally teach the reader what to say, placing the words before him that he yearns to speak to his Lord. Three consecutive times, separated by a few lines, the reader is urged to announce his or her faith: "Say: He is God, the One" (112:1), "Say: I seek refuge with the Lord of the dawn" (113:1), and "Say: I seek refuge in the Lord of mankind" (114:1).

The reader has now been brought to the edge of a new life and commitment, expressed, as I did years ago in the student mosque, in the words, *Ashhadu an la ilaha illa Allah, wa ashhadu anna Muhammadan Rasul Allah*—I bear witness that there is no deity except God, and I bear witness that Muhammad is the Messenger of God

For those whom Islam has embraced, the greatest witness to God's unremitting, pursuing, sustaining, and guiding love is the Qur'an. Like a vast, magnificent ocean, it lures you deeper and deeper into its dazzling waves until you are swept into it. But instead of drowning in a sea of darkness, as described above, you find yourself immersed in an ocean of divine light and mercy.[66]

In the days after becoming a Muslim, I tried to attend every congregational prayer at the mosque, but I was drawn especially to the dawn (*Fajr*), sunset (*Maghrib*), and evening (*'Isha'*) prayers, because during these three the Qur'an is recited aloud rather than silently, as in the other two. This soon caught the attention of one member of the congregation, who was curious as to why I made an extra effort to come to these prayers, as he considered them to be by far the more taxing and as the recitation was in a language that was totally foreign to me.

I had never given the matter any thought, but I responded almost instinctively, "Why is a baby comforted by his mother's voice?" For even though an infant does not know the words, it is a familiar voice that soothes, a voice that he feels he has known in a distant past and that has always known him.

There were times when I wished I could live within the protection of that voice forever, but the new believer must live and grow in faith in the real world.

---

[66]Schuon employs this simile in his *Understanding Islam.*

CHAPTER 3

Rasul Allah

The Prophet is closer to the believers than their own selves, and his wives are their mothers. (Qur'an 33:6)

The rumor was spreading rapidly through the city, and the crowd swelling in the courtyard was growing more restive by the minute. Even though there had been plenty of signs during the past few days, they were now in shock and on the edge of panic. Maybe this would be their greatest trial, greater than the suffering, the immigrations, the fighting, and the dying; for he had always been there—with his sure and steady leadership, his tremendous spirituality and compassion, his reassuring smile, and his kindly sense of humor.

"Awake, O Father of the Dust!" he had joked, as he brushed off the dirt from his startled cousin. And out of the deepest humility and respect, he had spread his mantle and made a place for the poor old woman to sit. How could they forget that rugged, determined gait of his, as if he was striding uphill, or his granddaughter riding on his shoulders when he led them in the prayer? And God was always with him: in the cave and on the field of Uhud and on the pulpit. It cannot be true! they thought. What are we going to do now?

'Umar bolted from his quarters into the courtyard. "They are lying!" he cried to the crowd, promising to cut down with his sword the pernicious fabricators. Towering over his audience, he was more fierce than ever, and his enraged eyes guaranteed his threat. He used to say that at the sight of 'Umar, Satan himself would reverse direction and flee!

At first they were relieved, for 'Umar had seen him only minutes earlier in the apartment. But they could still hear the crying of his wives inside their rooms, and there was something eerie and unreal in 'Umar's protest—like that of a boy that refuses to accept his father's demise. O God, it's true, they gasped. Our Lord, help us. Muhammad is gone!

Abu Bakr, his horse sweating and panting hard as he guided it toward the mosque, dismounted hastily and made his way toward his daughter's apartment. Parting the curtain, he asked permission to enter. "No need to ask today," was the reply.

69

He walked over to the mat where his son-in-law lay, his face covered with a cloak. Their friendship went back so many years—to long before he was a prophet, even before his marriage to Khadijah, back to when they were both bright young prospects in Makkan society. He bent down and kissed the face of his beloved: "Sweet you were in life, and sweet you are in death." He lifted his head gently between his hands while his tears fell onto the Prophet's face. "O my friend, my chosen one, dearer to me than my father and my mother, the death that God has decreed for you, you have now tasted. After this no death shall ever come to you." With great care, he lowered the Prophet's head onto his pillow, bent again to kiss his face, drew the cover over him, and left the room.

Abu Bakr, who was short, slight of frame, and best known for his tender heart and clemency, did not appear to be a natural leader. In fact, his own daughter had once disqualified him from leading the prayer because of his emotional nature. However, the Prophet had seen deeper into him. Reentering the courtyard, Abu Bakr went to the front of the crowd. He called for the people's attention, but 'Umar, who was still haranguing them, would not allow himself to be interrupted.

The crowd shifted its attention, for the people wanted to hear what Abu Bakr had to say. "For those who worshipped Muhammad. . ." he began loudly. 'Umar now turned toward him, and both he and the crowd fell silent. "Know that Muhammad is dead." He continued firmly: "But for those who worship God, know that God lives and never dies!" His voice rose in intensity as he recited

> Muhammad is but a messenger. Messengers passed away before him; if he dies or is killed, will you turn back on your heels? And whoever turns back on his heels will do no harm to God, and God will reward those who are grateful. (3:144)

'Umar, stunned by the realization that the Prophet was really dead, fell to his knees, releasing the bereavement that he had refused to accept. In the future, he would recount how, when Abu Bakr recited those divine words, it had seemed that they were hearing them for the first time. Although it would not become official until the next day, the question of who would succeed Muhammad politically (there could be no successor to his prophethood) was answered at that very moment in the hearts of many.

Abu Bakr's role was limited, for he died two years later. It was, however, the most sensitive time of all, for he had to steer the new Muslim community through one of its most difficult phases of development. The Revelation had been completed, its application had been demonstrated, and it was now time for the ummah to be cut loose from the security of life in the Prophet's company and to apply the Message in new and uncharted domains. The task was made easier by the fact that the outlook and personalities of the Prophet's closest companions had been molded by the events of the past twenty years. The Qur'an and Muhammad's example were not yet two separate bodies of knowledge that they had to study and research, for they were a part of their lives. But two gigantic dangers, which would forever challenge the community, confronted Abu Bakr from the start: sectarianism and the human tendency to elevate saints and heroes to divine rank, even those who were sent to combat that tendency.

The Western convert of today has to face these same issues, although from a somewhat different perspective. Somehow he must find his place in a community whose traditions and perspectives, at this time in his life, are largely alien to him. During the same process, he must also come to terms with the person of the Prophet Muhammad.

Beginning with the Qur'an

At present there are very few books in English dealing with the basic Islamic beliefs and practices.[67] As a result, most American Muslims' first contact with the person of the Prophet is through an English translation of the Qur'an with a commentary. And this is certainly appropriate, for the Qur'an has always been the principal fount of faith for the Muslim community.

For those from a Judeo-Christian background, the natural initial expectation is that the Muslim scripture should be, for the most part, about Muhammad and his community. However, this is not the case. The name "Muhammad," for instance, appears only four times in the entire text, while the name "Jesus" appears twenty-five times and that of "Moses" one hundred-and-thirty-six.[68] As discussed in the preceding chapter, the Qur'an is concerned mainly with those who read it and their relationship with God. It is true that one can find allusions to historical events related to the Prophet's time, but the references appear to be purposely vague so that the struggles and challenges referred to can be applied to the lives of almost any people of any time. Nonetheless, there

---

[67]Of an introductory nature: Hammudah Abdalati, *Islam in Focus* (Indianapolis: American Trust Publications, 1975); Sayyid Abul A'ala Maududi, *Towards Understanding Islam*, trans. Khurshid Ahmad (Indianapolis, Islamic Teaching Center, 1977); Muhammad Hamidullah, *Introduction to Islam* (Paris: Islamic Cultural Center, 1969).

[68]Hanna E. Kassis, *A Concordance of the Qur'an* (Berkeley: University of California Press, 1983).

are enough Qur'anic references to Muhammad's thoughts and feelings, hopes and disappointments, to allow us to form some picture of his personality.

Our approach to the Prophet will differ from that of the non-Muslim scholars of Islam, who search for material or psychological motives behind the revelations. We will attempt to come to know Muhammad from the standpoint of one who has become convinced of the Qur'an as the divinely revealed word of God, for this is the usual path taken by the convert: his convictions about the Qur'an develop more rapidly than his perceptions of the Prophet Muhammad. In addition to this, we will try to discern how the Qur'an wishes the believer to regard him.

The most salient point made by the Qur'an about Muhammad is that, although he was the recipient of the revelation and therefore possesses special qualifications, he is nothing more than a man. There is very little in the Qur'an that can be used to make more of the Messenger than the Message. We have already seen the verse quoted by Abu Bakr to announce the Prophet's death to the community. There are several others that make the same point:

Say [O Muhammad]: "I have no power to harm or to benefit myself except as God wills." (10:49)

We sent messengers before you, and appointed for them wives and children, and it was not for any messenger to bring a sign except by Allah's leave. (13:38)

And they say: "We shall not believe in you until you cause a spring to gush forth for us from the earth, or you have a garden of date trees and vines, and cause rivers to gush forth in their midst, carrying abundant water; or cause the sky to fall upon us in pieces, as you say [will happen] ; or you bring God and the angels before [us] face to face; or you have a house adorned with gold, or you mount a ladder to the skies. No, we will not even believe in your mounting until you send down to us a book that we can read." Say: "Glory be to God! Am I anything but a mortal, a messenger?" And nothing kept men from believing when guidance came to them except that they said, "Has God sent a mortal as a messenger?" (17:90-94)

And they say: "What sort of messenger is this, who eats food and walks through the streets?" (25:7)

And if We had not made you firm, you would have come close to inclining to them somewhat. In that case, We would have made you taste double [the punishment] in life, and double in death, and you would have found no helper against Us. (17:74-75)

The Qur'an parallels Muhammad's mission and struggles with those of former prophets, who are presented as equally human (14:11). They are tempted by sexual passion (12:24; 12:33), cherish earthly things (38:31-33), may seek out others of superior knowledge (18:60-82), and may be swayed by their emotions and act rashly (28:14-21; 7:150). They are also fallible (38:24-25; 37:139-144), subject to self-doubts (28:33-35), and seek God's guidance and forgiveness (7:151, 28:16; 38:24-25; 38:35; 6:77).

Muhammad's mortality is shown most effectively in the verses that address his psychological and spiritual needs, as well as in those that address the ordinary events of his daily life. While Muslim scholars search for eternal lessons in these, they also help to reduce the distance between the Prophet and ourselves. It would be unrealistic to expect a person who is subjected suddenly to overpowering spiritual illumination not to call his own sanity into question. Therefore, in the early stages of his mission, we find such assurances as: "Your Lord has not forsaken you, nor is He displeased" (93:3), "Have We not expanded for you your breast, and removed from you the burden which weighed down your back, and raised high your esteem?" (94:1-4), and "You are not, by the grace of your Lord, mad or possessed. No, truly for you is an unfailing reward, and you (stand) on an exalted standard of character" (68:2-4). We also see him being corrected in strong terms on a number of occasions—for example, when, in his attempt to fight the pre-Islamic prejudice attached to marrying former slaves, he persistently urged his cousin Zainab and his freedman Zaid to avoid divorce despite their mutual dissatisfaction with their marriage,[69] or when he disdainfully turned away from his blind disciple in his zeal to convert some Makkan aristocrats,[70] or when he imposed on his wives and

---

[69]Haykal, *Life of Muhammad*, 285-98. At that occasion, the following verses were revealed: And when you said to the one to whom God had shown favor and to whom you had shown favor, "Keep your wife with you and fear God," and you hid within yourself that which God was about to make manifest for you feared the people, but God has more right that you should fear Him. (33:37)

[70]The relevant verses are as follows: He frowned and turned away because the blind man came to him. But what could tell you but that he might be purified, or that he might be reminded and the reminder might benefit him. But to him who regards himself as self-sufficient, to him you give [full] attention, although his purification does not rest with you. But as for him who came to you in earnestness and who has fear, of him you were unmindful. No, but it is surely a reminder! Then let whomever wills be reminded. (80:1-12)

himself an unduly harsh restriction as a result of intermarital quarrels. (66:1).[71] Despite cultural differences, married readers should be able to recognize and appreciate the several allusions in the Qur'an to domestic tensions in Muhammad's life (33: 28-34, 50-55, 59; 66:1-6).

The affinity between ourselves and the prophets is counterbalanced in the Qur'an by the fact that although they are simply people, they are nevertheless truly exceptional ones. They are God's elect (38:47), raised to the highest degrees of human excellence (6:83), doers of good (6:84), in the ranks of the righteous (6:85), purified with qualities most pure (38:46), devoted and sincere (12:24; 19:52), and preferred above all other people (6:86). Muhammad in particular is described as being a most beautiful example (33:21) and as having an exalted standard of character (68:4). He deserves our respect (2:104; 4:46, 9:61) and God and the angels send down salutations upon him (33:56).

Even when a prophet is censured or repents, his error cannot be classified as an act of deliberate rebellion or transgression against the will of God, but rather it is a temporary mixing of his divine mission with his personal feelings and aspirations. This would seem almost unavoidable and, for an ordinary person, certainly excusable. While God demands the highest standard of conduct from a prophet, the Qur'an shows clearly how thin the line is between these two. Thus, Solomon blames himself for being distracted by the allurements of wealth and power (38:31-33), and David repents for allowing his personal feelings to impair his judgment (38:22-35). When Moses angrily accuses his brother of laxness (7:141) or Jonah abandons his people (37:139-147),[72] it is because of their intense emotional involvement in their missions and their terrible disappointment when it is stalled. And we would not be prone to fault Muhammad for his attempts to eliminate prejudice, or for his enthusiasm to deliver the message, or for trying to settle a family quarrel in an equitable way.

The Qur'anic depiction of God's messengers is midway between the Jewish and Christian understandings. They are exonerated of the gross sins attributed to them in the Old Testament, but are not raised to that level of divine perfection as Jesus often is in popular Christianity, despite his very

---

[71]Haykal, *Life of Muhamad*, pp. 438-42. The verses dealing with this incident are the following: "O Prophet, why do you forbid [for yourself] that which God has made lawful to you, seeking to please your wives?" (66:1)

[72]Muslim exegetes, relying heavily on Jewish and Christian sources, have attempted to produce explicit and detailed accounts of these incidents, which are alluded to only briefly in the Qur'an. Personally, I prefer the purposeful vagueness of the Qur'an, which includes only the basic outline, thus highlighting the most important lessons to be learned while preserving the utmost generality.

human image in the Gospels. Both of these tendencies may lead to excessive negativism and pessimism, for in the first, the examples are hardly worth following, and in the second, such an attempt would not be realistic. Islam has been criticized as being unrealistically positive and as not acknowledging adequately man's inherent weaknesses and proclivities towards evil. But, as argued in the preceding chapter, Islam, and in particular the Qur'an, takes into full account man's inclination towards self-ruin, although such a concern is not the whole message. The design of the Revelation is not limited to making us aware of our failings or informing us of God's grace and forgiveness; it is also to encourage and direct us to strive to overcome our defects and to reform ourselves. While this is never easy, the final verdict of the Qur'an is that we must never cease trying or give up hope. Surrender to God is not a single step; it is a continuous struggle. In the Qur'an, God does not insist that we reach infallibility or immunity from temptation, attributes that were not demanded of His elect. Rather, we are assured of the fact that God loves His servants and wants all individuals to submit themselves voluntarily to His will.

A frequent observation made by Western converts to Islam is that the Muhammad of the Qur'an is quite different from the Muhammad one encounters in the collections of Prophetic traditions, biographies, or in the usual Friday sermons at the weekly congregational prayer. This is not to say that one obtains an entirely incompatible view, but that the Qur'an appears to accentuate different qualities of the Prophet. In the sermons, stories, and traditions, much is made of the victories in battle, the miraculous happenings, the brilliant leadership, the unflinching obedience of his Companions, the promulgation of laws and rules, and the Prophet's great spirituality. These are aspects that would naturally impress people, especially the early Muslims, because for them they were proof that he is indeed God's Messenger.

When we read the Qur'an, however, much of that fades into obscurity, as does the character of the Prophet himself. What remains is a man who is very reluctant to insult his guests when they have stayed too long (33:53), who deals gently with his followers after their failure at Uhud (3:159), who perhaps too readily excuses others (9:43), and who prays for the forgiveness for his enemies (9:80). He is described as kind and compassionate (9:128), and as a "mercy" to believers (9:61) and to all beings (21:107). His anxiety and concern for the success of his mission and the fate of his fellow man (16:37; 16:127; 18:6) is such that he has to be reminded frequently that his duty is only to deliver the Message (6:107; 11:12), that only God guides people (2:272), and that it is not in his power to guide those he loves if God has decided differently (28:56). This is only a partial glimpse of Muhammad, but it is significant that this is the side of his character that is exposed in the Qur'an.

The desire to know him better, more intimately, is nearly irrepressible; especially if one had been raised on the Bible, where the prophets occupy center stage. The Qur'an refrains from dramatizing Muhammad's inner conflicts, leaving us instead with only brief hints and clues. We do not come to see so directly and vividly the fears, anguish, and doubts, as we do in Jesus, for example, when he fights temptation in the desert (Matthew: 4; Luke: 4), or during the night in Gethsamane before his arrest (Matthew: 26; Mark: 14; Luke: 22), or in his final agony on the cross (Matthew: 27; Mark: 15; Luke: 23). Even in the other Islamic sources of *sirah* and hadith, which will be discussed below, we learn of his statements and reactions, but seldom of his inner and private thoughts. By this I mean that we are seldom alone with the Prophet and given privileged access to his feelings. Instead, we always learn of him through an intermediary, whether it be God Himself or a Companion of the Prophet. Perhaps we were not meant to know Muhammad on such a personal level, so that we would no longer feel any need for a human object of veneration but direct all of our spiritual longings entirely to the All-Merciful. This may explain, in part, why Prophet Muhammad is most frequently referred to by his function in the divine scheme: the nearly anonymous designations of *al Rasul* [the Messenger] and *al Nabi* [the Prophet].[73]

In the Mosque

Almost a year had past since I said the Shahadah, and Mahmoud and I had become much more than friends; we were brothers in Islam. We drove together to Fairfield to hear a lecture sponsored by one of the Muslim student groups at the local masjid, which was a small house that had been converted into a place of prayer. We stood out in the large audience, not only because I was the sole American but because we were practically the only ones wearing Western clothing. Not long after we had found a space to sit on the floor, the first speaker began. Seeking to remind his listeners of the impotence of their faith as compared to that of the Prophet's Companions, he told the following story.

The Prophet met a bedouin in the desert and invited him to Islam. The bedouin was resistive and demanded proof of his claims.

---

[73]Later, we will see that the Qur'an does recognize the need for a human exemplar. Islam, however recognizes that this need, if unbridled, could lead to a form of idolatry. The tension between the two is maintained throughout the Qur'an.

Muhammad then asked if a witness would do. "We're in the middle of nowhere! There isn't another man for miles. Who could possibly serve as your witness?" The Prophet pointed to a nearby tree. "This will be my witness." At that moment the tree tore one side of its trunk out of the ground and took a step toward the two men; then it ripped the other side of its base from the ground and came another step closer. The bedouin watched in terror and then shouted, "I testify that there is no god but Allah, and I testify that Muhammad is the Messenger of Allah!"

Mahmoud saw the discomfort in my face and tried to redress the damage after the lecture. Of course, he was correct in saying that the audience was not representative of all Muslims and that the value of such a story lies not in its historicity but in its ability to inspire greater awe and consciousness of God. Indeed, many in the audience had listened transfixed to that and similar stories during the lecture, always following them with outbursts of praise. But I felt that Mahmoud's argument was more of a Western apology than an Islamic one. In my opinion, such stories violate the Qur'an's appeal to reason and its de-emphasis on the supernatural in favor of the wonders of nature and creation. However, Mahmoud, with his usual diplomacy, drove home a significant point: who are we to deny the legitimacy of another perspective simply because it disagrees with ours?

I now knew that, for my own sake, I needed a better understanding of the place of hadith (the Prophetic traditions) in the life of my new community. I was about to enter a maze of confusion, distortion, suspicion, and dogma, a field to be explored only submissively and superficially, in which there is little room for misgiving.

It is to this science that orientalism directs its most formidable criticism. Unfortunately, the literature written by Muslim scholars, whether originally in English or translated from other languages, to counteract this attack has been an entirely inadequate response.[74] And the need for an effective response is urgent for Muslims living in the West, because this subject plays an important role in directing and binding the community, and in meeting the challenge of self-maintenance in a radically foreign environment.

---

[74]There are a few very important exceptions: Nabia Abbott, *Studies in Arabic Literary Papyri*, vol. I: "Historic Texts" (Chicago: 1957), and vol. II: "Qur'anic Commentary and Tradition" (Chicago: 1967);Suhaib H. Abdul Ghafar, *Criticism of Hadith among Muslims with Reference to Sunan Ibn Majah* (IFTA: 1984); Muhammad M. Azmi, *Studies in Early Hadith Literature* (Beirut: 1968); Muhammad Z. Siddiqi, *Hadith Literature* (Calcutta: Calcutta University, 1961).

A convert to Islam quickly discovers the need to adopt a position on the role of the Sunnah and the hadith in his or her life. The problem is that the options presented are so extreme that many converts soon come to feel estranged from the community they have joined. In my opinion, this situation could be avoided if there were a real chance for honest and open discussion on this subject. Although I lack the expertise to rectify this problem, I will try to put forth, from my limited perspective, some of the main issues.

Let us begin by establishing some key terms.

Hadith, Sunnah, and Sirah

'Abd Allah ibn Salam related, on the authority of al Zubaydi: 'Abd al Rahman ibn al Qasim said: My father, al Qasim, informed me that 'A'ishah said: The Prophet raised his eyes and said three times: "In the highest company. . ." [75]

The above is an example of a hadith (plural, *ahadith*), which collectively comprise an area of knowledge that has been the subject of intense study by both Muslim and non-Muslim scholars since the earliest days of Islam. The primary meaning of the word hadith is "new." When it is applied to a verbal communication, it is usually classified as "news"—an account or report of what someone said or something that happened which was reported by witnesses or those who heard of it through reliable sources. In Islamic scholarship, the science of hadith is confined to the study of the words and deeds of Prophet Muhammad, which Muslims consider to be the second eternal source of guidance in their lives (the Qur'an being the first).

The word "sunnah" literally means "a way" or "a traveled path." When used in reference to the Prophet, it stands for his life example and his model behavior. It is therefore connected closely with the hadith literature, for it is chiefly through the latter that we come to know Muhammad's actions and sayings.

The many biographies of Muhammad are referred to as *sirah* (literally, biography). But for the moment, we will concentrate on the subject of hadith.

As in the above example, every hadith consists of two parts: the *isnad* (the chain of authorities through whom it has been transmitted, and the *matn* (the actual text). Muslim specialists in this area attach extreme importance to both elements. For example, two *ahadith* with the same *matn* but different *isnads* will be classified differently in terms of their

---

[75]Muhammad Asad, *Sahih al Bukhari: The Early Years* (Gibraltar: Dar al Andalus Publishers, 1981), p. 33.

78

authenticity. One may also note in the *isnad* the careful attention given to the precise method of transmission at each stage, which for Muslims testifies to the exactitude, integrity, and reliability of the individuals who were included in the process through which traditions made their way into the canonical collections of *ahadith*. This impression finds support in the many accounts of the great piety of the most respected collectors of *ahadith*, such as al Bukhari and Muslim, who often traveled great distances and underwent serious hardships to investigate new *ahadith* and substantiate the wording of the texts and the links in the chains of the already known ones. The canonical collections, produced in the third century of the Islamic era, are named after the scholars who compiled them: *Sahih al Bukhari, Sahih Muslim, Sunan Abu Daud, Jami' al Tirmidhi, Sunan al Nasa'i*, and *Sunan Ibn Majah*. While there are many other respected collections, such as *Sunan al Daraqutni* and *Sunan al Darimi*, most Muslim specialists regard these six as the most reliable, with the collections of al Bukhari and Muslim holding the highest claims to authenticity.

The work of these great *muhaddithun* (scholars of hadith, usually rendered as "traditionists") was necessitated in part by the prominent place the Prophetic traditions had gained in legal argumentation toward the end of the second Islamic century,[76] and by the ineludible fact that thousands of traditions had been fabricated for political, factional, pious, prejudicial, personal, and even seditious purposes.[77] The extent to which forgery occurred may be ascertained by the fact that, out of the six hundred thousand traditions examined by al Bukhari, he accepted only 2,602 (not counting repetitions) for his collection, *al Sahih*.[78] This is somewhat misleading, however, for al Bukhari never claimed that there were no authentic traditions outside of his collection. Moreover, the number six hundred thousand does not correspond to the number of distinct reports, but includes all the different channels by which reported *ahadith* came to him, including repetitions.

When al Bukhari accepted a specific hadith, he would often reject many others with an identical *matn* on the ground that their *isnad* did not meet his standards. For him and for all *muhaddithun*, the authenticity of a hadith was determined principally by its *isnad*, while the *matn* was considered only secondarily.[79] For a hadith to be accepted as authentic, it had to have a continuous chain of reliable and trustworthy authorities and have

[76] J. Schacht, *The Origins of Muhammadan Jurisprudence* (Oxford: 1953), 41-57.
[77] Abdul Ghafar, *Criticism of Hadith among Muslims*, 33-48.
[78] Azmi, *Studies in Early Hadith Literature*, 301.
[79] Ibid., 305.

no hidden defects. For example, a hadith would be rejected if it was known that a link in the chain of transmitters contained two persons that never had the opportunity to meet.

During the second Islamic century, this need to establish the reliability of *isnad* engendered the collection and compilation of volumes of biographical data on the narrators of traditions, as well as criticisms of their character, veracity, and intelligence.[80] This literature, known as the *asma' al rijal* (literally, "the names of the men), developed into an almost independent science of its own of such magnitude and richness that Sprenger calls it "the glory of Muhammadan literature."[81]

The science of hadith divides traditions into three classes: genuine (*sahih*), fair (*hasan*), and weak (*da'if*). This latter group is subdivided further: suspended (*mu'allaq*), interrupted (*maqtu'*), broken (*munqati'*), incomplete (*mursal*), forged (*mawdu'*), and having an error in the *isnad* or the *matn* (*musahhaf*). They are also divided according to the number of their transmitters during the first three generations of Muslims. The *mutawatir ahadith* were transmitted through the first three generations by such a large number of transmitters that there is little doubt as to their authenticity.[82] The minimum number of required transmitters varies, depending on the scholar, from as few as seven to as many as seventy. There are very few *ahadith* in this class. The *mashhur ahadith*, which are far more numerous, were transmitted by two to four transmitters in the first generation and a large number in the next two. These two groups have occupied an important position in Islamic law since its earliest days. The *ahad* traditions were transmitted in the first three generations by four or fewer transmitters and, due largely to the arguments of Imam al Shafi'i,[83] they became, together with the *mutawatir* and *mashhur* traditions, the second source of Islamic law for Sunni (commonly called the "orthodox" by orientalists) jurists.

From this short introduction, one can get a feel for the immensity and complexity of this classical Islamic science that, unfortunately, can boast only a very few true experts today. As Siddiqi remarks:

As a matter of fact, the whole system of teaching, particularly of Hadith, in India and (so far as I know) in the whole Islamic world

[80]Siddiqi, *Hadith Literature*, 126-27.
[81]Ibid., cited on page 170.
[82]G. H. A. Juynboll, *The Authenticity of the Tradition Literature: Discussions in Modern Egypt* (Lieden: E. J. Brill, 1969), 96-129. Here, he challenges this conception.
[83]Schacht, *Origins of Muhammadan Jurisprudence,* 11-20.

has been reduced to mere formality. Very few of the teachers possess any knowledge of the *Asma' al-Rijal*—a subject so essential for a study of Hadith.[84]

Converts to Islam, whose access to the hadith literature is much less direct than their access to the Qur'an, often find themselves in a bind regarding this field. In the absence of readily available experts, certain traditions are cited indiscriminately by the Muslim masses to justify almost any idea or behavior. The matter is further complicated by the convert's background. If he or she has come from the Judeo-Christian tradition, which has been rejected to some degree, he or she has already rejected a parallel heritage of testimonies that, at least until recently, were believed to have been faithfully preserved. It is also difficult to ignore the criticism of Western scholarship, which has so successfully exposed human intermeddling in the Jewish and Christian scriptures, and has arrived at similar conclusions regarding the traditions of Muhammad. It is also hard not to question the authenticity of those accounts that seem incompatible with what one might expect of a prophet or that endorse something that seems to be extreme and unreasonable behavior. On top of all this, a Muslim is expected to accept the assertion that all the *ahadith* accepted by the majority of earlier and contemporary Muslim specialists are true and accurate reports of Prophet Muhammad's statements and actions. This places many converts in the uncomfortable position of having to rationalize and then yield to a dogma that, because one is not supposed to question it, is very hard to believe in and often forces a compromise of one's commitment to the truth.

We will take up each of these issues one at a time, beginning with contrasts between the hadith and the Bible.

The New Testament and the Hadith

Most Muslim and non-Muslim writers consider the Qur'an and the Bible to be dissimilar scriptures, especially in terms of literary style, authenticity, and the manner in which they have come down to our own time. The same can be said of the collections of hadith and the Old Testament, for although the differences are perhaps not as great in this case as in the former, they are substantial enough to discourage comparisons.

While writers have suggested similarities between the canonical hadith collections and the New Testament,[85] a close examination uncovers many important differences. Admittedly, both serve to guide their respec-

---

[84]Siddiqi, *Hadith Literature*, 139.
[85]Kenneth Cragg, *Jesus and the Muslims* (London: George Allen & Unwin, 1985), 91.

tive communities in religious matters and contain teachings attributed to a divinely chosen messenger. In addition, each canon was established more than three centuries into the lives of their communities and depends on earlier transmitted testimonies. But the first two contrasts are very general, since almost all sacred writings share these attributes, and the last two are somewhat superficial, because different motives and methods were behind their compilation.

There were three principle impulses behind the collection of *ahadith*. First, Muhammad and his mission made such a deep impression on his contemporaries, and indeed all of human history, that it was only natural for the early Muslims to gather as much information as they could about him and his revolutionary movement. Second, his sayings were an important source of information for interpreting the Qur'an. Third, with the passage of time and as their empire expanded, the legal problems facing Muslim jurists grew in number and complexity. Jurists began to distrust their legal and moral instincts, with the result that the demand for explicit or analogous Prophetic precedents increased.

The New Testament writings were motivated by somewhat different circumstances. In common with all prophets, Jesus preached radical change. As best as we can tell, however, its direction was moral and spiritual and did not include the actual rules and institutions for governing his society. He demanded reform, but not a recasting of the existing social order. We could speculate as to what direction he would have taken had he lived longer, but this would only be conjecture. Perhaps it was due to his emphasis on the individual's inner spirituality over outward observances or the brevity of his mission, but for some reason almost no records of his sayings and actions were preserved. To the best of our knowledge, Jesus left no new scripture to interpret. As the early Christian churches were mainly concerned with organization and survival under a hostile government, and with teaching the new faith and correcting certain abuses, no real effort to construct a formal and comprehensive system of law based on the teachings of Jesus was undertaken. In their effort to shape the new community, early Christian writers made almost no references to the actual sayings of Jesus.

By the start of the third Islamic century, the science of hadith had become so prominent and influential that, at least in the sphere of law, authentic ahadith were fast becoming second in authority only to the Qur'an, taking precedence over argument from analogy (*qiyas*) and independent reasoning (*ra'y*).[86] The authors of the six canonical hadith collections, as

---

[86]Schacht, *Origins of Muhammadan Jurisprudence*, 98-137.

well as many other *muhaddithun*, responded to this development by arranging their material by topic, which facilitated legal investigation, and by approaching the authenticity of these reports with great care and caution. We thus possess abundant and detailed information regarding the development of this science and, in particular, on the reasons and methods of selection behind the formation of the canonical collections. As stated in the *New Oxford Annotated Bible with the Apocrypha*, the same cannot be said of the New Testament:

> Why, how, and when the present books of the New Testament were finally gathered into one collection are questions difficult to answer because of the lack of explicit information.[87]

This highlights a basic difference between the two canons: the formation of the canonical hadith literature in the third Islamic century represents the culmination of a systematic and critical scholarly investigation, while a comparable examination of the New Testament was not undertaken until approximately fifteen hundred years after its compilation. Nonetheless, orientalists have questioned the accuracy of the findings of Muslim scholars, an issue that we will discuss shortly.

The contents and forms of these two collections are also quite different. The New Testament can be divided into two distinctive sub-sections: the Gospels and the Epistles (or Letters). The New Testament letters were written by various teachers in the early Christian Church to provide instruction and encouragement to growing communities, and also sometimes to individuals. The letters fall into two main groups: those attributed to Paul and those attributed to other writers. Although it is now commonly accepted that Paul did not write all the letters ascribed to him by tradition,[88] undoubtedly the majority of them were his, allowing of course for later alterations by scribes. Paul's letters are probably the earliest New Testament writings, for his epistles and several of the other letters predate the Gospels. Collectively, the epistles contain only a handful of Jesus' sayings and a few very brief references to his life. However, such important Christian doctrines as Jesus' crucifixion and resurrection, vicarious atonement, and the New Covenant replacing the Abrahamic Covenant are already present.

The four Gospels of the New Testament, written in the last third of the first century, are designated by the pseudonyms of Matthew, Mark, Luke,

---

[87]Herbert G. May and Bruce M. Metzger, *The New Oxford Annotated Bible with the Apocrypha* (Oxford University Press, 1977), 1169.
[88]Ibid. See the introductions to 1 and 2 Timothy and Titus.

and John; the names of their actual authors are unknown. Mark, written in approximately 70 AC, is considered to be the earliest, and the Gospels of Matthew and Luke are believed to be based mostly on this Gospel and a no longer extant source of the sayings of Jesus called the Q-source.[89] The Gospels of Matthew, Mark, and Luke have so much in common that they are called the Synoptic Gospels (from the Greek synopsis: a seeing together). The mystical Gospel of John, which places a heavy emphasis on symbols and mysteries, stands apart from the Synoptic Gospels and, one can safely say, is the most popular of the four. The literary style of the Gospels is biographical and concentrates mainly on the last few months of Jesus' life and his public preaching. The books of the New Testament were written in the common Greek of that time, which was known and used by the peoples of the Roman Empire to whom the first Christian missionaries carried their message.

The canonical hadith collections are arranged according to their subject matter. Thus, they resemble more closely the recently discovered Gospel of Thomas, which consists of a listing of the sayings of Jesus with only the barest minimum of introduction.[90] The hadith are not arranged chronologically and contain practically no commentary or instructions from their authors to the Muslim community, although certain legal and religious positions can be ascertained from the chapter headings and the selection and arrangement of material. The six canonical hadith collections have many traditions in common, as individual traditionists often subjected those hadith accepted by a predecessor to their own critical standards.

Another major difference is the language in which the texts were written. The language of the hadith is always Arabic, which was the language of Muhammad. In the case of the New Testament, however, every specialist agrees that it was written in a language—Greek—that Jesus did not speak. The original language of his teachings was Aramaic, the common language of Palestine in his time.[91] This disparity between the spoken and written languages meant that one of the overriding goals of the writers of the Gospels and the Epistles of the New Testament was to translate the meaning of Jesus' life into another culture and language.

Thus, the hadith literature, in particular the six canonical collections, differs fundamentally from the New Testament writings in the ways they were collected, written, studied, and used. This being the case, it is rather

[89]Ibid., 1167.
[90]Jean Doresse, *The Secret Books of the Egyptian Gnostics* (New York: Viking Press, 1960).
[91]May and Metzger, *The New Oxford Annotated Bible*, 1442.

useless to suspect one of these on the basis of the other. However, it **is** the case that if one comes from a non-Muslim religious heritage, particularly a Christian one, then he or she is likely to already have definite expectations as to what is and is not saintly conduct, and these will at times conflict with the depictions of Prophet Muhammad in the hadith and the *sirah* literature.

Expectations

For my generation, the late sixties and early seventies was the era of peace and love. Young men grew their hair long and placed flowers in it, wore tattered clothes and disheveled beards, and walked barefooted. I think it was more than simply coincidence that we resembled closely the pictures of Jesus that we grew up with—the ones we saw in prayer books, paintings, icons, stained glass windows, and movies. If you used drugs, you could even get that sort of glazed, other-worldly look in your eyes. Those who openly professed the identification were known as "Jesus freaks," but most of the young were not interested in religion.

Yet I feel that the Jesus mystique was definitely there, affecting even the irreligious, not only in the way young people looked but in the calls for peace, love, and a new world order. Jesus was the ultimate activist-passivist: defending the meek and oppressed (especially women), denouncing the hypocrisy of the Establishment, taking on its persecution and, in the end, refusing revenge. There are recent challenges to the historicity of this perception, but for nearly two thousand years this is what he has been to Christians. In Western eyes, at least, it is the most alluring and sympathetic portrait in history—not because he was the greatest leader, politician, warrior, or orator, but because he loved and forgave like no other man or woman.

It is a portrait hard to match and, for Muslims, there is no need to try—although attempts have been made[92]—for the Qur'an has the believers say: "We make no distinction between one and another of His messengers" (2:285). The cardinal concern of the Qur'an is not with the messengers but with man's need to surrender himself to God alone.

If this were the end of the matter, potential converts would regard it as a positive point on the side of Islam. But it is not the end of the matter. By this I mean that one has to reconcile one's preconceptions of what is true saintliness with accounts in the biographies and traditions that portray the Prophet endorsing assassinations of poets who derided him, allowing the

---

[92]Sulaiman S. Nadwi, *Muhammad: The Ideal Prophet*, trans. Mohiuddin Ahmad (Lucknow, India: Islamic Research and Publications, 1977).

execution of the men of the Banu Qurayzah and the sale of their survivors into slavery, marrying the daughter of a tribal chief whom his forces had just killed, or pressuring women to hand over their jewelry for the war effort by reminding them of the inferiority of their sex and that they would be the majority of the inhabitants of Hell.[93]

Needless to say, in the very same sources there are a far greater number of exalting accounts. For instance, Watt's assessment of Muham-mad's life at the end of his book *Muhammad: Prophet and Statesman* includes the following perceptions that come very close to Muslim feelings:

Of the many stories illustrating his gentleness and tenderness of feeling, some at least are worthy of credence. The widow of his cousin Jafar ibn Abi Talib herself told her granddaughter how he broke the news of Jafar's death. She had been busy one morning with her household duties, which included tanning forty hides and kneading dough, when Muhammad called. She collected her children—she had three sons by Jafar—washed their faces and anointed them. When Muhammad entered, he asked for the sons of Jafar. She brought them, and Muhammad put his arms around them and smelt them, as a mother would a baby. Then his eyes filled with tears and he burst out weeping. "Have you heard something about Jafar?" she asked, and he told her he had been killed. Later he instructed some of his people to prepare food for Jafar's household, "for they are too busy today to think about themselves."

He seems to have been specially fond of children and to have got on well with them. Perhaps it was the yearning of a man who saw all his sons die as infants. Much of his paternal affection went to his adopted son Zayd. He was also attached to his younger cousin Ali ibn Abi Talib, who had been a member of his household for a time; but he doubtless realized that Ali had not the makings of a successful statesman. For a time a grand-daughter called Umamah was a favorite. He would carry her on his shoulder during public prayers, setting her down when he bowed or prostrated, then picking her up again. On one occasion he teased his wives by showing them a necklace and saying he would give it to the one who was dearest to him; when he thought their feelings were sufficiently agitated, he presented it not to any of them, but to Umamah.

[93]*Sahih al Bukhari*, trans. Muhammad Muhsin Khan, vol. 2, "The Book of Zakah" (24), Hadith no. 541.

He was able to enter into childish games and had many friends among children. He had fun with the children who came back from Abyssinia and spoke Abyssinian. In one house in Madinah there was a small boy with whom he was accustomed to have jokes. One day he found the small boy looking very sad, and asked what was the matter. When he was told that his pet nightingale had died, he did what he could to comfort him. His kindness extended even to animals, which is remarkable for Muhammad's century and part of the world. As his men marched towards Mecca just before the conquest they passed a bitch with puppies; and Muhammad not merely gave orders that they were not to be disturbed, but posted a man to see that the orders were carried out.

These are interesting sidelights on the personality of Muhammad, and fill out the picture formed of him from his conduct of public affairs. He gained men's respect and confidence by the religious bases of his activity and by qualities such as courage, resoluteness, impartiality and firmness inclining to severity but tempered by generosity. In addition to these he had the charm of manner which won their affection and secured their devotion.[94]

But it would be hard to say that the overall picture of Muhammad obtained from the hadith and sirah literature is more appealing than that of Jesus in the Gospels. Certainly a true search for God should be based on more than a competition between personalities, as these may not be represented historically. Still, incidents such as those that I first listed above are discomfiting, as evidenced by the fact that Muslim apologists have devoted considerable effort to rationalizing or glossing over them,[95] as was done by those who tried to respond to *The Life of Muhammad* by the orientalist William Muir,[96] in which his cultural and religious prejudices were quite conspicuous.

The defense by Muslim writers brought up many valid objections and, over the years, has caused Western writers to reassess earlier orientalist works and the career of the Prophet. These Muslim authors demonstrated that the orientalists had relied heavily on accounts that Muslims judged to be unreliable and that they had left key facts and historical considerations

---

[94]W. Montgomery Watt, *Muhammad: Prophet and Statesman* (London: Oxford University Press, 1978), 229-31.
[95]See, for example, Muhammad Ali, *Muhammad the Prophet* (Lahore: 1984); Haykal, *Life of Muhammad.*
[96]William Muir, *Life of Mahomet*, 2d ed. (London: 1894).

out of their presentations. One example, mentioned above and which we will discuss below in a different context,[97] is the issue of the so-called six assassinations, whereby Muhammad is supposed to have ordered the elimination of persons who composed poetry against him. Ali argues that four of these accounts are based on traditions that Muslim scholarship considers either weak or fabricated, and the other two involved cases of high treason committed during war by citizens of the city-state of Madinah.[98] With such examples, Muslim apologists were able to argue that earlier orientalists had exploited Muslim sources, however weak, when it suited their purposes, and ignored information that Muslims considered reliable when it was contrary to them. Such attitudes and behavior have caused many Muslims to consider orientalists as "enemies of Islam." More modern orientalist scholarship has tried to achieve a greater objectivity, but Muslims still approach the works of Western Islamists with considerable suspicion.

Apart from the issue of the veracity of sources is the problem of historical and cultural perspective: what is unacceptable in one place and time may be perfectly admissible, even desirable, in another. For Muhammad to offer his hand in marriage to the daughter of a slain chieftain seems terribly insensitive in our view, but in an era when intertribal skirmishing (*raziyyah*) was, as Watt points out,[99] a "normal feature of desert life" and something of an Arabian "sport," for Muhammad to do otherwise would have been less than chivalrous and somewhat dishonorable. Moreover, this was the customary way in Arabia of establishing bonds of peace and alliance with another tribe.

The work of Goldziher has shed much light on this matter.[100] He shows, through his extensive study of pre-Islamic poetry, that the seventh-century Arabs considered forgivingness of one's enemies a tribal liability and an invitation to future attacks, and that the most respected chief was the one who was the most swift and terrible in retaliation. On two earlier occasions, Muhammad had been willing to punish Jewish treachery with mere exile from Madinah, but during the Battle of the Ditch, when the perfidy of the Banu Qurayzah threatened the very existence of the city-state, he permitted their male combatants to be executed for treason.

In the same work, Goldziher includes a lengthy discussion of the tribal poets in pre-Islamic times.[101] He demonstrates the vital role they played

---

[97]See the discussion of apostasy in chapter 4.
[98]Ali, *Muhammad the Prophet*, 325-44.
[99]Watt, *Muhammad,* 104.
[100]Ignaz Goldziher, *Muslim Studies I* (London: George Allen and Unwin Ltd., 1967), 24-27.
[101]Ibid., 45-54.

in times of war, when a highly skilled poet was worth more than a multitude of seasoned soldiers, which may also explain why the poets mentioned above may have posed such a grave threat to the early Muslims, notwithstanding Muhammad Ali's argument.

In the United States, we consider slavery as one of the vilest of institutions, while Muslim jurists, basing themselves on the Qur'an and the sayings of Muhammad, sought to enact laws that insured fair and kind treatment of slaves. In many places, the Qur'an enjoins the freeing of slaves, going as far as to order the allocation of community funds to purchase their freedom. But, it does not ban slavery altogether, for this institution was necessary for dealing with prisoners of war in a humane way.[102]

Another example of this is the Qur'anic statement that, under certain conditions, a man can have up to four wives simultaneously. In modern times, such an institution is generally held by Westerners to be a means of subjugating woman, a less-than-obvious conclusion. But in seventh-century Arabia, there were specific needs that had to be met: due to the continuous intertribal wars, a higher infant mortality rate among males than females, and men's greater and more frequent exposure to danger, there were more women than men. Polygyny was a natural way to manage the imbalance and to insure the protection and maintenance of a tribe's women.[103]

Finally, it must be remembered that the message of the Qur'an is comprehensive and that it was more than simply revealed: it was framed in the lives and trials of Muhammad and the early Muslims. It taught the meaning of suffering, and the need for forgiveness and patience under persecution. In the years before the emigration to Makkah, the early Muslim community presented one of history's most stirring responses to this lesson. Even those unimpressed by Islam would have to credit Muhammad and his Companions during this period, for we have an instinctive empathy for the oppressed and humbled. In this sense, it is easier to be the victim than the victor. Many times we have to fight to defend ourselves or others from the Pharaohs and Quraysh of our time who deny basic human rights. Sometimes we win and gain authority, and consequently Islam is equally concerned with that part of our lives. It therefore instructs us in what is morally correct in such matters as fighting, law, justice, and punishment. While these have less of a romantic appeal than some others, they are at least as important. The mission of Muhammad was to live both lives, and, for Muslims, no man in history ever did it better.

---

[102]Muhammad Qutub, *Islam: The Misunderstood Religion* (Kuwait: IIFSO, 1982).
[103]See discussion on men's and women's roles in chapter 4.

This is more than simply sentiment on the part of most Muslims, for it has to do with their commitment to the second half of the *Shahadah*. To testify that Muhammad is the Messenger of God is to accept the Prophet's life-example as one's touchstone, and to affirm that his actions set the standard for mankind's conduct without regard to time and place. Therefore, if Muslims are to convince Western civilization that Islam provides a better way, they will have to either soften their commitment to Muhammad's example or invest the time and effort to argue this case convincingly. The first alternative is suicidal, and the second demands sincere and critical scholarship.

Western Criticism of the Traditions

When it comes to historicity, orientalist and Muslim scholars alike agree that the Qur'an presents the authentic utterances of Muhammad under what he assumed to be divine inspiration. Gibb writes that "it seems reasonably well established that no material changes were introduced [into the Qur'an] and that the original form of Mohammed's discourses were preserved with scrupulous precision."[104] Moreover, for many years, orientalists accepted the Muslim version of the development of hadith: that the study of hadith was an area of intensive activity while the Prophet was still alive, that fabrication began very early on, and that the institution of *isnad* was created, adopted, and formalized within a few decades of his death in order to deal with this problem. Orientalists were also willing to accept that, although this institution evolved during the succeeding years, it basically remained unchanged.[105] If this view is accepted, then Muir's conclusion that undetected fabrications would almost have had to occurred in the first Islamic century seems justified.[106]

Goldziher, in his landmark work entitled *Muhammedanische Studien II*, challenged the classical description of this science's development and the integrity of all of the hadith compilations, including the canonical ones.[107] With few exceptions, virtually all subsequent Western studies of this subject support his conclusions. Modern critical methods of literary and historical research have led Western scholars to conclude that:

---

[104]Gibb, *Mohammedanism*, 50.
[105]Muhammad Zubayr Siddiqi, *Hadith Literature* (Calcutta: Calcutta University, 1961), 134, in which several Western scholars who agree with this view are cited: Leone Caetani, J. Horovitz, and J. Robson.
[106]Muir, *Life of Mahomet*, xxxvii.
[107]Ignaz Goldziher, *Muslim Studies II* (London: George Allen and Unwin Ltd., 1971).

(a) The hadith literature is based largely on mere oral transmission for more than a century and that the hadith collections that have come down to us do not refer to any records of *ahadith* that may have been made at an earlier period.

(b) The number of *ahadith* in the later collections is much larger than the number of those contained in the earlier collections or in the earlier works on Islamic law. This, according to such scholars, shows that most of the hadith are of doubtful character.

(c) The *ahadith* reported by the younger Companions are far more numerous than those related by the older Companions, which, they assert, shows that the *isnad* are not quite reliable.

(d) The system of *isnad* was applied arbitrarily to hadith after the end of the first Islamic century. Therefore, it does not prove the genuineness of the tradition to which it is attached.

(e) Many of the *ahadith* contradict one another.

(f) There is definite evidence of large-scale forgery of *isnad* as well as of texts of *ahadith*.

(g) Muslim critics confined their criticism of hadith only to the *isnad* but never criticized texts.[108]

These and other criticisms have been addressed by Muslim and some Western scholars. The most widely-quoted books in English are those of Azmi, Abbott, Siddiqi, and Abdul Ghafar.[109] Some of these points can be defended in a natural way. For instance, (b) can be attributed to the process of passing the hadith from one generation to the next: the original transmitter reports it to his contemporaries, who then relate it to several of his younger listeners of the next generation, and so on. We would expect that the Companions who lived longest after the death of Muhammad would narrate more information concerning him than those, like Abu Bakr and 'Umar, who died soon after him; thus (c). Since the hadith record the Prophet's actions over a twenty-three year period which saw many transitions, and because he was dealing with a great variety of personalities and problems, it would not be unusual to discover disparities in his behavior; hence (e).

---

[108]Siddiqi, *Hadith Literature*, xxi-xxviii.
[109]Abbott, *Studies in Arabic Literary Papyri*, vols. I and II; Abdul Ghafar, *Criticism of Hadith among Muslims*; Azmi, *Studies in Early Hadith Literature*; Siddiqi, *Hadith Literature*.

Abbott and Azmi have argued convincingly concerning (a) and (d), and Muslim traditionists have been aware of (f) for fourteen centuries, as this was the reason behind their labor.[110] Although Muslim scholarship laid greater stress on the *isnad*, Siddiqui and Abdul Ghafar[111] document that (g) is simply untrue. Abdul Ghafar, for example, demonstrates that early traditionists would often reject a report if one of the transmitters was known to have certain personal motives which were supported by the tradition's text. In such cases, the *matn* and *isnad* were considered together. But in reality, examining the *isnad* with the tools developed by Muslim traditionists is to this day the more objective test of a hadith's genuineness, for how one judges the *matn* depends a great deal on personal predilections (a twentieth-century science student is more likely to distrust reports of miracles and prophecies than his seventh-century counterpart, for example), interpretation, and context. It is noteworthy that the greater part of current western hadith criticism concentrates on the *isnad*.

Many important issues that deserve further and careful consideration on both sides are obscured by such a brief summary. Orientalists are often so committed to the idea of the hadith literature's total unreliability that they appear to be blind to evidence that contradicts this and to other possible, sometimes more natural, interpretations of the data. There is a pronounced tendency to label all conflicting data as "unauthentic," "unreliable," or "unhistorical" without explanation, apparently because it does not fit with their views. The fact is that to discount Muslim scholarship so completely, almost all Muslims associated with the study of traditions have to be implicated, a view that is propounded by Goldziher and, to an

---

[110]See Abbott, *Studies in Arabic Literary Papyri*, vols. I and II; Azmi, *Studies in Early Hadith Literature*, 28-106. Here the authors provide extensive documentation of pre-classical hadith literature. Western critics have charged Muslim scholars with being naive in accepting the authenticity of the (abundant) early Islamic texts that they use to support their view of the development of hadith science. But such a criticism allows for a strange double standard on their part: the orientalists' arguments are also, out of necessity, built on studies of early Muslim texts. Thus, it seems that they expect their audience to accept the texts and the related interpretations that support their theories. Without a doubt, Muslim scholarship, like any other, has not been flawless. However, it must be realized that the Muslim understanding fits much better with **all** the data that has come down to us than does its Western counterpart. Of course, one could simply dismiss all early Muslim texts as a huge effort at fabrication that had the support, cooperation, and connivance of all of the proponents of the varied and divergent points of view of the first four Islamic centuries. However, this does not appear to be either humanly possible nor in accord with human nature. In addition, such a dismissal deprives Western scholarship on this subject of any claims to legitimacy.

[111]Siddiqi, *Hadith Literature*, 199-204; Abdul Ghafar, *Criticism of Hadith among Muslims*, 30-50.

every greater degree, by Schacht.[112] Such theories are nearly impossible for Muslims to accept, for they reveal an attitude toward religion that has not yet infected the Muslim mind.

Certain "specialists," seeking to judge the authenticity of the hadith, suppose that they can establish the following criteria, disregarding thirteen centuries of Muslim scholarship. First, if a hadith can be interpreted as favouring a particular group or school, it has most likely been fabricated. If it favors the spiritual life, for example, the Sufis must have invented it. If it provides an argument for literalists hostile to spirituality, then the literalists fabricated it. Second, the more complete its *isnad*, the greater the chance that it is false. The reason for this, according to them, is that the need of proof grows in proportion to the lapse of time. Such arguments are truly diabolical for, taken as a whole, they amount to this reasoning: if you bring me no proof it is because you are wrong, but if you do bring proof it means you need it, and so again you are wrong. How can these orientalists believe that countless Muslim learned men—men who feared God and hell— could have deliberately fabricated sayings of the Prophet? It would lead one to suppose bad faith to be the most natural thing in the world, were it not that "specialists" have almost no feelings for psychological incompatibilities.[113]

Gibb, writing in the same vein but with less passion, focuses on the difficulty, at least after the first few generations, of passing on fabricated traditions:

To Western scholars the technique of Hadith criticism by the examination of the chain of authorities seems to present some grave defects. A frequent criticism is that it is as easy for forgers to invent an *isnad* as to tamper with or fabricate a text. But this overlooks the difficulty that the forger would have in getting the *isnad* (with his name at the end of it) accepted and passed on by scholars of honest repute. And that the Muslim critics of tradition were generally honest and pious men must be allowed, even if some Muslims have themselves asserted the contrary. A more fun-

---

[112]Goldziher, *Muslim Studies II*; Schacht, *The Origins of Muhammadan Jurisprudence.*
[113]Titus Burckhardt, *An Introduction to Sufi Doctrine*, trans. D. M. Matheson (Wellingborough, UK: Thorsons Publ., 1976), 41.

damental criticism is that the *isnad* technique was elaborated only in the second century.

Following up this statement a little later on he concludes:

> The judgements and criteria of the early traditionists, whatever may be regarded as defects in their method, seem at least to have effectively excluded most of the propagandist traditions of the first century and all those of the second, such as those which supported the doctrines of the Shi'a or the claims of the 'Abbasids, or which foretold the coming of the Mahdi.[114]

Theories are often formulated in the extreme and inspired by definite biases. The researcher, based on certain hunches, begins with the strongest possible conjecture that the fragments of evidence allow and then presents it to his peers and the experts, either to be rejected or to be chiseled and smoothed into a better approximation of the truth as further research presents new considerations. At least this is how it is supposed to be. Naturally imperfect, there could be important observations in the initial findings and formulations to which we should be alert. Juynboll, after an assiduous study of modern Muslim discussions on the authenticity of the hadith literature, discovered in his later research what he believed to be a middle position between the Muslim and the Western scholars on this subject.[115] He includes in his work discussions of some conjectures by Goldziher and Schacht that are supported by his own investigations, together with quite a few new discoveries. Juynboll's presentation is detailed, thorough, cogent, and addresses the complaint of Muslim specialists that Western theories are built on studies of hadith that were judged spurious by Muslim scholars centuries ago.[116] Juynboll relies heavily on "authenticated" traditions to argue his views. What follows is a summary of a few of his conclusions:

---

[114]H. A. R. Gibb, *Mohammedanism* (London: Oxford University Press, 1969), 82, 85.

[115]Juynboll, *Muslim Tradition*. I must admit that ultimately I did not see Juynboll's position as a middle one. It appeared to me to be a significant attempt at salvaging and defending the main conclusions of Goldziher and Schacht in light of the works of Azmi and Abbott.

[116]Juynboll, *The Authenticity of the Tradition Literature*. While this objection has definite validity, some underlying assumptions in the methodology are not entirely unsound. For instance, once it is accepted that a large class of traditions are suspect, such as those dealing with the coming of the Mahdi, we may have reason to doubt other traditions of the same genre. Although the great traditionists were aware of the possibility of fabrication, as is evident from the scarcity of suspect traditions in the canonical collections, one may attempt to discover some flaw that they may have missed or deemed insufficient. On the other hand, if a large number of traditions in a certain class did not meet the standards =

1) Juynboll, after a careful survey of the role of the early judges (*qadis*) in the major centers of legal thought during the first three Islamic centuries, agrees with Goldziher's and Schacht's statement that during the first Islamic century, legal decision making, whether done by the ruling authority or by the Muslim jurists, was based on what they believed to be the spirit of Muhammad's teachings rather than a meticulous copying of his actions. At that time, a need for an explicit Prophetic precedent was not usually felt or sought. He also argues forcefully against the imputation that second-century judges were wont to fabricate traditions whenever it suited them.[117]

2) Juynboll argues in favor of Schacht's claim that "*isnads* have a tendency to grow backwards," meaning that legal decisions and maxims first arrived at by jurists were later projected back to the Prophet with complete isnads. He offers as an example the legal opinions of Sa'id ibn al Musayyab (d. 94 AC), showing how many traditions that appear in later collections with *isnads* containing his name can be found in other sources as his own sayings and not linked to persons older than himself. Muslim scholars account for such a phenomenon by explaining that the opinions of Ibn al Musayyab are based on previous examples set by either the Prophet or his Companions; they support this by the fact that there exist completely independent *isnads* of the highest quality that go back to the Prophet and do not involve Ibn al Mussayab at all. If, this argument goes, an opinion of Ibn al Mussayab were projected back to the Prophet, how did the fabricators get all the other transmitters of all the other chains, who belonged to rival and competing centers of law, to collude in falsely ascribing the statement to Muhammad?

While not addressing this most weighty question, Juynboll counters:

The reason why these legal decisions should be considered, in the first instance, as being Sa'id's own juridical insight, rather than as being traceable back to previously set examples, lies in the mere fact of them being quoted as Sa'id's decision at all. A legal decision that indeed does go back to the Prophet or one of his Companions **simply does not require** being put into the mouth of Sa'id as also being the product of the latter's reasoning. The numerous instances where Sa'id is credited with juridical opinions

_____

= of Muslim specialists, one cannot automatically assume that all traditions of that genre are fabricated. Also, if we put aside the matter of authenticity, the proliferation of various traditions may tell us something about the mind set of the early Muslim communities.
[117]Ibid., 77-95.

merous instances where Saʻid is credited with juridical opinions definitely point to one conclusion only. He thought of the problem in these terms first, **before** this decision was moulded into a saying attributed to authorities preceding Saʻid. There is indeed no **necessity** whatsoever for crediting Saʻid with merely having repeated a legal opinion of his predecessors, be they the Prophet or one of his Companions.[118]

Juynboll also mentions that there are many references in the early rijal works to the phenomenon of "raising" a report of a Companion or a Successor (Tabiʻi) "to the level" of a Prophetic saying. Thus, this practice was known to Muslim experts. Juynboll lists several transmitters, among dozens of others mentioned in the *rijal* works in connection with this practice, who have traditions occurring in the canonical collections.[119]

3) He believes that the great majority of hadith claimed to have been narrated by Anas ibn Malik—approximately two thousand three hundred—are suspect. He states that if one compares those that originated in Madinah with those that originated in Baghdad, one finds a considerable dichotomy. We would expect that such a highly respected and prolific figure would narrate pretty much the same reports when he traveled to both centers, but Juynboll finds that there is minimal overlapping in the traditions narrated in his name in these two centers. Juynboll uses similar reasoning in criticizing the traditions claimed to have been narrated by Abu Hurayrah.[120]

4) One device that Juynboll believes helped fabricators construct perfectly sound *isnad*s was what he calls the "age trick," or the ascribing of fantastic ages to transmitters to give *isnad*s greater authority. This could be used, for example, when two successive transmitters in an *isnad* were known to have lived sometimes as much as a century apart. The apparent conflict could be smoothed over by noting that the elder one had lived an extremely long life, often long past a century. He believes that this technique was also used to raise some transmitters to the status of "Companions," hence giving them and their traditions greater authority. Juynboll notes:

The following Successors, otherwise not such important transmitters, supposedly reached incredible ages: Qays b. Abi Hazim (died

[118]Ibid., 15-16. Emphasis is the author's.
[119]Ibid., 31-32.
[120]Ibid., 62-64, 104.

84-98/703-16 at the age of well over one hundred), Ziyad b. 'Ilaqa (died 135/752 at the age of almost one hundred; another report has it that he was born in the Jahiliyyah), Abu 'Amr Sa'd b. Iyas (died 95-98/714-717 at the age of 120), al Ma'rur b. Suwayd (when al A'mash saw him he believed him to be 120), Suwayd b. Ghafala (died 80-82/699-701 at the age of 120 or 130; he claimed to be just as old as the Prophet), Zirr b. Hubaysh (died 81-83/700-702 at the age of 127), etc. The *tarajim* devoted to these centenarians in the rijal works are on the whole very favorable without a shadow of a doubt being cast on the ages they claimed to have reached. This must have greatly facilitated the manipulation with *isnad*s, whether they did that themselves or whether this occurred at the hands of anonymous people. Furthermore, traditions supported by *isnad*s including their names occur, without exception, in all the canonical collections.[121]

5) Goldziher,[122] in *Muslim Studies II*, asserts that the *mutawatir ahadith* in which the Prophet is reported to have said that the one who falsely ascribed anything to him had made his place in Hell, and other similar sayings, were fabricated in order to put a stop to such fabrication. Muslim scholars have cited this as an example of the unsubstantiated claims that orientalists have made in the past, for Goldziher supplied no supporting evidence. Juynboll includes a lengthy discussion of these traditions and produces evidence in favor of Goldziher's position. He also uses this example to argue that the characterization of *mutawatir* is no guarantee of a hadith's authenticity.[123]

6) Finally, we should mention that Schacht's "common link theory" is also given a careful treatment.[124] This theory posits that one can detect both the fabrication and the time of fabrication of a particular tradition if its different *isnad*s intersect at a common intermediary point, a "common link." Schacht gives an example[125] of a hadith with three different chains of authorities that have the same narrator at precisely the third link in the chains and then differ elsewhere. According to his theory, this common link is either the fabricator or the point at which the fabrication was made.

[121]Ibid., 46-8, 61-2.
[122]Goldziher, *Muslim Studies II*, 131.
[123]Juynboll, *Muslim Tradition*, 96-129.
[124]Ibid., 206-17.
[125]Schacht, *The Origins of Muhammadan Jurisprudence*. Schacht seems to sense this concerning his own investigation (page 228).

I chose to cite Juynboll's work because it is more recent and thorough, and for its clear exposition. I sketched findings of his that seemed to me most significant, and yet are either unknown to or dealt with inadequately by Muslim authors in English. Let me, as a layman, share a few impressions that came to me immediately, beginning with (2), since finding (1) is unlikely to excite much Muslim opposition.

Schacht's "projecting back" theory is given a full treatment only in Azmi's text. Although Azmi does not discuss in detail all of Schacht's examples or anticipate explicitly the objection of Juynboll, he does make use of some general strategies against Western hadith criticism that apply to this theory and many others. He demonstrates consistently that the conclusions of orientalist hadith critics are often: (a) far from necessary; (b) based on fragmentary data that conflicts with the bulk of available evidence; and (c) founded on a fundamentally faulty approach.

Concerning (c), he makes a relevant observation that Juynboll did not take fully into account: that Western theories depend on comparisons of legal and hadith literature. These two disciplines have always been related yet autonomous sciences, for the subject of hadith science is exclusively what the Prophet said and did, while the ultimate interest of Islamic law, although it applied the conclusions of the former science, is to develop systems of law. The standards of the traditionists were naturally more exacting than those of the legal scholars when it came to traditions. One has to be cautious when drawing conclusions about one of these sciences based on a study of the other. In the twentieth century, for example, it would be inappropriate to theorize on the development and standards of mathematical research by concentrating on advances and methods employed in the related science of physics. This, Azmi holds, is the fundamental error in all recent Western investigations.[126]

In their arguments in favor of "projecting back," Western writers exhibit a disquieting impreciseness in their terminology. We discover frequent mixing and equating of such key words as "alike," "identical," and "similar" with regard to the texts. The impression given is that the opinions of scholars, which are identically formulated, are projected back to Prophetic sayings. But when we compare the two, they frequently involve different phrasings altogether. In these instances, the scholar's statement could easily be taken as an opinion based on previous examples or on a practice that was well-established at that time. In regard to this, it may be helpful to understand why chains of transmission of scholarly opinions were preserved at all. In other words, why was the trouble taken to trace

---

[126]Azmi, *Studies in Early Hadith Literature*, 221.

statements back to **any** authority other than the Prophet or his Companions?

At a time when statements from authorities were used in legal circles, it seems to have been necessary to establish a chain of transmitters back to the original source, regardless of who the authority was, for it to be accepted as evidence. Today we can quote a publication, but that luxury was not available in the past. Juynboll's retort then really boils down to: Why did jurists quote authorities other than the Prophet when the statements of their opinions were either **similar** or **identical** to statements made by Muhammad? A number of explanations are possible.

It is often more convenient to quote an opinion of a respected authority than to refer back to his original arguments and evidence. Argument from authority is a common tactic and is only one of many strategies used to argue a case. A position is supported by demonstrating that an expert, after considering the evidence available to him, has arrived at the same conclusions. For example, if someone were to ask me—as people often do—whether, based on 2:34, a husband has the right to slap his wife in the face because she does not obey him in some matter, I might reply, "No. In Islam, a husband should never use physical force against his wife, except under the most extreme circumstances. Even then, he is not permitted to strike her in the face."

In the back of my mind I have several sayings, similarly phrased, of the Prophet commenting on this verse. However, I may or may not resort to quoting them to support my reply, depending on the circumstances and the questioner. As a matter of fact, contemporary Muslim speakers most often quote the opinion of the third-century scholar al Tabari, who based his judgment on reported sayings of the Prophet, on this issue. The fact that my understanding conforms to some sayings of Muhammad, even if I arrived at it independently, says nothing about the authenticity of the related saying, since I am discussing an immediate, practical behavioral problem.

This may explain the case when a scholar's statement has a **similar** sense as a saying of the Prophet's. But what of those statements traced back to a scholar whose wording is **identical** to a statement of the Prophet's in a hadith? Juynboll's remark in (2) cannot be so easily dismissed here, as such cases arise most frequently as statements of legal maxims or slogans. Indeed, why would persons make the effort to trace a statement back to a jurist when, in fact, it originated with the Prophet?

It is conceivable that legal scholars did not always specify that the legal maxim employed originated with the Prophet, even when they were aware that it had. When it comes to establishing rules of behavior, Muslim speakers and writers to this day do not always establish the source of the practices that they enjoin.

A convert can find this quite frustrating. What will invalidate your prayer? When is ritual washing (*wudu*) required? What does one do if one joins a congregational prayer already in progress? Who can inherit from a Muslim? These are just a few of the multitudinous regulations that we are taught, often without being informed of any explicit corresponding Prophetic precedent, for the simple reason that these practices are so well-established and accepted that the writer or speaker sees no need to provide this information. The new convert soon finds himself/herself searching for the source of every new ordinance he/she hears, because for all he/she knows this practice could be nothing more than the opinion of the writer or speaker.

Also, as Azmi avers, not every Muslim lecturer of the first three Islamic centuries was an al Shafi'i and not every student was an al Bukhari. Some were extremely exacting in their scholarship, while others were less stringent. Thus, some were likely to mix Prophetic statements with scholarly opinions. This happens even today. For example, one often hears or reads that Muhammad said: "Work as if you will never die and pray as if you will die tomorrow." It is known that the Prophet never said this, but uninformed speakers and writers often ascribe these words to him. Therefore, in cases in which a statement linked to someone other than Muhammad comes very close to a Prophetic saying, it does not exclude the possibility that the originator of the statement was misunderstood, that the lecturer assumed the audience's familiarity with the report, or that he had made sure to specify his source on other occasions.

Above all, we should not forget, as orientalists are eager to point out, that during the first century-and-a-half of the Islamic era, in most centers of legal thought it was deemed sufficient in legal disputes to demonstrate that a particular regulation was the established local practice from the time of the Prophet. It was not until the end of the second Islamic century that explicit Prophetic precedents became necessary. Until that time, it was enough for those involved in legal argumentation to establish a maxim by quoting a local authority without having to trace its origins. This fact is well established in orientalist literature. Later advances in the science of hadith and other factors brought about a change in the criteria of arguing legal cases. Once again, Azmi's caution against making inferences about one science by studying the development of another applies.

As Juynboll observes, Muslim traditionists were well-aware that even honest transmitters could be mistaken in attributing a statement to the Prophet when it had in fact originated with someone else at a later period.

However, they did not always assume, as does the "projecting back" theory, that someone, usually assumed to be a jurist or traditionist, consciously completed a chain in order to falsify information. They saw that the most effective means to check for possible mistakes was to compare and cross reference all of the known data on the matter. The traditionists felt that the methods of *isnad* criticism were the most effective guard against errors of this type.

Juynboll's conclusion concerning Anas ibn Malik and Abu Hurayrah, as stated in (3), is unconvincing. In his examination of some thirty-six traditions reported by Anas that appear in the *Muwatta'*, he realized that those of Madinan origin and those narrated through his Iraqi students did not show, in his own judgment, a "considerable overlap."[127] This surprises Juynboll, for, in his opinion, the information narrated by Anas in Madinah should be more or less the same as what he narrated during his stays in Basrah.

Putting aside the question of exactly what would constitute a "considerable overlap," why should we expect such an overlap in the first place? How and what a teacher teaches over the years depends on the individual and many other factors. Unfortunately, we do not have such precise information about Anas, but I would hope that my own work would not be considered as fabricated by a future researcher just because I lectured on different problems at different stages in my career. More importantly, while Anas is credited with some twenty-three hundred narrations, Juynboll derives his opinion after studying only thirty-six that are found in the *Muwatta'*. Such a small sampling raises the question of whether those traditions studied are at all representative of the others. Juynboll's discussion of Abu Hurayrah is even more cloudy, for he indicates neither the percentage of the traditions that he studied nor the percentage of those that ended up in the canonical compilations.[128]

The "age trick" theory mentioned in (4) is, to my knowledge, original. Unfortunately, only ten examples of it are given: four other explicit illustrations in addition to the six I quoted above. Since there are approximately ten thousand biographies in the extant *rijal* works,[129] it is difficult to place confidence in a theory based on so few examples. But in all fairness, any modern student of ancient Islamic literature cannot help but be skeptical of the advanced ages attached to so many individuals. Many Muslim writers have attributed this to the notorious imprecision with which those living in the Middle East, especially the Arabs, kept track of

---

[127]Juynboll, *Muslim Tradition*, 67-8.
[128]Ibid., 204.
[129]Siddiqi, *Hadith Literature*, 165-88.

a relative's or even their own ages. The use of the lunar calendar and the almost complete non-commemoration of birthdays and deaths throughout much of the Muslim world may also contribute to this phenomenon. Strangely enough, however, almost every Middle Eastern friend of mine knows a family member who has lived more than a century.

Muslim scholars generally consider the birth and death dates found in the biographical works to be very rough estimates. In addition, this consideration is only one of a multitude of other factors considered by traditionists. Azmi shows the large disparity in life span estimates in the various biographical works and, due to the fact that very often no estimates are provided at all, he has to guess as to the person's dates of birth and death.[130] The biographical literature makes no pretense at perfection, for its purpose was to present all of the available data concerning individuals involved in the transmission of hadith that Muslim scholars felt could be of use.

My major objection to the "age trick" theory and, for that matter, much of the Western research done on the traditions, is what I like to call a fabrication phobia. By this I mean the obsession with sifting through the mass of data collected by the Muslim specialists working in this area and to label as a fabrication every peculiarity or inconsistency, rather than entertaining the possibility that they might arise as a result of estimates or human error. I wonder if this compulsion to see dishonesty or stupidity wherever possible is not a reflection of the type of underlying Western prejudice and arrogance discussed by Edward Said in his book, *Orientalism*.[131]

Juynboll admits that his arguments against the authenticity of two *mutawatir* traditions (5 above) generally are considered weak by historians.[132] Here and throughout his text, almost all of his crucial arguments are *argumenta e silentio*. The premise is that, if a number of scholars omitted what eventually would become a widely-accepted hadith from their own collections of traditions, this may indicate something negative about its authenticity. Muslim authors continue to be exasperated by this type of argument, since it assumes that each scholar would have heard of and collected all the traditions in existence at his time. This view, in effect, makes no allowances for human limitations and outside constraints. One of Juynboll's key sources is Malik's *Muwatta'*, even though it is known that Malik was first and foremost a jurist and not a traditionist. While his *Muwatta'* does contain a fair number of traditions, it was not intended to serve as a collection of hadith. Also, it must be remembered that Juynboll himself, on

---

[130]Azmi, *Studies in Early Hadith Literature*, 32-3.
[131]Edward Said, *Orientalism* (New York: Pantheon Books, 1978).
[132]Juynboll, *Muslim Tradition,* 98.

a number of occasions, stresses the incompleteness of his sources. Thus, Juynboll's arguments cannot be taken as conclusive.

Schacht's "common link" theory (6) has been bypassed in most subsequent Western and Muslims investigations of traditions and is, once again, based on scant evidence. Let us assume that we have several *ahadith* with identical texts and *isnad*s that all contain a common transmitter at some intermediary stage. In such a case, Schacht sees "a strong indication in favour of its [the hadith's] having originated in the time [of the common transmitter]."[133] There are only a handful of illustrations of this so-called "common link" in Western orientalist literature; one is given by Schacht[134] and a few others by Juynboll,[135] who mentions that this phenomenon is relatively rare. Schacht's example is shown to be inappropriate by Azmi,[136] and the explanation of this phenomenon by both Schacht and Juynboll is by no means the only, or the most obvious, one. In cases where the tradition is known to have been fabricated, as in the cases discussed by Juynboll, the common link would certainly suggest a possible time of falsification.

In general, however, the existence of a common link did not necessarily imply a fabrication. Muslim scholars, who were aware of this phenomenon centuries ago, allowed for other possible interpretations. For example, certain scholars were known to have investigated all the current sources of a given saying of Muhammad's, sometimes quite obscure sources. As a result, every once in a while we find a scholar who, at a particular point in time, has a saying from several sources and, especially if his knowledge is in demand, passes it on to his many students. As Juynboll shows, it is likely that Muslim traditionists were aware of the possibility that a common link could indicate a fabrication,[137] but, unlike Schacht, they required additional evidence before making such a claim.

In conclusion, I must say that I do not find Juynboll's views on the authenticity of hadith literature to be midway between the orientalist and Muslim positions. He seemed, at least to me, to belong quite comfortably to the Goldziher-Schacht school. Although his exposition is more careful and lucid than Goldziher's and Schacht's, I do not see in what way his approach and discoveries departed fundamentally from theirs, or why argu-

---

[133]Schacht, *The Origins of Muhammadan Jurisprudence*, 172.
[134]Ibid., 171-5.
[135]Juynboll, *Muslim Tradition*, 206-17.
[136]Azmi, *Studies in Early Hadith Literature*, 232-6.
[137]Juynboll, *Muslim Tradition*, 214-6. Juynboll views this need for corroborating evidence on the part of traditionists in a negative light, but to my mind it should be seen as an attempt to consider all of the available data and arguments.

ments against their theories could not be applied with equal effect against his. In my opinion, Juynboll's study does not contribute to a lessening of the distance between the Muslim and Western viewpoints on this area of study.

As a new Muslim, for reasons I mentioned earlier, I was extremely suspicious of the Prophetic traditions. It was not until four years after my conversion that I came across a book in English on hadith criticism by a Muslim author. Many Muslim writers briefly touch on this subject, but their presentations are usually very dogmatic; moreover, I had read orientalist works that were more scholarly and persuasive. Yet even though their judgments supported my skepticism, I was actually **less** sure of my doubts after studying them. The orientalists' conjectures were daring and interesting, but the overall picture presented lacked coherence, and, like Titus Burkhart whom I quoted above, I found their conclusions unrealistically cynical.

Some time later, through a lot of digging and some good luck, I found scholarly writers who defended classical hadith scholarship and whose accounts of its development seemed more sober and had fewer contradictions and psychological leaps than those of the orientalists. I also came to appreciate the immensity of the Muslim effort in collating great volumes of material on the Prophet and his Companions. In addition, I came to respect the statement that the authenticated hadith are, after the Qur'an, the most faithful source of information ever compiled on the life of any prophet or teacher of any of the great world religions. But more importantly, I discovered that the claim of the early Muslim experts was not to have arrived at a flawless record of Muhammad's sayings and deeds, but rather to have collected a body of information whose **authority** for deriving rules of Muslim conduct is second to the Qur'an. We will come back to this point shortly.

I do not wish to leave the impression that Western hadith scholarship is useless or unimportant. All the authors I cited above, who defend the integrity of this classical Muslim science, maintain otherwise. Although I do not agree with every Western criticism, I learned much from Western writings that I could not find in Muslim sources about the science of hadith. Moreover, Western scholars have made significant contributions to its study. They are reviving interest in the classical *rijal* and *awa'il* (reports containing information about who was the first to do something, or when certain institutions were first introduced) works, and such important legal texts as Imam Malik's *al Muwatta'*, Imam al Shafi'i's *al Risalah*, and Imam Ibn Hanbal's *Musnad* are being translated into European languages. The *Concordance and Indices of Muslim Tradition*, which represents the combined effort of about forty scholars from different countries spanning more than half of this century, is of immense value. It consists of all of the important expressions occurring in the six canonical collections, as well as the *Sunan al Darimi*, Imam Malik's *al Muwatta'*, Ibn Hanbal's *Musnad*, arranged in alphabetical order. In addition, new critical methods that may be of use to Muslim scholars, and which they should assess, have been developed.

A Question of Need

Obey God and the Messenger. (3:32; 3:132; 5:92; 8:1; 8:46; 9:71; 24:54; 33:33; 58:13)

Whoever obeys God and His Messenger, He will admit him into Gardens. (4:13)

O believers, obey God and obey the Messenger. (4:59; 8:20; 47:33)

And whoever obeys God and the Messenger. . . (4:69; 24:52; 33:31; 33:71; 48:17)

Whoever obeys the Messenger, obeys God. (4:80)

And if they had referred it to the Messenger and to those in authority. . . (4:83)

You have in God's Messenger a beautiful example. (33:21)

Whatever the Messenger gives you, take. (59:7)

A messenger from among themselves, . . .teaching them the Book and the Wisdom. (2:129)

A messenger from among yourselves, . . .teaching you the Book and the Wisdom. (2:151; 62:2)

An unlettered messenger from among themselves, . . .teaching them the Book and the Wisdom. (3:164)

God has sent down upon you the Book and the Wisdom. (4:113)

It is only for the Messenger to deliver the clear Message. (24:54; 29:18; 64:12)

Grant had only a half an hour for lunch. He had to use the bathroom, wash, pray, and eat. He made for the men's room, remembering to recite the correct formula as he entered it with his left foot—or should it have been his right? He was not sure; it had something to do with the possibility of tripping and falling dead.

He sat down to urinate, doing his best not to soil himself or his clothes. If only his ex-Marine buddies could see him now, going to the toilet like a woman! He tried not to think any thoughts about religion, but trying not to was self-defeating. As he left the stall, he recited another supplication and then headed for the sink. He quickly took off his shoes and socks, careful to step on the coarse brown paper towels he had placed on the floor by the sink so that no part of his feet would touch the bathroom floor. He turned on the water and recited another invocation.

He began the ablution ritual, repeating each action three times: washing his hands, gargling with water, sniffing water in and out of his nostrils, washing his face, washing his right and then his left arm up to the elbow, wiping the inside of his right ear with his wet right index finger, followed by the left, wiping the top of his head and the back of his neck with his wet hands, and finally, washing his right foot and then his left up to the ankle, each time returning his foot to the paper towel from which it came. He recited another supplication. Time was running out, so he picked up his shoes and socks and, making certain that his feet were still on the paper towels, started scuffling on them towards the door.

Just at that moment his manager came into the bathroom. The two men stood face to face: Grant, his bare feet resting on two paper towels and water dripping from his face and arms, and his manager, wide-eyed and dumbfounded. Grant suddenly noticed the coolness of the bathroom floor underneath the heel of his right foot; in the encounter, he had inadvertently let it slide slightly off the paper towel. He gritted his teeth and threw back his head in frustration: now he would have to repeat his ablution.

Of all believers, converts can be the most severe and rigid in their ideas and practices. The new force in which they are immersed and the inner struggles to make sense of it and to respond to it can easily precipitate excesses. Established believers are likely to see them as paradigms of true faith, while they are keenly cognizant of their own weaknesses and temptations. The dual needs to be accepted and to be honest with oneself and others will frequently pull them in opposite directions and will be at the root of many compromises and contradictions. It seems almost unfair that the most dramatic tests of faith come so quickly. The most common reaction is to become a cardboard cut-out Muslim; that is, in outward actions and behavior to adopt what one hears and sees around oneself. This is not born of insincerity but of insecurity, of the need for a new identity, assumed in totality according to the norms of the adopted community. And there is plenty of idiosyncratic behavior—little pieces of advice, kindly shared—to integrate into one's practice, more often then not loosely tied to the Prophet's Sunnah.

As one who has lived through it, the best advice that I can offer a new Muslim is not to adopt any behavior or position unless and until you feel certain of its necessity. Otherwise, you may end up trapping yourself in a corner, unable to be yourself and unable to unload the burdensome behavior without attracting disappointment and suspicion—not only from others but from yourself as well. The escape is usually to leave the community—not to renounce Islam, but to exist anonymously on its fringes. The justification and target of the anger and the feelings of failure is the Sunnah and hadith, or more precisely, the importance that Muslims attach to them. The result is that one has gone from one extreme to another.

How a believer applies the example of Muhammad to his/her own life is almost entirely a personal matter, since very few Muslims are going to be jurists who will contribute to the formulation of rules of conduct for the wider Islamic community. For the common Muslim, the Sunnah guides his or her moral, ethical, and spiritual conduct: the way one relates to one's children and parents, other relatives, friends and neighbors, performs one's prayers and other rituals, and conducts one's business. How successfully it shapes one's life, how great a benefit or burden it yields, depends on individual interpretation and application. For some, the Sunnah requires the wholesale adoption of all of the recorded practices of the Prophet, without considerations of context—his and theirs—to be followed as precisely as possible. As a result, American Muslims can sometimes be found making supplications in Arabic, having practically no idea of what they are saying, or can be seen wearing turbans, robes, and sandals on American city streets. For them, even the most minute detail of the Prophet's example has a spiritual or ritualistic significance, and they testify to the well-springs of faith that they discover in imitating him. For others, the Sunnah is interpreted with the utmost liberality and is disregarded unless it conforms to preconceived ideas. For these, the Prophet was no more than a tool who, for all practical purposes, was to be ignored after the revelation was completed.

Between these two, there are a myriad of responses to Muhammad's example, but almost universally the first approach is adopted towards the rituals. This is in part because the rituals are seen as the believer's door to the Unseen and to mystical converse with the Almighty. Since we are not privy to the realities and truths that Muhammad was shown, we acknowledge, especially in spiritual matters, our blindness and dependence on his prophetic vision. Also, the rituals are the great leveler of the Muslim community, transcending time and place, race and language. While standing in all humility before God, together with fellow Muslims, the ritual of each disciple of Muhammad is the same as that of every other one throughout history, an acknowledgment of the essential spiritual equality with which each of us has entered this world. But a fair number of American Muslims have questioned even this role of the Prophet's example.

On the community level, the Prophet's Sunnah has supported differing interpretations and applications. As the career of Muhammad saw a great diversity of trials and opportunities, Muslim communities have stressed different aspects of his life example according to their circumstances. In this respect, the extent of Muhammad's Sunnah has been wide enough to meet the needs of diverse Muslim groups and flexible enough to serve approaches as dissimilar as the literalist and the Sufi. In the United States, the atmosphere in the Islamic centers located in such big cities as New York and Chicago, which serve the indigenous communities, is quite different from that found in centers run by Muslim student groups at American universities. It would be wrong to conclude from this that, in reality, Muslims are unaffected by the Sunnah, for, despite differences of understanding, the Qur'an and the Sunnah (and both must be included in this) have stamped the character and bearing of all Muslims, regardless of time and place, with qualities and outlooks that are readily recognized as distinctively Islamic. Denny gives a simple and poignant example:

They were Japanese, about twenty men and women, all dressed in white and standing in straight rows behind a stocky, older man with close-cropped hair. This leader recited the first chapter of the Qur'an in perfect Arabic with a resonant voice. The setting was Karachi, Pakistan's international airport transit lounge during the Muslim pilgrimage season, when believers from all over the world make their way to Mecca, in Arabia. The little group of Japanese Muslims was waiting to board the plane for the final leg of their long journey to Jedda, the Red Sea port of entry for the Holy city of Mecca. The Japanese performed their prayers in a small mosque in the terminal, near duty free shops and refreshment stands.

Japan does not have many Muslims, of either Japanese or other descent. But the Japanese Muslims I saw at prayer in Karachi were clearly Japanese—in language, manner, and physical appearance

—but they were also something else. That "something else" is a special style or pattern of behavior and comportment that sets observant Muslims apart from other people, regardless of ethnic, linguistic, cultural, or racial identity.[138]

The upshot of this discussion is that there is no need to see the Prophet's Sunnah as a millstone. People will differ in their understanding of it according to their experiences and circumstances. This may be frustrating for Western converts, since they constitute only a tiny minority in a huge Muslim melting pot. As the Muslim community, especially in the West, combines so many different cultures and traditions, a great deal of maturity and sophistication is needed when dealing with the question of respecting the viewpoints of others. From my own observations, the Western convert is often among the least tolerant.

It is now time to ask the principle question, which I have tried to avoid: Why does the Qur'an need a supplement? We can esteem the labor of the traditionists and the adaptability of the Sunnah, but why complicate our lives with an additional source of guidance? Is not part of the purpose of the Revelation to provide the essentials of guidance and to leave the rest open to the time-bound changes that are certain to occur? By including the Sunnah, are we not narrowing the Qur'an's applicability? Does not the Qur'an itself insist that "it is only for the Messenger to deliver the clear Message"(24:54; 29:l8;64:l2)?

The answers will depend on one's approach to the Qur'an, for that is where the question originates. Muslim exegetes uphold the importance of knowing the occasion of a particular revelation—the historic incident(s) that the verses of the Qur'an addressed—in order to gain a fuller understanding of its message. But this has not prevented them from reading additional meanings (that is, levels of meaning) that reach far beyond the occasions that gave rise to them. This is supported by the personal experience of the believer, who, in his/her daily reading of the Qur'an, discovers new directions and import in passages read many times before. Traditionally, Muslims have been extremely cautious about attaching a final meaning or set of meanings to any verse, for "None but God knows its final meaning (4:134)" and "Though all the trees in the earth were pens, and the sea were ink, with seven seas after it to replenish it, the words of God would never be exhausted, for God is All-Mighty, All-Wise" (31:27, 18:109). Based on this understanding, Muslims have been opposed to the idea that the Qur'an contains verses that are outdated.

---

[138]Fredrick Denny, *Islam and the Muslim Community* (San Francisco: Harper & Row, 1987), 5-6.

Even those who assume the theory of abrogation (i.e., that some verses annul others) usually say that this means that certain verses focus or narrow the meaning of other verses on the same subject, and then admit the possibility of additional lessons, meanings, and interpretations to be drawn from them.

The idea that verses of the Qur'an are obsolete, in the sense of not having any application beyond the historic incident addressed, is a hazardous one. If we assume that there are Qur'anic passages that have no relation to the present or the future, then the wisdom of God and the concept of the Qur'an as universal guidance is diminished. That God would include obsolete information within the final Revelation imposes limitations on His power and knowledge. In addition, it would be up to each individual or community to decide what parts of the Revelation to ignore or apply. In this way, humanity would guide the Qur'an instead of the Qur'an's guiding man. Since Islam has no clerical hierarchy, it goes without saying that with such an approach the unity of the Muslim community would be jeopardized. The alternative is to assume that the Qur'an is a universal message in its entirety, and that each generation of believers is duty bound to seek, interpret, and apply its lessons and directives. This approach is difficult, although appealing. But, it must be asked, does it stand up to scrutiny?

There are Qur'anic passages that, at first glance, appear historically, culturally, or geographically fixed. However, a deeper analysis reveals that the Qur'an instructs in a very natural way, imparting lessons of general import by considering concrete examples, such as those that relate to the following verses:

1. Make ready for them whatever force and bands of steeds you can muster, that you may strike terror in the enemies of God and your own, and others beside them not known to you, but known to God. (8:60)

2. O Prophet, why do you forbid [for yourself] what God has made permissible for you, seeking to please your wives? Yet God is forgiving and kind. Surely God has made permissible for you the dissolution of your vows. And God is your Protector, and He is the All-Knowing, the All-Wise. And when the Prophet confided a matter to one of his wives and when she disclosed it, and Allah made it open to him, he made known part of it to her and avoided part of it. Then when he told her about it, she said: "Who has told you about this?" He said, "I was told by the All-Knowing, the All-Aware." . .O you who believe, save yourselves and your families from the Fire whose fuel is men and stones. . . . (66:1-3, 6)

3. O you who believe, let your dependents and those who have not yet reached the age of puberty, ask permission [to enter your presence] on three occasions: before the dawn prayer; when you disrobe for the midday siesta; and after prayer at night. These are the three times of nakedness for you.(24:58)

4. The expiation for it [breaking an oath] is feeding ten poor people with such average food as you feed your own families, or clothing them, or freeing a slave. (5:89)

5. Have you not seen how your Lord dealt with the People of the Elephant? Did He not make their plans go astray, and sent against them hordes of birds, pelting them with stones of hardened clay, and made them like eaten-up stubble? (105:1-5)

6. For the journeys of the Quraysh, their journeys by winter and summer: then let them worship the Lord of this House, who feeds them against hunger and gives them security against fear. (l06:1-4)[139]

In the first passage, Muslims understand that, although God helps those who struggle in the cause of right, they should not engage in battle unprepared. Rather, they should seek and employ weapons and strategy that will give them a military advantage, such as, for the early Muslim community, a skilled cavalry. The aim is more than to secure victory: it is to create a deterrent, to "strike terror" in the hearts of potential enemies, whether known or unknown, in order to discourage aggression and bloodshed.

The second example, related to the Prophet's family life, demonstrates vividly that our families provide one of the greatest and most challenging opportunities for growth and decline, as well as one of the most difficult tests of the intention to serve only God. First of all, the Prophet is criticized for forswearing any contact with his wives, apparently too drastic a response to what had taken place. His wives are reprimanded severely for violating their husband's confidence, thereby giving rise to petty and damaging domestic tension. Throughout, God reminds us of His forgiveness, for these trials are bound to occur. The general admonition follows.

From the third passage we discern that although not all cultures observe an afternoon siesta, we should follow certain principles of privacy and modesty within our families. As for the fourth passage, many Qur'anic reg-

---

[139]See Asad, *The Message*, 22-23, for an argument against the theory of abrogation. See also Ali, *The Religion of Islam*, 31-45; John Burton, *The Collection of the Qur'an* (London: Cambridge University Press, 1977), pp. 234-40.

ulations clearly allude to the abolition of slavery, and the Muslim community will forever have to live with the embarrassment of its being the last to formally dissolve this institution. While slavery has finally been eliminated, many modern Muslim writers have read in the verses enjoining the freeing of slaves the analogous requirement to free a fellow human being from the bondage of severe debt as one means of atoning for breaking an oath.

Finally, regarding the fifth and sixth examples, surahs 105 and 106 may seem to have little relevance today, but these are among those most often recollected by pilgrims as they proceed along the dusty roads of Makkah toward the Holy Shrine. Surrounded by that stark and threatening landscape stands the simple yet exquisite Ka'bah, like a beautiful jewel set in stone, prepared, preserved, and protected by God Almighty, in the most unlikely of places, to be visited and shared by all pilgrims. Here, the Muslim comes to experience personally and poignantly the sense of being truly a part of God's eternal plan.

Muslims have always been able to read the verses of the Qur'an into their lives—not only out of desire but also out of deep necessity, for its message penetrates faithfully and profoundly into their immediate needs and ordeals. Hence we find that as the temporal separation of Muslim commentators from seventh-century Arabia increases, the more they stress the transcendence and coherence of the Qur'an in its entirety.

If this approach is taken, then how does one react to the verses with which I began this section? For the relatively small but significant hard core of pious enthusiasts in the first generations of Islam, it is hard to imagine how they could have responded in a way that differs substantially from that recorded by history: the zealous collection of thousands of major and minute details concerning the Prophet's life and conduct. This was the most natural and obvious response for those inclined to scholarly investigation at that time.

The Qur'an itself appears to foresee this early development, and not only in the verses I have quoted. Take, for instance, the following somewhat back-handed references:

> O wives of the Prophet, **you are not like any other women**. If you are mindful of God, do not be too soft in your speech, so that the one in whose heart there is disease feels desire, but speak honorable words. And stay in your houses, and do not deck yourselves out as did the pagans of old. (33:32-33)

> O Prophet, We have made permissible to you your wives to whom you have given their dower and those whom your right hand possesses out of what God has assigned to you [from among the

female prisoners of war], and the daughters of your paternal uncles and paternal aunts, and the daughters of your maternal uncles and your maternal aunts who migrated with you, and any believing woman who bestows herself [in marriage] to the Prophet if the Prophet desires to marry her. **This is for you exclusively—apart from the believers.** We know what We have ordained for them about their wives and what their right hands possess. (33:50)

Both of these verses seem to anticipate the idealization of Muhammad's example, while at the same time cautioning that this should be done carefully and intelligently and with due consideration of the special status of Muhammad, his family, his nearest Companions, and his times. As for the verses that assert that it is "only for the Messenger to convey the clear Message," they follow exhortations to obey God and the Messenger, and stern warnings to those who do otherwise: "And if you turn your backs, it is only for the Messenger to deliver the clear Message," indicating that the responsibility for one's future course is solely upon one's own shoulders, now that the Message has been communicated clearly.

These verses should be understood in the context of the more abundant references stressing obedience to the Messenger and the several statements designating Muhammad as being charged with teaching and receiving the revelation of "the Book and the Wisdom." Teaching involves more than transferring a text: it requires explanation and demonstration as well. In general, Muslims have considered the example and teachings of Muhammad as part of his guiding legacy, and they view the need to study and understand that heritage as being just as important now as it was to earlier generations. This approach is, I feel, the most consistent with the Qur'an, which, while warning against the deification of men, appears to acknowledge the need for a human exemplar. Yet there remains another related question: Is every hadith adjudged to be authentic by scholarly consensus really true?

A Question of Truth

"I find it hard to believe that the Prophet said that."
"But, brother, that hadith is sahih!"
"Yes, I know, but do you think it's really true?"
"It's sahih! If you don't accept a hadith that has been classified as sahih, you're not a Muslim."
"Why didn't anyone tell me that before I converted?"

Most new Muslims soon learn that to harbor any doubt about the veracity of a hadith accepted by the consensus of scholarly opinion is tantamount to a breach in faith. In this way, they are pushed to rationalize too severe a doctrine. It is a radical tenet that no error whatsoever could have slipped by Muslim traditionists in their centuries of research, and it comes close to equating the integrity of their human effort with that of the revelation of the Qur'an. Strangely enough, the notion of the inerrancy of *sahih* traditions is countered by both the formal doctrines and actions of Muslim jurists and scholars throughout Islamic history.

The very fact that those who specialize in Islamic jurisprudence consider the authority of the authenticated traditions as second to that of the Qur'an admits the possibility of imperfections in the traditions. Equally significant is the fact that although the *sahih* traditions enjoy a position of high honor in Islam, qualified experts have felt the right to challenge those traditions generally believed to be genuine without jeopardizing their Islam. This continues until this day.

For example, Abu al Hasan 'Ali al Daraqutni (d. 385 AH), in his *Criticism and Investigation*, challenged the reliability of two hundred tradtions in the canonical collections. The incident of the "satanic verses," in which Muhammad supposedly compromised his message to suit the pagans of Makkah, has been judged by Muslim orthodoxy as entirely fictitious, even though it appears in *Sahih al Bukhari*. Such eminent scholars as al Baqil-lani, al Juwayni, and al Ghazali reject a saying in *Sahih al Bukhari* and label it untrue.[140] Ibn al Mulaqqin (d. 804 AH) said of a certain tradition in al Bukhari's collection: "This is a strange saying. If al Bukhari had spared his book this, it might have been better."[141] Recently, Muhammad 'Ali challenged the hadith in *Sahih al Bukhari* that deals with the stoning of adulterers.[142] Fazlur Rahman attacked the tradition, found in the same source, about women being the majority of the inhabitants of Hell.[143] Yet none of these scholars is viewed as having renounced Islam due to their criticisms.

The inerrancy of the traditions is a popular belief among the Muslim masses. It could be a legacy of the era of *taqlid* (imitation), when the doors to independent reasoning in jurisprudence were closed in favor of the unquestioning adoption of legal decisions arrived at by the four

---

[140]Al Qastallani, 7:173.
[141]Ibid., 8:40.
[142]Ali, *The Religion of Islam*, 756-58.
[143]Fazlur Rahman, *Health and Medicine in the Islamic Tradition* (New York: Crossroad Pub., 1987), 105-106.

schools of Islamic law.[144] However this came to be, the fact remains that Muslim scholarship always has exercised the freedom to challenge individual authenticated sayings, while recognizing the overall high integrity of those hadith that have been classified as *sahih*.

Given the above, one can with some legitimacy raise the following questions: If we admit that there are possible flaws in the canon of hadith, does it not decrease their validity as a source of guidance? Does such a possibility not open the way to errors based on inaccurate information?

First of all, we must accept that any response by human beings to divine revelation runs the risk of being flawed, simply because of our inherent limitations. In conjunction with this, we must realize that the massive and vigorous action of Muslim scholars, undertaken since the earliest days of the community, to collect, disseminate, and test information on the Prophet's example was indeed a **response** to the Qur'an, particularly the injuction to "obey God and the Prophet." This was not a scattered and individual reaction, but a collective response that incorporated cross-examination, comparison, and criticism. Certainly not one of us, if we had lived during the first few centuries of the Islamic era, would have doubted that this effort was valid and in harmony with the Revelation.

That early response to "obey God and the Prophet" decidedly affects us today, for we have inherited the methods, tools, and results of the early scholars, and because no interpretation that avoids careful consideration of that first response can be taken seriously. Classical Islamic law was aware of the above objection and thus formulated a hierarchy of approaches to the decision-making process. It gave priority to the Qur'an, then to Muham-mad's Sunnah, then to analogies drawn from these, and, lastly, to independent opinion (*ra'y*). The lines between these priorities are sometimes obscured in practice, as there is some overlap. Moreover, the Muslims of one generation will criticize and review the activities and conclusions of scholars of preceding generations with regard to their application of this model. But by this hierarchy, they understood that there was a gradation of means to get to and follow the spirit of the Revelation, and that the observance of these precedents was the best possible insurance against error. This formulation became the standard Islamic praxis in the beginning of the third Islamic century and has held sway ever since by force of argument, for it was the one that comformed most perfectly to a coherent approach to the Qur'an and to the history of the Muslim community's response to it.

---

[144]Ibid., 115-16.

Who Is Muhammad?

This chapter shares some ideas on the implications of this question for all Muslims and how it may be approached by new converts.

In order to emulate the qualities and behavior of another, we have to be able to identify with him to some extent. Such an identification is so tied to our personality and his, that answers to this question will depend on the believer and the stage that his/her life has reached. All answers may intersect in a common understanding, but many unique perceptions will continue to exist. Certainly my own perceptions of Muhammad are deeper and perhaps more real than they were eight years ago, although I am sure there is yet much more to understand.

Right now, I would say that if I were to describe the Prophet, my description would be close to that of Watt quoted above. My guess is that for Muhammad to have won the great respect of his followers, they must have seen him as the most perfect personification of the traditional ideal of what it meant to be an Arab leader: one who "keeps good relations with kith and kin, helps the poor and the destitute, serves his guests generously and assists the deserving calamity-afflicted ones."[145] He must have been, as tradition reports, a man of great integrity, forbearance, and courage, for the Arabs could have accepted no less. His word must have been as hard as steel to have captured his Companions' total confidence. When he decided on a course of action he unwaveringly saw it through.

But to have been the elect of God, to have won the love of his disciples so effortlessly, to have changed society and history to the extent he did, he was surely much greater than merely the Arab ideal. He must have possessed the kind of concern, compassion, and spirituality that we can only poorly approximate in ourselves. To be sure, he was no flower child: he would dispense God's law swiftly and impartially. When some of his Companions pleaded that he make an exception in the law for a noble woman who committed theft, he responded that if his most cherished daughter Fatimah did the same, he would see to it personally that her hand were amputated.[146] On the other hand, when there was the smallest room for doubt or excuse, or a way open for forgiveness, he would seize it, as when he gave an adulterer three opportunities to withdraw his

---

[145]Asad, *Sahih al Bukhari*, 207. This is Ibn al Daghinnah's description of Abu Bakr. But Khadijah, the wife of the Prophet, comforted him in identical terms after he had received the first revelation. Apparently this was a commonly held definition in pre-Islamic times of an "upright man."

[146]*Sahih al Bukhari*, trans. Muhammad Muhsin Khan, vol. 5, "The Book of Military Expeditions (59), Hadith no. 597.

confession or when he declared a general amnesty after his conquest of Makkah.[147]

Muhammad also had the sensitivity to know when and how to upraise and humble those around him, including himself, with perfect honesty. After the victory at Hunayn, it came to his attention that the Ansar, who had given refuge and support to him when no other community would and who had risked their lives defending his Message during the most critical years, felt slighted when the Prophet "bypassed" them in favor of the newly-converted Makkans, who had been his most implacable foes, in the distribution of spoils. The feeling spread among them that after this final victory, Muhammad's attention and affection would return completely to his Makkan kinsfolk. At that, he immediately called for a private meeting with the Ansar and addressed them thus:

> "I have been told that you are dissatisfied at my ostensible partiality towards the Quraysh chiefs." "Yes," they replied, "there are some amongst us who are talking like that." Then the Prophet said: "Is it not true that I came in your midst while you were misguided; so God guided you to the right path. You were indigent; God made you prosperous. You were ever at daggers drawn with one another; God created mutual affection in your hearts." Lowering their heads in embarrassment, they replied that all that was true. "You could also reply differently and you would be justified. You could say that I came over to you when I was belied and rejected by my own people and you accepted me. I came to you when no one would help me, and you stood by me. I was turned out of my home, and you gave me shelter. O Ansar! Did it make you suspicious that I gave a portion of worldly riches for the purpose of conciliation, thinking that Islam was already ample reward for you? O Ansar! Are you not satisfied to take home with you the Messenger of God, while others drive home goats and camels? By God, in whose hands is my soul, if all the people go one way and the Ansar take another, I will tread the path of the Ansar!" Needless to say, the moment he finished, there was a spontaneous outburst of joy and tears in the audience.[148]

---

[147]Ali, *Religion of Islam*, 214-21.
[148]*Sahih al Bukhari*, trans. Muhammad Muhsin Khan, vol. 5, "The book of Military Expeditions, (59), Hadith nos. 614-25.; Ali, *The Religion of Islam*, 227-28.

After eight years, these are among the perceptions of Muhammad that have become a part of me. If his wives are like mothers to the believers, then maybe the Prophet is like a father to them. This would be, at least for me, the most appropriate one word symbol for the combined feelings of respect, awe, and love that I have come to hold for Muhammad, the Messenger of God.

CHAPTER 4

The Ummah

And hold fast, all of you together, to the rope of Allah and do not be divided. And recall Allah's favor upon you: how you were enemies and He brought about reconciliation between your hearts so that you became, by His grace, brothers; and you were on the brink of an abyss of fire and He saved you from it. (3:103)

It was nearing the end of summer and I would soon be going off to college for the first time. I sat in the school yard by the fence, waiting for my team to play the winners of an ongoing half-court game. On an average night, there would be around fifty kids from our mostly Italian neighborhood hanging out at Sheridan school. Tonight there were about ten. A young black boy rode up to me on his bicycle. "You better go home, Jeff. There's gonna be trouble tonight."

I needed no further explanation. Three days earlier, several young men from our neighborhood had attacked a black teenager from Beardsley Terrace in retaliation for the night during which one of ours was jumped and had his nose broken. It was our turn to face requital—and then it would be theirs, and then ours, and then theirs again, going back and forth forever. I couldn't wait to escape from all this.

Maybe our urban areas have always been a dumping ground for the waste products of our society's unrelenting greed and neglect, for a refuse that is incinerated in the fear, violence, and rage of our cities' children, and which our nation isolates and contains rather than corrects, due to economic considerations. I have heard it said many times that these kids are hardly children—they are criminals. But what did we possibly expect? For have they not been robbed of their childhoods, raped of their innocence, hardened by our dereliction? Someone has to pay the price. How many times does the Qur'an warn us of the needs of the yatim, the poor lost and abandoned children?

Hastily I tried to talk one of my teammates into leaving. But it was too late. The fences and walls surrounding the schoolyard were now being scaled adeptly by lean young black warriors numbering more than one hundred. The idea in such situations is to try to drastically outpower the other side, to catch its members off guard. Tonight we miscued. Several cars screeched to a halt in front of the playground fence. Car doors and trunks flew open. A shout of "We got fire and we know how to use it!" rang out in the darkness.

Guns were tossed into nervous hands, their barrels gleaming beneath the street lights. At moments like this, fear is not the right word; numbness and shock are closer to the mark. You aren't thinking of getting hurt because you are now relying on your instincts. It was not yet time to run since running too early could spark a nervous reaction that could be fatal. We were centered around the basketball net. It would all be over soon.

Furman Jackson, the victim of last week's assault, defiantly marched into the schoolyard. He was pointing out his attackers: "It was him, and him, and him!"

His judgment was precise and accurate. City violence is usually very efficient. There's no use in creating new enemies and vendettas. But how bizarre this all was! I remembered how these same kids, who were about to face their judgment, a few months earlier had initiated a new Jewish fellow into our neighborhood by beating and kicking him, leaving him lying and crying in the snow, begging and pleading while they cackled and jeered. They say that what goes around comes around.

Furman turned toward me. I had known him since fourth grade, and even then he was always trouble. Children have a natural affinity and attraction to each other, but already, in fourth grade, we had sensed out the barriers that barred us from one another. Somehow I saw in his face the boy of eleven that I could never get to know. I wonder what he saw in mine.

"He's all right!"

I stepped slowly backwards, making my way toward the only exit. Dennis, another of the vindicated, followed close to me. The crowd parted and let us through. No one wanted to be there. We have to overcome all kinds of resistance and compassion in situations like this, to dig down once again into a deep reserve of brutality. It may look easy but it actually takes considerable practice.

When I stepped outside the gate, I turned around. There was movement in the crowd, something like a dancing motion, like a swirling breeze rustling through tall grass, as they maneuvered for position. Then came a loud clapping sound and within seconds, an angry cyclone had ripped through, leaving several bodies uprooted on the hot schoolyard tar. I ran—like everyone else, I ran. Running, scattering. From the police? From the pain? From the horror? Who knows? We all ran!

That night, and other days and nights like it, kept coming back to me while I listened to 'Abd al 'Alim Musa's lecture to the Muslim students at the University of San Francisco. Confused emotions—learned reflexes—

120

were colliding with my impressions of the speaker. He was a tall, strong, imposing black American, clever and sharp-witted. Ten years earlier, he could have been a dangerous opponent. I was told that once he had been a member of the Black Panthers and that he had gone to prison because of it. It was hard to see that in this man, who was so much at peace with himself and others.

A few questions into the question-and-answer period, he was asked, "Do you feel Islam has affected your life?"

His expression changed, as if he were surprised or impatient with the question, like when I have to explain an idea to one of my students for the tenth time.

"People just don't realize—they really can't believe the power of Islam," he said, shaking his head. Then he aimed his finger at Grant and me on the other side of the room and proclaimed: "The very fact that you have white men like these sitting together with black men like us" (referring to the Afro-American Muslims who had accompanied him from Oakland) "as brothers, when just ten years ago we were killing each other in the streets, tells you how much impact Islam can have on a life!"

It was as if he were reading my mind.

'Abd al 'Alim walked over to me after the program and extended his hand. I could not remember the last time I had shaken hands with a black man—I mean, really shaken hands, with warmth and love. Had I ever? And it hurt deeply, because it hurts to release our pains, for we first have to wrench them out and face them again. And pains that we have gotten used to—that we have even come to depend on—can be difficult to release and forget.

At that time, I had only been a Muslim for about a month. I would learn a great deal from 'Abd al 'Alim during the next five years that I spent in San Francisco. However, the deepest lesson I took from him was of the brotherhood of man.

There is great celebration in the Muslim community at the news of a new believer, something like when a family receives a newborn. That comparison is made frequently, for a new Muslim is reminded repeatedly that his/her past sins are now behind him and that his/her soul is white as snow, like that of a baby at birth. One Muslim friend used to tell me how fortunate I was and that he was even a little bit jealous of me. The outpouring of affection could be overwhelming at times, as is the lengths to which the community will go sometimes to help you make the transition successfully.

Just like a child, the newcomer is bombarded with advice, tips, and instruction. He/she has adopted and been adopted by a new family and has acquired brothers and sisters from all corners of the world—from very different cultures like Saudi Arabia, Pakistan, Malaysia; from such "enemy" lands as Iran, Iraq, Libya, and Palestine; and from such unknown places as Mali, Tanzania, Yemen, and Nepal. And he/she begins to empathize with their triumphs, sufferings, and dreams as they become more and more his/her own. The Prophet once said that the believers are like a person's body: if one of its members get sick, the whole body suffers.[149] So when a Palestinian home is demolished, or an earthquake kills thousands in Iran, or Muslims die fighting in Afghanistan, the believers everywhere feel insult and anguish, because "the believers are indeed brothers of each other" (49:10) and "the believing men and believing women are protectors of one another" (9:71). This sense of mutual responsibility is fortified by the sayings of Muhammad, among which we find: "You do not truly believe unless you love for your brother, what you love for yourself,"[150] "No one may call himself a believer who eats his fill while his neighbor remains hungry,"[151] and "You should help your brother whether he is wronged or doing wrong. If he is wronged defend him, and if he is doing wrong prevent him."[152]

Islam has long been recognized for its egalitarianism, and many occidental scholars have attributed the relatively recent peaceful spread of Islam throughout Africa to it. For upon entering the ummah, one discovers that a single standard applies to all members and, beyond that, to all humanity:

O mankind! Lo! We have created you male and female and have made you nations and tribes that you may know one another. Lo! the noblest among you in the sight of God is he who is best in conduct. (49:13)

This verse succinctly summarizes the Qur'an's universalism. It begins —as the Qur'an so often does—by addressing all humanity. The summons, "O mankind!" appears about twenty-five times throughout the Qur'an and indicates that the call is intended for all. The next sentence maintains the essential equality of all people, whether male or female. In many places, the Qur'an tells us that in our families and close relations there are critical opportunities for personal and spiritual growth. This verse rounds out that idea by informing us that human diversity provides us with

---

[149]*Sahih al Bukhari*, trans. Muhammad Muhsin Khan, vol. 8, "The Book of Good Manners" (71), Hadith no. 40.
[150]Ibid., 3:6.
[151]Asad, *Road to Mecca*, 297.
[152]*Sahih al Bukhari*, trans. Muhammad Muhsin Khan, vol. 3, "The Book of Oppressions" (43), Hadith nos. 623-24.

important tests as well, for justice, love, and compassion grow in another dimension when applied to those we view as different from ourselves. This concept can also be found in 30:22.

Such concepts presented the greatest challenge to Muhammad's pagan contemporaries, who were convinced that nobility depended only on one's descent. In pre-Islamic Arabia, one of the main features of the annual pilgrimage was the holding of poetry contests so that the participants could boast of their tribal and ancestral greatness, as well as their family's name, which, albeit with less emphasis, still plays a considerable role in determining one's status and opportunities in Arabian society. Thus, 2:200 admonishes the Arabs to remember God at the pilgrimage with as much devotion as they remember their ancestors, or even more than that. The principle that nobility depends on piety, and that tribal, national, racial, and linguistic differences are not reasons for division and hatred among individuals and groups (30:22), was certain to upset the entire established order of pre-Islamic society, especially if there were enough individuals daring enough to put it into practice.

This is why the Prophet's exodus to Yathrib (the pre-Islamic name of Madinah) and his subsequent establishment of the city-state of Madinah posed such a serious threat to pagan Arabia. It must have been clear to astute minds that the two systems—tribal and egalitarian—could not coexist. For twelve years in Makkah, this conflict had expressed itself primarily as a war of words and wills, as Muhammad and his followers were persecuted and boycotted by the powerful Quraysh. Then, when the representatives of the two opposing systems met on the battlefield of Badr one year after the migration to Madinah, sons fought against fathers, nephews against uncles, cousins against cousin—something unthinkable in tribal society. At the conclusion of the battle, after the Muslims had repulsed an army three times the size of their own, all of Arabia realized that the winds of change had arrived.

For Muslims, the community of believers is where Islam's equalitarian principles are to be implemented in practice, where those committed to its worldview are to participate—through faith, government, and law—in translating them into a socio-political order. But Islam's concern is not exclusively with its adherents, it extends to all mankind. It is important to observe that when the Qur'an enjoins giving charity to the needy, caring for orphans and widows, dealing justly, defending the oppressed, freeing slaves, and helping the wayfarer, no mention is made of the sufferers' religion. The Qur'an describes the Muslim ummah as the "best community" (3:110). For serving the one God? For worship? For believing in the correct dogma? No. They should be the "best community brought forth **for**

mankind": defending right, opposing wrong, and fighting against tyranny and oppression as servants of God.

What ails you that you do not fight in the cause of God and the helpless men, women and children who say, "O our Lord, bring us out of this land whose people are oppressors, and appoint for us from Yourself a protector, and appoint for us from Yourself a helper." (4:75)

In the words of the Qur'an (i.e., 2:30; 6:165; 10:14; 27:62; 35:39), human beings are the *khulafa'* (vicegerents) of God on earth and are to look after the unfortunate and oppressed.

The five pillars of the Islamic faith, which are the ritual embodiment of Islam's ideology, conspicuously unite humanity's duty to God and the individual's obligations to humanity. The *Shahadah*, the testimony of faith that an individual must repeat before being considered a Muslim, has always represented for Muslims much more than a statement of belief; it is a socio-political commitment as well and hence must be witnessed by at least two members of the community. The *Shahadah* also represents a person's acknowledgment and acceptance of the divine trust of acting as God's vicegerent on earth.

The zakah, usually translated as a poor-tax and consisting of a fixed percentage of a Muslim's wealth, must be given every year to those entitled to it: those in various kinds of need. The humanitarian concern behind such an institution is obvious. The month long fast of Ramadan, during which Muslims abstain from food, drink, and sex between dawn and sunset, creates intense feelings of solidarity among the believers. But it also has another purpose: to produce in each Muslim a strong sympathy for the world's poor and hungry, and an incentive to translate that sympathy into action. Two examples will suffice to make this point.

This past Ramadan, as I was out walking just before sunset, I heard a voice yell from a passing car, "Hey, Jeff! How's the fasting going?" It was another American Muslim—and to be honest, it was not going very well that day at all, for it was a very hot day and I was terribly thirsty. I called out, "I'm hanging in there!" As he drove away he held a thumbs-up outside his window. This gave me a big emotional boost and made me feel very close, not only to this man but to all Muslims, because it reminded me that several hundred million Muslims around the world were "hanging in there" with me that day as well.

One day during another Ramadan, I had overslept a bit and hence had missed the time of the light pre-dawn meal. Therefore, I would, in effect, have to go for twenty-four hours without food or drink. While this is not the end of the world, it is not easy, especially on a work day, as this was. I grew increasingly thirsty and fatigued as the hours of the day crawled along, and, at about five in the afternoon, I began to have some soreness in my stomach and a headache. By eight o'clock, a little more than an hour before sunset, I was nauseated and my head was pounding. My eyes burned as if someone had knotted them in their sockets. I lay down and tried to nap the last remaining hour but I was too uncomfortable. It was too painful to open my eyes, yet I could not sleep. Through the last half hour of the fast, I was counting every minute. Finally, it was 9:15 p.m. But even then I could not eat; I was too sick.

My wife brought me a small cup of light broth, and I began to sip it a little at a time. Sure enough, my headache began to dissipate, my stomach returned to normal, and my eyes slowly unwound. Within several minutes I felt perfectly normal. We were watching the news while eating, and there was a report on the starvation in Ethiopia and Somalia. The pictures of the gaunt, near-dead victims reminded me of the films we see of the Holocaust. I thought of how simple it had been for me to end my anguish, while men and women my age had to live in infinitely greater, permanent agony with no relief in sight and to stand by helplessly while their naked infants with bloated, ulcerated stomachs lay kicking weakly in the dust. Maybe at that moment I should have felt blessed, but I saw in their terrible suffering that I had failed a test.

Hajj, the pilgrimage to Makkah, has changed many a Muslim's life. Perhaps the most dramatic day is when the mass of pilgrims throng to the Plain of 'Arafat. There they gather, clad in the identical pilgrim's garb, speaking hundreds of languages, in the often blinding heat, rededicating themselves to their faith and humanity. It is a foreshadowing of the Day of Judgment, when all human beings, of every time and place, will be gathered on an endless plain, to face what they have truly become in this earthly life. For Malcom X, the Hajj represented a tremendous turning point, which he expressed in these words:

For the last week, I have been utterly speechless and spellbound by the graciousness I see displayed all around me by people of all colors. . . You may be shocked by these words coming from me. But on this pilgrimage, what I have seen, and experienced, has forced me to rearrange much of my thought patterns previously held, and to toss aside some of my previous conclusions . . . Perhaps if white Americans could accept the Oneness of God, then perhaps, too, they could accept in reality the Oneness of Man—

and cease to measure and hinder and harm others in terms of their "differences" in color. . . Each hour in the Holy Land [Arabia] enables me to have greater spiritual insights into what is happening in America between black and white.[153]

The only pillar still left unmentioned is the ritual prayer (*salah*). While individual prayer is encouraged, congregational prayer has priority. Of course, communal prayer, as Jesus is reported to have stated in the Bible, can be performed as much for show as for true piety.[154] Although the Qur'an warns of such hypocrisy (4:142, 107:1-7), the Prophet told his followers that prayer observed in congregation has over twenty times the value of prayer performed alone, a statement that stresses once again the importance of the community.[155]

The members of the congregation arrange themselves in tight formation, standing shoulder to shoulder and foot to foot at the start of the prayer, which consists of a number of cycles of standing, bowing, sitting, and prostrating. In the first two cycles (*rak'ats*) of the dawn, sunset, and evening prayers, the Qur'an is recited aloud by the prayer leader (imam), while in the remaining cycles of these three prayers (the dawn prayer has two cycles, the sunset three, and the evening four), as well as in all the cycles of the noon and afternoon prayer, the imam and the members of the congregation recite the Qur'an silently. Typically, the movements of the worshippers are slightly out of synchronization in the first cycle, but with each additional cycle they become more fluid and uniform, so that by the last cycle the worshippers seem to unconsciously anticipate one other's movements and the entire congregation moves as one. The experience is close to hypnotic. The prayer ends with the greeting of peace to those on one's right and left. Thus the Islamic prayer is a glorious and graceful confluence of recitation, instruction, movement, rhythm, and ritual, drawing the believer first outward to the community, then inward to private communication with God, and then back outside again with the greeting of peace at the prayer's end. In fact, that rhythm of mystical converse and community interdependence is maintained throughout the salah in the synchronous movements of the congregation.

A Muslim student I knew in San Francisco found that aspect of the Islamic prayer disturbing. "Why do we have to pray so close together, in

---

[153]CharrisWaddy, *The Muslim Mind* (London: Longman, n.d.), 113-16.
[154]May and Metzger, *The New Oxford Annotated Bible*. See the Sermon on the Mount, in Matthew 6:5-8.
[155]*Sahih al Bukhari*, trans. Muhammad Muhsin Khan, vol. 1, "The Book of the Call to Prayer" (11), Hadith no. 618.

such close proximity to each other? Here I am, trying to concentrate all my attention on God, and yet I am constantly conscious of someone's body brushing against me on my right and left!"

I told him that I thought he had arrived at an important observation that uncovers a fundamental precept of Islam: even in your most intense worship, you are not to forget your brother or sister on your right and on your left. In other words, your personal and spiritual welfare and salvation is inseparably linked to your response to your fellow human beings.

Recently a great deal of literature has been published in the West on the current Islamic "resurgence," with attempts to explain the underlying causes. The effects of modernization, colonialism, neocolonialism, the defeat and partition of the Ottoman empire, and the Muslims' frustration and Third World status are frequently cited. Undoubtedly these have played a role. But the current global Islamic revival is fueled mostly by young people, for whom the above-mentioned historical experiences are part of a distant past in their homelands. To understand the present calls for pan-Islamism and the establishment of Islamic states, it has to be understood that most of these longings are now being born and nurtured in the Islamic centers and student-run mosques in the United States and Europe.

If we listen to the Friday sermons, we can see that at the heart of these aspirations is the Qur'anic vision of the unity of humanity under the unity of God. In these Muslim communities, believers from numerous and diverse cultures have had to cooperate in building an Islamic lifestyle in the West. Tensions often are high due to disagreement over the ways this should be done and old prejudices surface every now and then. But the communities stick together, for the vision of Islamic brotherhood is more powerful than the racial and cultural obstacles. And through it all, Muslims have come to know that somehow that Islamic vision could become a reality, and that the chance to make it one may be greater now than it has been for several centuries.

And those who came after them say: "Our Lord, forgive us and our brothers [and sisters] who preceded us in faith, and let there not be in our hearts any ill-will toward those who have believed. Our Lord, You are most kind, most merciful." (59:10)

QUESTIONS

Her young voice echoed over the loud-speaker in the huge auditorium: "Many Muslim women feel that the separation of the sexes at conferences like this does more harm than good. The sisters are trapped back up here in the balcony, two thousand feet from the stage, while the men

127

occupy the main floor. Therefore we have unequal access to the speaker and we have to fight to get our questions heard and addressed. This is the situation regardless of whether the lecturer is male or female. It leaves us with a feeling of inferiority and secondary status. My question to each of the speakers is: Do you not feel that, in our present day, the detriments of segregation outweigh the benefits, and does there exist enough room in Islam to allow, at meetings like this, the men and women to sit on the same floor, trusting them to observe modest and respectful behavior?"

The audience at the youth session tensed, so much so that you could here the moderator's breathing in the microphone. The three young male American Muslim speakers, sitting behind the table on the stage, looked at each other to see who would take the question. The two on the extreme ends of the table shook their heads, passing the burden to the moderator. He cleared his throat and began slowly and cautiously.

"This is more. . . a question that. . . should be decided in your local masjid (mosque). Uh. . . uh . . . by a scholar. I remember one time we tried to run a session like that at a conference and because of the behavior of a few of the men, some sisters got really angry. Are there any more questions?"

"I thought the purpose of the youth conference is to open questions and discussions." It was the same faceless voice from above. "How are we ever going to find answers to our problems if we don't discuss them, and why is this a question for our local communities when it has to do with practices at our nationwide gatherings? What I am trying. . . ."

"I'm sorry, sister, but we don't have much more time, and we have another question on the floor!"

The youth sessions at the many Islamic conferences held throughout the year are by far the most exciting and interesting of all the programs offered. Questions of vital importance to the future of Islam in the West are put forth boldly and courageously, more often than not by the young women. This may be because the future of the Muslim community rests so heavily on the convergence of those two forces: women and children.

While the duty of Muslim men has been primarily to protect and maintain the system, the shape of tomorrow's Islamic society depends ultimately on the Muslim mother and child. I always come away from the youth sessions reinvigorated with hope, because they demonstrate that many of our young people are not afraid to stand up and raise issues that need to be raised. But I am also aware that this hope may be unwarranted, for intrepidity is a characteristic of youth, which could give way in adulthood, as this incident also shows, to the impulse to protect one's position by avoiding sensitive issues and thereby upholding the status quo.

The intention of this chapter is to confront some of the problems facing American Muslims. The selection of topics is based on the many communications, both by letter and conversation, that I have had with fellow American believers. I have tried to stick to the issues that arise most frequently, but the order in which they appear is more or less random. And I have agonized over two concerns. First, I wondered if I should discuss some of these problems at all, because any conclusions that are reached are bound to upset a good number of Muslim readers. This led naturally to my second concern: Should I present **any** conclusions? Would it not be better simply to list the different sides of a given controversy and omit any personal opinions?

My decision is contained in my reflections on the youth conference. We cannot continue to avoid discussing matters of current concern, for this very avoidance might cause the Muslim community to adopt the most convenient solutions to its problems, even if they were not developed in an Islamic context. We can then expect two divergent trends among our scholars and thinkers: liberal interpretation that rationalizes established Western cultural practices on religious grounds, and the formulation of "ideal" Islamic solutions that are far-removed from the daily realities of the Muslim masses. Both of these are certain to occur anyhow to some extent, as has happened frequently in the past, because, firstly, religion has a certain flexibility that allows for its adaptation to different cultures, and, secondly, because it is necessary to have an ideal in mind to which the community aspires. But, there is a danger of taking these trends too far, and this must be guarded against by all Muslims. This is why we must discuss sensitive issues openly now, especially during this rooting stage of Islam in the West.

Similarly, I feel that as Muslims we have to be willing to take and defend positions. No one wants to be subject to doubt and criticism, but this is the most effective and honest way to confront issues. It is true that very few of us have the authority to render a decisive judgment, and the more we are aware of this the better off we are, because in this way we will be forced to solve our community problems collectively by employing the Islamic principles of *shura* (mutual consultation) and ijma' (consensus). With this in mind, I remind the reader that this author is not a scholar of Islam, and that it is my hope that my opinions will be challenged freely and critically.

FAMILY

The best of you is the best to his family and I am the best among you to my family.[156]

The most perfect believers are the best in conduct, and the best of you are those who are best to their spouses. (Tirmidhi)[157]

"We aren't going to let you starve, mom. I know Kansas isn't paradise, but you can always come and live with us."

I found it awkward trying to console my mother over the phone. Consoling others had always been her role. She had seen her husband and five sons through terrible troubles. Time and time again she had shouldered our anxieties and failures with undaunting mercy and self-sacrifice. Maybe once too often, for it appeared that overnight her sixty-five years had caught up with and overtaken this once young and vibrant woman. This was the first time that I had felt hopelessness in her voice.

"Mom, we love you! You have to trust that."

The intervals of silence were killing me. I wished she would say something.

"We're your sons! It's our duty to take care of you now. And it's more than that. It's a gift from God that we have the opportunity to help the people that we love most."

I could hear her now, faintly. She was crying, a punishing, silent cry that tries to hide, that rains down in tears over clenched lips, that aches out in heart-stricken sighs.

"I have to go now, son."

"I love you, mom!"

"I know you do."

My mother is obsessed with the idea of never letting herself become a burden to her five sons, so much so that she will not even allow herself to cry in front of them. She is horrified at the idea of having to some day depend on her children. "You have your own families now," she will say.

"But you are our family too!" I will counter. "Doesn't raising five children count for something?" I think that, for my mother, it is more than just having to depend on us financially, although that alone is a scary predica-

---

[156]Gamal Badawi, *The Status of Woman in Islam* (Indianapolis: American Trust Publ., 1972), 18. This saying of Muhammad was quoted by Dr. Badawi.

[157]Quoted from the collection of Tirmidhi (10:11) in Muhammad Ali, *A Manual of Hadith* (London: Curzon Press, 1977).

ment, because it is far from clear that we can really be depended on now that our parents need us. It has to do with admitting that she has entered the class of the "elderly"—that awful word that signifies feebleness, uselessness, utter dependence, and isolation; the ones who get in the way; who move and think too slowly.

My mother knows their plight better than most. She worked for twenty years as a nurse in a health facility, a home for the "elderly" or "aged" or "senior citizens" (we cannot seem to find a word for old people that has a positive ring to it). It serves a wealthy clientele and is one of the finest retirement homes in the area, although by the time its residents make their way to the hospital wing to spend their final days, not much can be done to make it pleasant. To be sure, the nurses do their best, but they cannot eliminate the ever-present sense of death closing in, and, above all, they cannot become the family that never comes to visit.

My mother used to remind us again and again of the horrible loneliness of her patients as they faced death by themselves, and how her prayer was to die as her father did: on his feet, working, self-sufficient. But her health has taken a bad turn and her doctors doubt that she will ever return to work.

My father has also been forced into retirement. My parents now rely on social security, a third of which goes to pay their property taxes, and the precarious help of their sons. My father suggested selling the house they have lived in for almost forty years, but my mother could not deal with that nightmare. Their "golden years" are reduced to a daily struggle to subsist, and they are very conscious that if either of them should require extended medical care, their financial reserves could disappear.

Cultures much poorer than ours treat their elderly with more dignity and respect than we do. Of course, socio-economic factors have to be taken into consideration. In traditional cultures, the extended family strengthens mutual ties and feelings of responsibility for its members. The nuclearizing of the family unit, which began in the West and is becoming a global reality, was brought about mostly by unavoidable social transformations; industrialization, for example, played a big part. But natural and necessary changes in social structures do not account fully for the sad predicament of our aged, nor for the disintegration of the Western family. We have to concede a prominent place to plain old-fashioned selfishness and greed.

Parents of American converts usually have many reservations about their children's new commitment, but a frequently mentioned positive side effect is that the bond between them and their child has grown noticeably stronger after their acceptance of the faith. Indeed, after becoming a Muslim, I was consistently advised by fellow believers of my obligations to my parents.

This was more than the sharing of a traditional cultural perspective, for, as mentioned in a number of places previously, Islam places a great deal of importance on one's relations with one's family members. The paramountcy assigned to the family unit, including grandparents, aunts, uncles, and cousins, in the making of Muslim society can be grasped by considering that copious volumes on Islamic law are dedicated to inter-family relations. And while governments in Muslim lands were often willing throughout history to ignore much of classical Islamic law, Islamic family law was usually enforced.[158]

Modern society is said to be youth oriented, for its fashion, food, music, art, advertising, and many other elements cater to the young. It tries to stay abreast of the latest youthful trends, from which it gains abundant energy, fluidity, and vitality. This is certain to grate against cultures that depend upon tradition, in particular Islamic culture, which cannot possibly be conceived of as youth-oriented, at least not in the way I have just described. To be sure, the vast majority of Muhammad's earliest disciples were young men and women, mostly in their twenties,[159] and the Qur'an sharply censures those who blindly follow destructive cultural conventions (2:170; 5:104; 7:28; 21:53-54; 31:21). But the wisdom and experience of Muhammad and of such older Companions as Abu Bakr, 'Umar, and 'Uthman were indispensable to the movement's success.

Furthermore, the Qur'an puts great stock in wise and correct traditions, as it traces the essence of its message back through history to all of the prophets. Islam ended many degenerate cultural practices, such as infanticide, usury, and drinking, but it also modified certain other practices (for example, the pilgrimage, polygamy, divorce, and rules of inheritance) and endorsed still others. In this last category is the obligation to treat one's elders with the greatest respect, especially parents. In common with Judaism and Christianity, honoring one's parents is an Islamic requirement and exhibiting the slightest impatience or annoyance towards them is forbidden:

And worship Allah and do not associate anything with Him, and be good to parents and relatives. . . (4:36)

And your Lord has decreed that you worship none but Him and that you be good to parents. If one or both of them reach old age by your side, do not say "Uff!"[an expression of impatience] to

[158]Esposito, *Islam: The Straight Path*, 88-89, 149-52.
[159]Watt, *Muhammad at Mecca*, 86-99.

them nor repulse them, but address them with gracious words, and, out of kindness, lower to them the wing of humility and say, "My Lord, have mercy on them, as they cared for me in childhood. (17:23-24)

Show gratitude to Me and to your parents. To Me is [your final] goal. But if they strive to make you join in worship with Me things of which you have no knowledge, do not obey them, but keep them company in this life with goodness. (31:14-15)

As already noted, on joining the Muslim community I was quite astonished that so much emphasis was put on my relationship with my parents. Here are a few of the many sayings of Muhammad on this subject to which I was exposed almost immediately:

He said: "May his nose be rubbed in the dust! May his nose be rubbed in the dust" [an Arabic expression denoting degradation]! When the Prophet was asked whom he meant by this, he replied: "The one who sees his parents, one or both, during their old age but he does not enter Paradise [by doing good to them]." (Muslim)

A man came to Muhammad and asked permission to go to battle. The Prophet asked him, "Are your parents alive?" The man said, "Yes." The Prophet responded, "Then strive to serve them." (al Bukhari and Muslim)

When asked which action is most acceptable to God, Muhammad answered, "Performing the salah at its due time." When asked what next, he responded, "Showing kindness to parents." When asked what next, he replied, "Fighting in the cause of God." (al Bukhari and Muslim)[160]

It would be difficult to assess the esteem in which motherhood was held by the pre-Islamic Arabs. Available evidence gives us no clear idea, but it is almost certain that the Arab mother had her portion of parental respect. The verse referred to earlier (2:200) concerning the pilgrimage, and the fact that female infanticide was practiced more regularly than male infanticide, would lead us to believe that pre-Islamic Arabia, like

---

[160]*Riyad al Salihin of Imam Nawawi*, trans. Muhammad Zafrulla Khan, 73-76.

other cultures at that time, generally saw men as superior to women and the father as more honored than the mother. Moreover, a comparison with Jewish, Christian, and Persian writings of that period would support this conjecture.[161] If this be the case, then Islam not only enjoined respect and responsibility towards one's parents, but added an important dimension by singling out the mother for the larger share.

> And We have enjoined upon man goodness toward parents. His mother carries him in distress and gives birth to him in distress. (46:15)

> And We have enjoined on man concerning his parents—his mother carried him in weakness upon weakness, and his weaning was in two years: "Be thankful to Me and to your parents. To Me is the [final] destination." (31:14)

> A man came to the Prophet and asked, "Who among people is most entitled to kind treatment from me?" He answered, "Your mother." The man asked, "Then who?" He said, "Your mother." "Then who?" the man insisted. The Prophet replied, "Your mother." The man asked, "Then who?" The Prophet said, "Then your father."[162] (al Bukhari and Muslim)

Any truly religious society depends heavily on tradition, and it is the responsibility of the parents to pass on its traditions and teachings to the next generation. In such a system, deference towards parents and elders is a natural requirement, as it is with Islam. We would not expect an Islamic system to have the same fluidity as present-day Western culture, which Muslims tend to interpret as social instability rather than something positive. Islamic society seeks continuity and harmony with its past and with what is permanent and immutable. The bridge between its past and future are its parents and their young children, and thus they are charged with the heaviest burden. They must insure dignity and honor for their elders and pass on enduring guiding principles to their young. Such an effort demands of them a selfless involvement in the lives of both, and there is little place for "me first."

[161]Badawi, *Status of Woman in Islam*; Afzalur Rahman, *Role of Muslim Women in Society* (London: Seerah Foundation, 1986); Nabia Abbott, *Aishah: The Beloved of Muhammad* (Chicago: University of Chicago, 1942).
[162]*Sahih al Bukhari*, trans. by Muhammad Muhsin Khan, vol. 8, "The Book of Good Manners" (71), Hadith no. 2.

Having already discussed the believer's relationship with parents, I will say a few words on his/her duty to children. There are few direct pronouncements in the Qur'an concerned exclusively with parental behavior towards children. Rather, such obligations are contained in the many exhortations to be responsive to the needs of kinsmen in general. That the welfare of children is a community responsibility is unmistakable in the Qur'an's persistent warning to all believers not to ignore the needs of poor children and orphans. But it is mainly through example that the Qur'an instills in the reader deep-seated feelings of urgency about his/her children's future.

When such holy personages as the mother of Mary (3:35) or Zakariya (3:38) or Abraham (14:35; 14:41) ask God for a child or pray for their offspring, their first plea is for righteous and God-fearing children. The Qur'an presents several examples of parents urging their children to commit themselves to God and sharing with them moral lessons (2:132; 11:43; 12:18; 12:64-67; 12:98). A most tender instance is the conversation between Luqman and his son:

And when Luqman said to his son, advising him: "O my dear son, do not ascribe any partner to God; surely ascribing partners to Him is the worst of wrongs. . . .O my dear son, if there were but the weight of a mustard seed, and it were hidden in a rock or in the heavens or the earth, God would bring it forth; truly, God is Most Subtle, All-Aware. O my dear son, establish the salah and enjoin goodness, and be patient in whatever may befall you; that surely pertains to steadfastness in [dealing with] affairs. And do not turn your cheek in scorn toward people, nor walk insolently upon the earth; truly, God does not love the braggart boaster. And be modest in your bearing and lower your voice; surely the harshest of all sounds is the sound of the donkey." (31:13-19)

In the Qur'an we see that believing parents, in contrast to such nonbelievers as Abraham's father, are not harsh or impatient with their children. Instead, they are forbearing, caring, and ever-mindful of their children's progress in faith. The religious quality of their parental love and concern arouses in Muslim readers the same pressing sense of responsibility toward their own offspring, echoed in the Qur'anic warning: "O you who believe, save yourselves and your families from a Fire whose fuel is men and stones" (66:6).

Already mentioned is the fact that Muhammad's example was one of great tenderness toward children. Once a bedouin said to him that his people never used to kiss their children. The Prophet's response was: "I cannot put mercy in your heart if God has taken it away."[163]

From several references in the Qur'an, we obtain a mixed message as to how pre-Islamic Arabian society viewed parenting. The Qur'an contains passages that comment on parental sentiments, which would indicate that, like people of all times, they cared very much for their children. There are also many places in the Qur'an that reveal that, for Muhammad's contemporaries, the size of one's family was a measure of a man's prowess and success (3:10, 14; 9:55; 18:46; 19:77; 26:88; 34:35). It seems that this pride was based only on the number of sons without reference to daughters, for several verses indicate that female offspring were considered a liability. The following two references bring this out clearly. The first derides the pagan belief that the angels were "daughters of God," although the pagans themselves viewed the birth of a female as contemptible, while the second condemns both this attitude and one of its darkest manifestations: female infanticide.

> What! Has He taken daughters from among what He creates, but chosen sons for you? When news is brought to one of them of [the birth of] what he sets up as a likeness to the Most Merciful, his face is covered with darkness and he is grieved inwardly.(43:16-17)

> And when one of them is given news of [the birth of] a female, his face is covered with darkness and he is grieved inwardly. He hides himself from the people because of the evil of that which he has received tidings. Shall he keep her in contempt, or bury her in the dust? Ah, how evil is what they decide on! (16:58-59)

This inequity is the theme of several sayings of the Prophet. Although in many Muslim cultures the birth of a male is still more celebrated than that of a female, the last traces of this favoritism may finally be disappearing in this century's Muslim reawakening, at least among the educated. Muhammad is reported to have said:

> Whoever is blessed with two daughters or is taking care of two sisters, and treats them well and patiently, he and I shall be in Paradise like these . . .," gesturing with his index and middle fingers.[164] (Muslim).

and

---

[163]Ibid., 78:18.
[164]Badawi, *Status of Woman in Islam*, 15.

Whoever has a daughter and he does not insult her, and does not favor his son over her, God will enter him into Paradise.[165] (Ibn Hanbal, No. 1957)

In this vein, I have been reminded on countless occasions by fellow Muslims of how fortunate I am to have three daughters.

The great importance placed on family relations in Islam is a natural corollary of the precept that faith is acted out and matures within society. Since the family exacts the largest investment of our emotional and material resources, it becomes the key setting for teaching and learning justice and virtue. Little wonder that Prophet Muhammad called marriage "half of one's faith"[166] and that the Qur'an enjoins the believers to "marry the single among you" (24:32).

All of this, we might say, sounds well and good, perhaps ideal, but how does it stand against the values of contemporary society, Western society in particular? Is it practical, even possible, for young adults to invest themselves so fully in the lives of their children and parents? Exactly where would this lead? Today many couples feel the need for two-career households. The bottom line is: "Toward what changes or sacrifices, if any, are we heading?"

PERSPECTIVES

I am not leaving a greater trial for men than women. (al Bukhari and Muslim)[167]

Our viewpoints do not originate in a vacuum; they are a synthesis of our environment, background, experience, and personality. These are reflected in any human attempt to derive comprehensive guidelines for society, for the applicable results are always limited to a certain time and place. One of the miracles of divine revelation is that it communicates, through a particular community, a message that is relevant to very different peoples. Our part is not restricted to learning how earlier communities understood the divine word, for we are expected to communicate it visibly by how **we** live and conduct our affairs. To do any less would be to ignore its universal character and to distance ourselves—and even

---

[165]Ibid., 15.
[166]Ali, *Religion of Islam*, 603.
[167]*Sahih al Bukhari*, trans. Muhammad Muhsin Khan, vol. 8, "The Book of Wedlock" (62), Hadith no. 33.

more, all succeeding generations—from the revelation's perpetual relevance.

I am very much aware of the fact that my views on the roles of men and women in Muslim society, and indeed on all the topics I have been discussing, are affected a great deal by my peculiar circumstances, as is true of anyone. And this is exactly why the process of review and interpretation must never cease. Virtually all Muslim revivalists, whether traditionalist or modernist, are convinced that through the ages many superfluous, burdensome, and cultural accretions have infiltrated Muslim thought and practice, and that we must reestablish the "true" Islam. Most insist on a return to the Qur'an and the Hadith. However, this also involves interpretation, and we are bound to differ on how we read them. So how are we to separate the true interpretations from the mistaken or false, the legitimate from the illegitimate, the admissible from the inadmissible?

Those who come from traditional Muslim societies have an extremely important role to play here because they have witnessed from inside the debilitating effects of the contamination, and because they have also experienced the adoption of Islam, admittedly imperfect, on a societal level. Thus they have a better understanding of the consequences of implementing different perceived aspects of Islam.

But coming from within the Muslim world also has certain disadvantages, for those who originate in it are in part a product of the society that they are attempting to purify, a fact that makes objectivity difficult. Criticism from outsiders might be valuable (I have the work of Western Islamists in mind here), but they are often prejudiced and, even when they are less so, they lack the most essential ingredient for understanding Islam: any personal experience with it, for Islam is a way of life and it must be lived to be truly understood. This is where the convert comes in, as he has come in frequently in Islamic history, for such a person combines commitment with skepticism, sometimes leading to important and inspiring insights. Since converts are not grounded in the traditions of the faith, they are also likely to bring with them radical, alien ideas that will be tested by the larger community.

In no sphere of Muslim life is this tension between traditional and modern ideas so pronounced as in that of the roles of men and women. Most commentators who discuss Muhammad's saying, "I am not leaving a greater trial for men than women," believe that it refers exclusively to sensual temptation. But this may be too limited an understanding. Many modern Muslim thinkers lament that the rights of Muslim women have been obstructed by powerful cultural forces. If this is so, then perhaps Muhammad had this in mind as well, for, without a doubt, the issue of the status of woman in Islam stands today as the biggest barrier between Islam and its acceptance in the West. In addition, many Western converts will live apart from the Muslim community until this matter is resolved to their satisfaction.

Before my conversion, I had given some half-hearted support to a few campaigns of the national women's movement, but for the most part, like many of my contemporaries, I was straggling along with all kinds of ill-defined and contradictory notions about contemporary sex roles. I knew that there was something wrong with the way things had been formerly, but there were no clear or practical alternatives. The women's movement gradually went the way of so many movements of the sixties and seventies: it generated a lot of initial excitement and some important and positive results, but then everybody got tired of it and it withered away. For many, it was too extreme, for it appeared to advocate not only equal rights but total equality.

Many theories were constructed to explain that there are no essential differences between the sexes, although daily experience suggested otherwise. Maybe the women's movement failed to communicate its message effectively, or perhaps there was a lack of consensus on what the message was. It sounded like a call for some sort of sexual communism, a forced homogenization of men and women, that involved women becoming like men more than the converse. Even though the women's movement failed to provide direction, it argued convincingly that society oppresses women, a position of which I was convinced when I became a Muslim in 1982.

I did not know too much about Muslim male-female relations back then. I knew about polygamy, veiling, and segregation, but these did not necessarily imply oppression. In segregation, for example, each sex may prefer to restrict intermixing, and if women are barred from male functions, the opposite is equally true. Besides, I knew that these practices could be based more on culture than on religion. Nevertheless, I did believe that Muslim women were among the most male dominated in the world. This is simply a given in contemporary Western thought; it was the understanding in the past, as portrayed in novels set in Muslim lands, and it is accepted today in movies and television.

There is a scene in a recent movie in which Goldie Hawn, a representative of the American liberated woman, takes a group of beautiful (of course!) doe-eyed, veiled Middle Eastern women on a tour of the nation's capital, culminating in her reading to them, accompanied by inspirational music in the background, the Constitution of the United States.

That scene may result in a false picture of Middle Eastern women but it accurately represents the average American's perception. Now, even if you are conscious that what you are presented is not reality, it does have an effect, and if you are presented with no alternative view, you are likely to believe that there must be some truth to it. In any case, I entered the Muslim community with low expectations on this score.

Eight years of daily involvement in the community and travel to the Middle East has forced me to entertain other perspectives. While for Americans the veiling of Muslim women is a sign of male domination, Muslims, on the other hand, view women's dress in the United States as exploitative. Since many Muslim women prefer to be housewives, they must be oppressed/since many American women work full time, they must be unprotected. Families have too much to say in the marriage of young people in the Muslim world/American families treat their children irresponsibly. Thus what one side interprets as subjugation, the other sees as freedom. That in itself is not difficult to understand. But what if you are caught between the two cultures?

TO THE ISLAMIC CENTER

"A few weeks after my conversion, I decided to go to the Islamic center for the first time in order to celebrate my new-found faith with people whom I knew would understand. I took great pains to dress appropriately and rehearsed the opening chapter of the Qur'an as I drove across town.

"I quickly found a place in the big parking lot. The main door opened to the rear of a large prayer room. The floor was covered with what had to be at least one hundred oriental rugs. The walls were freshly painted white and reached up some forty feet to a beautiful expansive white-domed ceiling. The front wall contained a prayer niche decorated with calligraphy. This is how I had always imagined it should be!

"The faces that turned to see me looked astonished. They were clearly uncomfortable, so I did not advance any further. I sat down about twenty feet behind them, thinking I would give them the chance to make the first move. No one did. Not one introduced himself; not even an "Al salamu alaikum" or a smile. I wondered if I had done something wrong.

"As the rest of the congregation, which consisted only of men, arrived, various individuals embraced each other and sat down, joking and talking. Yet no one gave me more than a single glance. I felt as though I had leprosy.

"Then the call to prayer was made. We prayed—but I prayed alone, where I had been sitting. When we had finished, I walked toward the front of the room in order to exit by a side door. I tried to make eye contact with some of the "brothers" to get a response, but they turned their heads.

"I could not believe it! I thought perhaps more time was needed to break the ice; after all, I was clearly different from the rest and a stranger. I returned to the center on two other occasions. Each time the response was the same. I decided never to go back again."

This, of course, was not my experience. It was shared with me by a forty-five year old American divorcee with two young adult Christian children. I have heard similar tales from other American women too many times, but there were several aspects of Nicky's account that were unusual.

Most converts come to Islam searching for something because they are unhappy with their lives and the act of conversion is a huge emotional leap. Nicky told me that she had not been unhappy at all. She had a wonderful career and home in Santa Barbara, and an extremely close relationship with her two daughters; she enjoyed being single and did not feel the need for a male companion at this stage in her life. She had formed a close friendship with a Saudi woman living in Santa Barbara and had come to believe in her religion. She entered joyfully, full of great expectations. Her ordeal at the Islamic center has not dampened her spirits nor her joy at being a Muslim. She has since met some other American Muslims and some less conservative Middle Eastern friends, who have together formed their own little Islamic community: meeting, fasting, and praying together regularly.

The congregation that Nicky encountered was certainly not trying to be mean. They were simply reacting in the way they had always been taught to react in such a situation: when a covered Muslim lady comes to the mosque, one does not look at her or approach her. In other words, it is proper to ignore her. Not every congregation in North America would have behaved this way, for much would depend on how deeply rooted its members were in American culture. But more often than not, the impression relayed to me by American Muslim women, converts or otherwise, is that they are not wanted in the mosque.

My daughter, now four years old, has already gotten this impression. Our neighbors, who are Christians, have a little girl of approximately the same age, and Jameelah and she are good friends. Her friend tells about how her family attends church together, how they sing, and where she sits with her mom and dad, and so forth. The little girl went so far as to innocently invite my daughter to one of their Sunday services. When Jameelah and I discussed the issue, she inquired, "Why aren't ladies allowed in our mosque, daddy?" I told her that they are, but had a difficult time explaining why they don't actually come.

I am not sure how or when the mosque acquired an atmosphere just barely tolerant of women; it obviously happened in another time and different cultural context. Other cultures may provide other avenues for enriching the faith of Muslim women. However, in this culture, to offer women an alternative to attending prayers at the mosque, such as a weekly women's gathering, is to offer them second-class status. If we do not encourage women to come and participate in our community meetings on equal footing with men, the existing atmosphere in our mosques is likely to change very slowly, and we are almost certain to lose many of our children. I am not advocating changing the forms of the rituals; I am advocating that we encourage, facilitate, and welcome family participation in all of our community functions.

WOMEN IN THE QUR'AN

And their Lord answered them: "Truly I will never cause the work of any of you to be lost, whether male or female. You are of another." (3:195)

And the believing men and believing women are protectors of each other. They enjoin the right and forbid the wrong, and they observe regular salah and give zakah, and obey God and His Messenger. On them God will have mercy. Truly, God is All-Mighty, All-Wise. (9:71)

Whoever works righteousness, whether male or female, and is a believer, We shall give him [or her] a good life, and We will give them their reward according to the best of what they did. (16:97)

Truly, the surrendered men and surrendered women, and the believing men and believing women, and the devout men and the devout women, the patient men and the patient women, and the humble men and humble women, and the charitable men and the charitable women, and the men who fast and the women who fast, and the men who guard their private parts and the women who guard [their private parts], and the men who remember God much and the women who remember [God much]—for them God has promised forgiveness and a tremendous reward. (33:35)

The tone of the Bible as regards women is set from the start in the allegory of the first man and woman. Eve, the temptress, is held more accountable than Adam and must therefore bear the curse of childbirth. It was she who first surrendered to the evil prompting of Satan and then helped him to seduce Adam. No match for this alliance, Adam learned the bitter lesson that man must always maintain authority over woman and be on guard against her guile.[168]

This ancient symbol of the relationship between the sexes reflects a definite male bias and the dominance of religious institutions; no doubt it would accurately represent the relative positions of men and women in most world societies over several thousand years. This male bias and control is also evident in the commentaries of past Muslim scholars on the parallel accounts contained in the Qur'an, commentaries which suggest strong Jewish and Christian influences.[169]

From the vantage point of the twentieth century, we are in a fairly good position to distinguish between what the Qur'an says about the sexes and what past commentators assumed. Yet orientalists in the recent past have often confused the two and, when filtered through their own preconceptions, concluded that Islam takes an abject view of womanhood. Fortunately, this is slowly changing. For example, in her introduction to Margaret Smith's *Rabi'a the Mystic*, Anne Marie Schimmel writes:

The Western reader who is inclined to accept uncritically Margaret Smith's remark on p. 127 that "Islam is responsible for the degradation of Muslim women" should understand that the "degradation" was more the result of social forces than of Islam itself. or the Qur'an speaks repeatedly of the *muslimun wa muslimat, mu'minun wa mu'minat*, "Muslim men and women, believing men and women," and the same injunctions are valid for men and women when it comes to prayer, fasting, pilgrimage, etc. The oft-repeated claim that women in Islam have no soul cannot be verified from the Qur'an nor from the traditions.[170]

The Qur'anic version of the story of the first man and woman (2:35-39; 7:19-25) is distinguished as much by what it does not say as by what it does. No mention is made of Eve's tempting Adam, or that childbirth is a punishment for women, or that this incident is the basis for man's "rule over" woman, or that woman was created for man. The issue of who was

---

[168]May and Metzger, *The New Oxford Annotated Bible*, 1169.
[169]Gordon D. Newby, *The Making of the Last Prophet* (University of South Carolina Press, 1989,) 1-28.
[170]Margaret Smith, *Rabi'a the Mystic* (Cambridge, UK: Cambridge University Press, 1984), xxvi-xxvii.

created first seems to have been avoided on purpose. The Qur'an states that both Adam and his wife were tempted and sinned, and that they both repented and were forgiven. Based in part on this account and on such verses as those above that explicitly uphold the spiritual equality of men and women, contemporary Muslim writers have been able to argue convincingly that Islam recognizes no sexual differences as regards virtue and piety.

Unfortunately, there are two disturbing considerations that are frequently glossed over or ignored. The first is that this equality has not always been upheld by Muslim scholars.[171] Even today, there are Muslims who claim that women, because of their inherently weaker nature, are more prone to sin. This thinking is not too difficult to dismiss as a deviation antithetical to clear affirmations in the Qur'an, and it can find support only if verses of a practical legislative nature are employed to infer something negative about feminine spirituality. The second consideration is that there are a small number of authenticated prophetic traditions that present a contrary picture. I have already mentioned one of the most influential of these:

> The Prophet once passed by some women and said, "O you women! You must be extra careful to be good for I have seen most of you in Hell. I have not seen a creature more lacking in reason and religious observance than you, who yet overpowers the wits of a man of sound reason." "How are we lacking in religious observance?" one of the women in the group insisted, and got the reply, "Is it not the case that when you menstruate, you are required neither to pray nor to fast?" "Yes," she said, "but how are we lacking in reason?" "Is not the evidence of one of you half that of a male's?" "Yes," she replied.[172]

Of all of the traditions of Muhammad, this is the one that American Muslims questioned me about more than any other. One convert told me that it caused him considerable pain and greatly deflated his faith.

Some Muslim scholars, such as Jamal Badawi, who have confronted this hadith, maintain that what the Prophet intended here was not a judgment on women's spirituality, but rather an exhortation to work harder on their faith due to certain disadvantages.[173] Badawi points out that Islam's requirement that women not observe the salah or fast during menstruation

---

[171] Abdelwahab Bouhdiba, *Sexuality in Islam*, trans. by Alan Sheridan (London: Routledge and Kegan Paul, 1985), pp. 116-40; Smith, *Rabi'a the Mystic*, 111-36.

[172] Rahman, *Health and Medicine in the Islamic Tradition*, 105.

[173] Jamal Badawi, *Islamic Teaching Series*, Halifax, NS, Canada.

and the forty days after childbirth is a compassionate concession of temporary immunity from these demands (2:222 characterizes menstruation as a hurtful condition). Badawi also mentions that women are encouraged to make private supplications during these times.

The reference to two female witnesses being equal to one male witness in business transactions is a reflection of the fact that, according to Badawi, women generally have less aptitude for business dealings than men, especially, in his opinion, in a Muslim setting, where their talents will generally be diverted to other societal needs.

Thus, Badawi sees Islam's concession to women during menstruation and the ruling on witnessing a contract not as statements of female inferiority, but as a tender gesture in the first case and an acknowledgment of distinctive male and female strengths in the second. However, this seems to strain against the tenor of the hadith, which appears to be saying that these stipulations exist **because** of certain flaws in the feminine character that make a woman a more likely candidate for Hell. It could be argued, and I understood as much from Badawi's remarks, that such a negative conclusion results from forcing a too literal interpretation. Indeed, the Prophet's descriptions of his Night Journey to Heaven (the *Mi'raj*, which included this vision of Hell) may not have been meant to provide empirical data on the Unseen, but rather to encourage and warn.

Fazlur Rahman, in his *Health and Medicine in the Islamic Tradition*, is more critical of this hadith.[174] He finds it opposed to the Qur'an's position on the spiritual equality of men and women, and believes it was imposed on Islam, via the hadith, from the ethos of the non-Arab cultures that entered Islam after their conquest. The statement that speaks of the evidentiary value of female testimony as being half that of a man's, he posits, presupposes the later development of the law of evidence in Islam. Like Badawi, he argues that the corresponding reference in the Qur'an speaks specifically about a business transaction and is not enacting a general law. The Prophetic saying, he continues, appears to be upholding the later formulated generalization.

While I admit that the wording in the saying does appear to be general, it is impossible to prove that that is what was intended. We will continue the discussion of a woman's testimony shortly. For the present, we will simply agree that one of these viewpoints is probably correct, for the weight of evidence from the Qur'an and other authentic traditions is indisputably in favor of male-female equality.

---

[174]Rahman, *Health and Medicine in the Islamic Tradition*, 105-6.

Another important way to discover Qur'anic viewpoints is to study its dramatizations. In other words, when people are portrayed in the Qur'an—for example, when we see them praying, talking, or acting—we may ask what elements of their character are highlighted. We used this approach earlier when we discussed parenting.

Some of the most sympathetic and gripping personality portraits in the Qur'an are of women: the Queen of Sheba, the exemplary leader; the mother of Moses, about to surrender her son to the will of God; the wife of Pharaoh, begging God's protection from the oppression of her husband; and the mother of Mary, dedicating her unborn child to the service of God. The story of Mary, mother of Jesus, is one of the most arresting, so much so that the surah in which it appears is named after her.

An interesting observation is that while the men portrayed in the Qur'an range from utterly despicable disbelievers to noble prophets, all of the dramatizations involving women are ultimately positive. Now, I am not referring to a mere statement of fact—for example, that Abu Lahab's wife will suffer damnation or that Noah's and Lot's spouses were disbelievers, for we are not shown these women's personalities. I am referring to what we are shown of a specific character at some moment in his or her life. Whenever this occurs with a woman in the Qur'an, she is a believer; indeed, in all cases but one, they are unswerving believers, but even this exception, the woman in the story of Yusuf (Joseph), eventually repents and mends her ways. In comparison to the scriptures of other religions, this stands as a unique and remarkable feature of the Qur'an.[175]

---

[175]Verses 12:29 and 43:16-18 are sometimes cited to show that the Qur'an places women on a lower intellectual and moral plane than men. They read: This is from the cunning of you [women]. Truly, your cunning is great! (12:29) What! Has He taken daughters from among what He creates, but chosen sons for you? When news is brought to one of them of [the birth of] what he sets up as a likeness to the Most Merciful, his face darkens and he is grieved inwardly. Then, is one brought up among finery and unclear in argument [to be likened to God]? (43:16-18)

Unfortunately, I have heard Muslim men use this argument on many occasions. The word *kayda*, translated above as "cunning," means the ability to outwit, outmaneuver mentally, or deceive through subtlety. The second verse describes a woman as someone who, when involved in an argument or a verbal dispute is unclear (*ghayr mubin*; lit., other than clear). Thus we are presented with two somewhat contrary statements about feminine intelligence. If we take these statements at face value, they need to be reconciled. But this poses no problem if one simply considers the context of their occurrence.

The first statement is uttered by Potiphar, whose wife has just attempted to seduce Joseph. The second is presented as the insidious thinking of the pagan Arabs, which, in another verse (16:58-59) is associated with the crime of female infanticide. To ignore the contexts of these would be similar to arguing that the Qur'an is nothing more than poetry, since such an assertion, on the part of non-Muslims, appears in the text.   =

146

The Male and the Female

And the male is not like the female. (3:36)

Each one of you is a trustee [lit., shepherd] and is accountable for that which is entrusted to him. A ruler is a trustee and is accountable for his trust, a man is a trustee in respect of his family, a woman is a trustee in respect of her husband's house and children. Thus, everyone is a trustee and is accountable for that which is entrusted to him.[176] (al Bukhari and Muslim)

In the past, it was clear to men everywhere that, as a general rule, males were more intelligent, more rational, and less emotional than women. In the recent minute ensuing interval of history during which women have been granted equal access to education and political life, we have seen many of these ancient assumptions challenged. Today in the United States, the differences in national test scores between males and females are negligible. Although a slight advantage goes to women in verbal skills and to men in mathematical skills, even this trend may be changing as more women are now preparing for careers in the sciences. Women have infiltrated the worlds of politics, business, higher education, medicine, and other formerly male-only domains with remarkable speed and success. And it is now frequently argued that men are not less emotional than women, but that they display their feelings

---

= In the story of Yusuf, when the husband of his seductress learns of Yusuf's innocence and his spouse's guilt, he does not initiate any action against her, which he would be totally justified in doing. Rather, in order to avoid a public scandal and jeopardize his high standing in society, he simply excuses the entire matter with the above exclamation. Later, when his wife's passion for Yusuf is blatantly obvious, he imprisons Yusuf to avoid embarrassment. Such early Muslim commentators as al Tabari, who viewed Potiphar as an example of moral impotence, saw his character as most reprehensible and far from the ideal of true manliness. Thus they would often weave legends around the story that detailed what they saw as a rather despicable personality. Hence many accounts connect his moral weakness with his sexual impotence. The same commentaries tended to be very sympathetic to Potiphar's wife and defended her attraction to Yusuf because of her husband's failings.

Whatever the actual case may be, the Qur'an seems to present two common and opposing attitudes that are used by men against women to justify their own moral shortcomings. Both statements are connected to patently unjust deeds, and this should not be overlooked when interpreting them. It is quite unfortunate and remarkable that Muslim men still quote these verses out of context in an effort to denigrate women. I am not denying that women can often outwit and mentally outmaneuver men—this is stated elsewhere in the same surah—but men should not use this fact as an excuse for their own weaknesses.

[176]*Sahih al Bukhari*, trans. Muhammad Muhsin Khan, vol. 2, "The Book of Friday" (13), Hadith no. 18.

in different ways: resorting to violence and shouting more often. Men commit many more violent crimes and crimes of passion, for example, than women.

Yet, with all the changes in roles and perceptions that have taken place in modern society, it does not appear that men and women relate to each other on a personal level very much differently than did their parents or grandparents. Men, I believe, still search for partners who are warm, nurturing, supportive, and gentle—what are traditionally held to be feminine characteristics—and women, for male companions that are self-confident, stable, strong, and dependable—so-called masculine qualities. Sensitivity in men is highly valued by today's women, but I am frequently told that this is rarely found.

Despite the experiments of the sixties and seventies, students inform me that the young man is now once again expected to pay the bills on a date—something I never had to worry about when I was in my teens and early twenties. In marriage, wives have become less economically dependent on their husbands, but they have also had to pay a price for this: if the couple is to have a lifestyle similar to that of their parents, often both must contribute to the maintenance of the family.

This in itself could be viewed positively, except for the fact that very often the burden of care for the household and children continues to fall almost entirely on the wife. The idea that women are better suited to care for young children endures in Western society. This is strongly reflected in various laws and customs: for instance, the mother is generally given custody of her children in a divorce situation and parents almost always prefer female baby-sitters. Therefore it appears that when it comes to sex roles, Western society may continue to be in a state of transition, searching for definition. This is even more true of Muslim society, which, in its confrontation with the West, has had to reexamine its positions.

Muslim authors often make the case that pre-Islamic Arabia was submerged in barbarism and ignorance and that Islam radically inverted the entire socio-political structure of the peninsula. In addition, it is claimed that, at that time in history, a more depraved environment could not be found to receive the revolutionary ideals of Islam. While it must be admitted that the pre-Islamic Arabs were unrefined and that signs of higher civilization were scarce, I believe that the simplicity of their lives and their codes of honor, nobility, and freedom made them prime candidates for the reception of the ideas contained in the Qur'an. The ideals of democracy, fraternity, equality, and magnanimity were firmly implanted in tribal values that now needed to be extended beyond the tribe.[177] The precept that one could become a full-fledged citizen by mere acceptance of an ideology would have met stiffer and better organized resistance in the powerful neighboring Persian and Roman empires. Thus, while the message of Islam was indeed revolutionary, I feel that the Arabian peninsula was the most fertile soil for its advance, in particular with reference to the status of woman.

It is easy to document that the position of woman in ancient Hindu, Greek, Roman, and Persian culture was one of utter subservience.[178] Deprived of an independent legal status, she was treated as a minor under the tutelage of her nearest male guardian. The situation of women in pre-Islamic Arabia was considerably better in comparison. From the Prophetic traditions, we learn that there were Arab women who inherited, initiated divorce, proposed marriage, participated in battle, and conducted business. These rights were apparently not uniformly recognized in Arabia, for the Qur'an had to enforce many of them. However, this shows that precedents for many Qur'anic enactments protecting women did exist at that time. The existence of numerous examples of women possessing a measure of independence exceeding that of their counterparts in neighboring lands would lead one to believe that the Qur'anic reforms might have been accepted more easily in Arabia than elsewhere.

At the center of Islam's conception of the male-female relationship is the statement in *Surat Maryam* that "the male is not like the female" (3:36). This pronouncement is made after the mother of Mary expresses disappointment at having given birth to a daughter, after her prayer for a son. God then issues a mild rebuke, informing her that He knows full well what was to be born and that the male and the female are not the same— and, implicitly, that they were not meant to be.

It is interesting that this criticism of male favoritism should appear in the story of Mary, the mother of Jesus, one of the Qur'an's most exalted personalities. Thus, at one and the same time, and through an explicit statement and an example, emphasis is placed on the differing natures of men and women and on the potential of women to surpass men in excellence.

In the divine scheme, men and women were not meant to be the same, but to complement and support each other. This is expressed in a variety of ways in the Qur'an.

---

[177]Asad, *Sahih al Bukhari*; Goldziher, *Muslim Studies* II.
[178]Badawi, *Status of Woman in Islam*, 5-11; Rahman, *Role of Muslim Women in Society*, 237-47.

149

They [your spouses] are your garments and you are their garments. (2:187)

And the believing men and believing women are protectors of each other. They enjoin the right and forbid the wrong, and they observe regular salah and give zakah, and obey God and His Messenger. On them God will have mercy. Truly, God is All-Mighty, All-Wise. (9:71)

And among of His signs is that He created for you, of your kind, spouses, that you may find repose in them, and He has put between you love and mercy. Truly, in that are signs for people who reflect. (30:21)

This concept is fundamental to Islam's treatment of the roles of men and women. The idea is that men and women do not have to be coerced into accepting a certain pattern of relationship, but rather that they have been created in such a manner that they will generally relate to one another according to definite behavioral patterns. The Qur'an and sayings of Muhammad do not need to insist that husbands adopt a particular posture of authority in the family, for the clear assumption is that most often the husband, because of various strengths and weaknesses that exist in both partners, will have greater freedom and authority in marriage than the wife. To be sure, a man will be inclined to resort to what he perceives as his advantage by brute force when he sees fit. Knowing this to be the case, Islam then proceeds to curtail male authority and protect women from its abuse, while at the same time stressing the minimal obligations owed by both sexes. Thus, when Muhammad stated that men are the shepherds of their families and women of their households, he was not introducing a rearrangement of authority in the family; rather, he was assuming a general pattern and pointing out that each in his/her role was responsible for his/her dependents. In other words, he was emphasizing obligations and responsibilities, not advantages.

The axiomatic declaration of distinctive male and female personality types is made without assigning superiority to either one, thus leaving the issue of exactly how the female differs from the male mysteriously open. We are told that men and women protect each other, are garments for one another, and fulfill each other's need for mercy and love. This reciprocity is a small part of a universal balance (55:7; 57:25) that runs through all creation. The Qur'an informs us that everything is created in pairs (36:36;

43:12; 51:49). In fact, the Arabic word for "pair" (*zawj*) is the same word as that used for "spouse." Hence the relationship between the sexes is a single element in the vast and complex systems of parities. Islam claims to facilitate this harmonizing of male and female forces, and the themes of complementarity and balance stand out in its approach to men's and women's rights.

Rights and Responsibilities

And for them [women] is the like of what they [men] have over them with kindness, but men have a degree over them (2:228)

While the Qur'an most often addresses the believers collectively with the words, "O you who believe," at times it make a special point to address both men and women, as in (33:35). However, in several passages, pronouncements are directed specifically either at men or at women, although in these cases there are usually parallel statements for the other gendeßr close at hand. In *Surat al Nur*, modest behavior is prescribed:

Say to the believing men that they should lower their gaze and guard their private parts: that is more pure for them. Surely God is well-acquainted with whatever you do. And say to the believing women that they should lower their gaze and guard their private parts, and that they should not display of their adornment except what [ordinarily] appears thereof, and that they should draw their head coverings over their breasts and not display their adornment. (24:30-31)

When the Prophet was asked to elaborate on these verses, he explained that to "lower one's gaze" was to "avoid the lustful look." It is worth noting that **both** men and women are commanded to do so, for during certain phases of Western history women were believed to be lacking in sexual desire or even to be asexual.

When I was an undergraduate student, research was undertaken to disprove this assumption. But the Qur'an and sayings of Muhammad are quite frank in admitting a powerful sexual drive in women. Consider, for example, the reaction of the Egyptian women when they saw the prophet Joseph (12:30-34). One also notes in 24:31 that the command to women includes stipulations on proper dress, and this occurs in two other passages, namely, 24:60 and 33:59. There are no similar statements directed towards men. The concern of the Qur'an here appears to be that society is more likely to exploit a woman's sexuality than a man's.

The problem of how to react to a spouse's immoral conduct is taken up in two places in the fourth surah of the Qur'an. The first discusses the case of a degenerate wife:

As for those [women] on whose part you fear rebellion [*nushuz*], admonish them; then refuse to share their beds; then beat them. But if they return to obedience, do not seek a way against them. Truly, God is Most High, Most Great. (4:34)

All authorities on the Arabic language agree that the verse lists a prioritized series of steps which are not to be taken simultaneously, and that the rebellion (*nushuz*) must be of an extreme and criminal nature. Most jurists cite promiscuousness as an example, but such other violations of Islamic law as drunkenness may be included. That the rebellion is against God's will and not merely the whim of the husband is proven by the fact that the same word (*nushuz*) is used in 4:128 to describe the steps a wife should take in cases of rebellion on the part of a husband. Muslim scholars (i.e., al Tabari, al Razi, and al Shafi'i) have always agreed that the third step, beating, is just barely permissible and should preferably be avoided. Due to the limits imposed by the Prophet, they understood that this action, if resorted to at all, should be more or less symbolic. The earliest authorities saw this reference more as a strong signal of the extreme repugnancy of immoral acts, not as a license for husbands to strike their wives, which all traditions testify, was never the practice of the Prophet and which he strongly discouraged.[179]

Instructions for wives in similar circumstances also are provided:

And if a woman fears rebellion (*nushuz*) or desertion from her husband, there is no blame on them if they arrange an amicable settlement between themselves. And amicable settlement is best, but greed is ever-present within oneself. (4:128).

As is clear from 4:130, in addition to trying to work out the problem with her husband, a wife is reminded of her option to seek a dissolution of marriage. Indeed, many jurists hold the opinion that if the husband persists in his reprehensible behavior, this may actually be required of her. A woman's options in this parallel situation are different from a man's for

---

[179]Rahman, *Role of Muslim Women in Society*, 407-408.

obvious reasons. Since he may already have another wife, and because he can remarry immediately, while a woman must complete a waiting period of three months before remarriage, it would not be to her advantage to threaten a cessation of conjugal relations or, for that matter, physical punishment, even if it were only symbolic in nature. Her best alternative, if her husband proves recalcitrant, may be to begin the process of dissolution. Since the first step, according to 4:35, involves bringing in family members from both sides to help mediate the crisis, the best interests of both individuals may be served by her taking this initiative.

The Qur'an's treatment of inheritance reflects its concern for insuring a large degree of autonomy to women, while balancing their needs and responsibilities with those of men.

God directs you as regards your children: for the male is a portion equal to that of two females (4:11)

And do not covet that of which God has given more to one than the other. Men shall have a portion of what they earn and women shall have a portion of what they earn. And ask from God out of His bounty; truly, God has full knowledge of all things. And for all We have appointed heirs from whatever is left by parents and relatives. And to those with whom your right hands have made a covenant, give them their portion; truly, God is witness over everything. Therefore men are charged with the full maintenance of women in that God has given more to the one than to the other and in that they support [them] from their means. Therefore the righteous women are obedient, and protect in his absence as God has protected them. (4:32-34)

Inheritance allocations are shown here to be a key feature in the economic arrangement of the Muslim family. Although there are some exceptions, in general a woman's share of inheritance is half that of a man's. The next passage connects this rule of inheritance to family responsibilities. According to Islamic law, the husband is entirely responsible for his family's maintenance. Although his wife is guaranteed her inheritance and may have several other sources of income, she is not expected to assist him in providing for either herself or her children. In addition, he cannot try to force her into doing so. Thus, in marriage and society, Muslim women are assured an independent economic status.

This is also true of men, but with some modification. Islam recognizes a husband's independent ownership of wealth and property, but it is subject to greater limitations. For example, he is legally obliged to provide for all his family's needs. His wife, out of necessity, is given some say as to how his money and property are used, especially in his absence. At the same time, she is reminded that, in her husband's absence, she should remain obedient to God in the most general sense and, in particular, not misuse her husband's property or violate his express wishes concerning it. While both men and women are likely to see that this arrangement in some ways favors the other sex (in early Islamic history, men felt that it placed them at an economic disadvantage[180]), the Qur'an warns each not to covet what God has given the other, since in the end a workable balance is achieved.

It is hard to say how far such a system can be implemented in the United States. More career opportunities are available to women than ever before, and a woman's financial independence is widely accepted and acclaimed. Moreover, it is almost impossible for most one-income families to survive. Indeed, American couples are accustomed to viewing marriage as a union and a joint venture.

In traditional Muslim cultures, couples have less difficulty with this notion. The wife of an Egyptian friend of mine runs a successful catering business here in Lawrence, the profits of which she is using to buy a condominium that she intends to rent. She is completely comfortable with the fact that her income, which may be beginning to exceed her husband's, is entirely her own and not to be spent on her family. And this example is not atypical.

If couples, out of necessity or otherwise, were to combine their incomes, some of the protections built into this arrangement would certainly weaken. The economic autonomy of the wife is supposed to be a safeguard in case of a crisis, such as divorce or death. Hence, if couples consider their incomes as joint, arrangements should be made to provide equivalent reasonable and practical legal protection to each of the spouses.

At this point, it might be useful to consider how medieval Muslim jurists envisioned the minimal requirements of a Muslim husband and wife toward each other. In my opinion, it seems that these scholars often limited the privileges of women as much as the texts would permit, while extending the rights of men as far as possible without blatantly contradicting the textual sources. Coming from a different viewpoint, one would expect —and this is currently happening—that today's Muslim thinkers would to some degree reverse this trend.

---

[180] A. R. I. Doi, *Shari'ah in the 15th Century of the Hijrah* (Islamic Trust Pub., n.d.). See the chapter on inheritance.

154

Nonetheless, aside from the fact that in the past the husband was usually given nearly incontestable control over where his wife could go and whom she could see, it is quite illuminating to discover the paucity of explicit obligations imposed upon each partner. Both had conjugal rights over the other, with some advantage going to the husband. The husband had to provide full maintenance for his wife and children, and sometimes his near relatives as well, while the wife's income was her own. She was **not** obliged to do housework, cook, or even care for her children. Moreover, if it were within her husband's means, he had to provide his spouse with a housekeeper (to this day, women in the Arabian peninsula assume what practically amounts to a legal claim to having a housekeeper or servant when they marry). It was also the husband's duty to pay for his spouse's religious instruction.[181] The wife was to manage her husband's estate responsibly and according to his wishes in his absence. She was not to invite onto his property individuals, especially males, of whom he disapproved. Although I do not feel that Muslim American couples will agree that blanket control by a husband over his wife's comings and goings or choice of friends is something necessary or desirable, they may be surprised by early Islamic opinions on domestic duties.

Beginnings and Endings

Their friendship had reached the stage where they could be straightforward, and so the business woman unleashed in her questions all the resentment and annoyance that she had held back for so long.

"Why do you wear that horrible scarf?"

"Because of my faith. And I don't believe that women should be sexually exploited."

"You have a bachelor's in mathematics. You should have a career."

"I do have one, and my education helped prepare me for it. I'm a mother and I'm raising three children."

"I meant something useful, something you could earn money with."

"What's of greater value than love? You can't see it or measure it, but it grows inside yourself and between you and those you love."

"But if you worked, you'd be more independent financially."

"I do work very hard, and my husband gives me ten percent of his take-home salary to use as I like. He also pays for a housekeeper who comes twice a week."

---

[181]For discussions on this topic, see: Rahman. *Role of Muslim Women in Society*; Keith Hodkinson, *Muslim Family Law* (London: Croom Helm Ltd., 1984).

"If you had a paying job, you wouldn't have to depend upon his generosity."

"But that money is mine. It and the maid are part of our marriage agreement. Even though I love my children and my home, my efforts are valuable and I deserve what we agreed upon!"

"But if you had more money, you could do more. For instance, you could travel more often."

"My goal in life isn't Europe."

The Muslim approach to marriage is boldly pragmatic. After the candidates have given their required consent, family representatives from both sides will get together to iron out the details and draft a contract. If all parties agree, the groom will give the bride an agreed-upon marriage gift (*mahr*). A brief religious ceremony will then take place, to be followed soon thereafter by a joyous celebration.

Among Arab Muslims, the practice is that quite often the young people will not live together immediately: each will continue to reside with his or her own family for a while as they get to know each other better, hopefully allowing stronger bonds of affection to grow. At this stage, the bride and the groom, for obvious reasons, are encouraged not to consummate their union. However, they would not be in violation of the religious law if they did, for they are now legally married. Much of the romance of marriage, as it is conceived of in the West, is removed by the formal and strict legal proceedings leading up to the union. The candidates, however, especially if they are young, will frequently base their choices on more or less romantic considerations. It is then the task of the family representatives to take up the harder negotiations. The rationale is to consider at the very outset the difficulties that may arise later and to agree before the marriage is finalized on a future divorce settlement if this unwanted action were to become unavoidable. That the possible dissolution of the marriage is taken into consideration during these negotiations is seen clearly in the two Islamic institutions of the dower or marriage gift (*mahr*) and the marriage contract.

And if you divorce them before consummation, but after fixing of a dower for them, then the half of the dower [is due to them] unless they remit it. (2:237)

And it is not permissible for you [men] to take back anything of what you have given to them [your wives], except if both parties fear that they will be unable to keep the limits ordained by God.

And if you fear that they will be unable to keep the limits ordained by God, there is no blame on either of them concerning what she gives [him back of his gifts] to secure her release. (2:229)

But if you decide to take one wife in place of another, even if you have given one of them a treasure for dower, do not take back the least bit of it. Would you take it back by slander and a manifest wrong? (4:20)

In these verses concerning the marriage gift that a man gives to his future wife, the possibility of divorce is clearly anticipated. Accordingly, Muslims have recognized two kinds of dowry that are to be settled upon during marriage contract negotiations: an initial dowry, to be paid before the couple wed, and a deferred dowry, to be paid in installments or in full on demand if the husband violates his part of the contract (4:20). If he seeks divorce before consummation, he is only obliged to pay half of what was originally agreed upon (2:237). If the wife should seek dissolution, she may be required to return some or all of her dowry, depending on the degree of blame the court attaches to her husband (2:29).[182]

Very often, the dowry is in the form of something that will appreciate in value, such as jewelry or real estate. The dowry settlement can, as 4:20 suggests, be quite large. As an example, an American friend, who married a woman from Egypt, bought his bride, as part of her dowry, an apartment in Cairo that she rents out; the money that she accumulates is reinvested. Another friend from Saudi Arabia recently negotiated a marriage contract giving his wife one hundred thousand dollars worth of diamonds.

Similarly, deferred dowries may involve some arrangement that takes into account inflation, such as a fixed percentage of the husband's annual salary for a number of years and/or some fraction of his accumulated estate. For example, the wife might be entitled to half of his immovable property. Interestingly, I am often asked by young foreign Muslim men if I know any American Muslim women who are interested in getting married. When I advise them that it may be easier to find someone in their home country, I am frequently told that American women ask for much smaller dowries. Personally, I am not comfortable with introducing my friends to men who wish to take advantage of their unfamiliarity with this institution.

---

[182]For discussions on this topic, see *Rahman*, Role of Muslim Women in Society, and Hodkinson, *Muslim Family Law*.

The dower is only one factor that must be settled by the marriage contract, which is the chief means of protecting the rights and needs of both partners. In the contract, each partner may specify any demand as long as it is not in opposition to some aspect of Islamic law. Thus, a woman can insist on the right to have a career outside the home, to have her husband fund her education, to have a servant for the housework, or to have a nanny for the children. Jurists in Pakistan acknowledge that she could require that her permission be obtained in case her husband wants to take another wife.[183] It may appear superfluous to claim privileges that the law already allows, but the marriage contract attempts to settle from the start possible points of contention, and, in case of divorce, rather than remaining a neutral consideration in the eyes of a judge, a breach of the contract will work against the guilty party.

For a Muslim, divorce, especially if children are involved, should be avoided at all costs. Not even under the best of conditions is divorce truly fair to those it touches. The Prophet is reported to have said that in the eyes of God it is the most hated of all permissible things.[184] Islam's attitude toward divorce is similar to its attitude toward war: at times it may be necessary, but only as a last resort. This is why family mediators are to be called in (4:35) and why divorce should be pronounced on three separate occasions, following a three-month waiting period before the divorce becomes irrevocable:

> Divorce is [only permissible] twice, after which [the parties should either] stay together in a goodly manner or separate with kindness. And it is not permissible for you [men] to take back anything of what you have given to them [your wives], except if both parties fear that they will be unable to keep the limits ordained by God. And if you fear that they will be unable to keep the limits ordained by God, there is no blame on either of them concerning what she gives [him back of his gifts] to secure her release. These are the limits ordained by God, so do not transgress them. And if anyone transgresses the limits ordained by God, then those are wrong-doers. Then if he divorces her [irrevocably for the third time], she is not lawful for him thereafter until after she has married someone other than him. Then if he [the second husband] divorces her, there is no blame on either of them that they come together again if they think they can keep the limits ordained by God; He makes them clear for people to know. (2:229-30)

---

[183]Hodkinson, *Muslim Family Law*, 150-51.
[184]Ali, *Manual of Hadith*, no. 284, from the collection of Abu Dawud.

After three unsuccessful attempts, the wife is told to put her marriage behind her and sincerely seek another marriage. This may result in a more harmonious union, and at the same time it forces each partner to consider soberly their decision to end the first marriage. As the dissolution of any marriage is usually charged with mixed passions and emotions, there is always the danger that individuals will attempt to violate the spirit of these commands while obeying the letter. This explains why a woman's new husband must initiate divorce before she may return to her former spouse (2:230), for this will insure genuineness on her part in seeking a second marriage.

Ironically, in the past, many Muslim jurists have allowed a husband to divorce his wife irrevocably by issuing three divorce pronouncements on a single occasion, which is clearly opposed to the intent of the Qur'an. In many Muslim countries, in an effort to forestall such abuses, governments now require all marriages and dissolutions to be officially registered. This may be seen as a positive action, in conformity with the Qur'an's admonition not to "make a mockery of God's revelations" (2:131) which occurs in the midst of a lengthy discussion of divorce.

Based on 2:229 and several incidents occurring during the time of the Prophet, Islamic lawyers have always recognized a woman's right to divorce her husband. In legal manuals, the technical term for divorce at the instance of the husband is *talaq*, and for divorce at the instance of the wife it is khul'.[185] The following case is often cited:

> Jameelah bint Salul complained to the Prophet about her husband, "By God! I do not dislike him for any fault in his character or faith, but I dislike his ugliness. By God! If I had no fear of God, I would have spat in his face when he came to me. O Messenger of God! You see how beautiful I am and that Thabit is an ugly man. I don't blame him for his faith or character, but I fear disbelief in Islam." Muhammad then inquired, "Will you return his garden that he gave you?" She answered, "Oh Messenger of God! If he asks for more, I am prepared to give him even more." The Prophet said, "Not more, but return the garden." Then he ordered that Thabit should accept the garden and the separation.[186] (al Bukhari)

Unfortunately, even though the evidence could plainly be interpreted liberally, many jurists did the opposite and chose to restrict a woman's

---

[185]Hodkinson, *Muslim Family Law,* 275-76.
[186]Rahman, *Role of Muslim Women in Society,* 150-52.

rights in this regard as much as possible. It is a widespread practice in some places not to allow a woman to exercise this privilege unless she requests it in her marriage contract, and, in other places, unless her husband commits one of a very limited number of extreme abuses.

The Qur'an's regulations concerning divorce—and this is true of men's and women's rights in general—are not the same for both sexes. For example, women must observe a waiting period of three months before remarrying in order to determine if conception has occurred and to establish paternity if it has, while men can remarry immediately. It does assure, however, that equivalence and equity prevail. Once again, this is one of the fascinating aspects of the Qur'an: it is alert to challenges that were unlikely to be raised at the time of the Revelation and, indeed, for centuries thereafter. In the seventh century, it was simply unnecessary to justify any disparity between the sexes as regards religious regulations, beyond the argument that men are innately superior to women. Yet the Qur'an offers this defense at the end of a passage on divorce:

> And for them [women] is the like of what they [men] have over them with kindness, but men have a degree over them (2:228)

And we have the previously mentioned verse:

> And do not covet that of which God has given more to the one than to the other. Men shall have a portion of what they earn and women shall have a portion of what they earn. And ask from God out of His bounty; truly, God has full knowledge of all things. And for all We have appointed heirs from whatever is left by parents and relatives. And to those with whom your right hands have made a covenant, give them their portion; truly, God is witness over everything. Men are charged with the full maintenance of women in that God has given more to the one than to the other and in that they support [them] from their means. (4:32-34)

Thus we sense a cognizance on the part of the Qur'an that Muslim women's rights will remain as a point of contention. Its answer seems to be that one must consider the larger context within which the individual pronouncements are made. If Muslim men and women have almost identical rights and obligations, while men have been given a somewhat larger degree of both, it is because the Author has taken into account the whole temper of society.

Ways to Paradise

I stood watching the two of them as they found each other again. They took such soothing comfort in their rejoining that it seemed as if the torture they had just survived had never been, and that they were long accustomed to the love they were now sharing. If God does give us something of His spirit, I thought, women must have gotten the greater share of mercy and compassion. It was right then, seconds after the birth of my third daughter, that I felt that I had been granted a special glimpse of the great creative impulse that brings us into being.

The Qur'an is unequivocal in affirming that men and women are of the same spiritual essence and that neither has an advantage over the other in terms of goodness. Yet, also in this area, Islam recognizes differences in the ways which best suit the spiritual progress of each. My mother always insisted that there is no love on earth like the love of a mother for her children, and this opinion of hers surely finds support in Islam.

We have already observed that, in a number of places, the Qur'an couples man's dependency on God with a child's dependency on its mother (31:14; 46:15), and that there are several sayings of Muhammad's that compare God's love to the love of a mother for her children. On one occasion, he pointed to a women caressing her infant and asked his Com-panions if they thought she would ever throw her baby into a fire. When they naturally said that that was impossible, he told them "And God loves you even more than that."[187]

Not only may it be that a mother's love is the nearest thing on earth to God's love, but it may also be her greatest strength and one of her main roads to spiritual excellence. The saying of Muhammad that "Paradise is under the feet of the mother"[188] might well be rephrased as "Motherhood is a woman's steppingstone to Paradise." And while we should not be misled into believing that fatherhood plays a minor role in a man's moral development, for there are verses in the Qur'an and sayings of the Prophet that underline its importance, it would have to be said that the same sources hold the risking of his life for a just cause to be the greatest act of self-surrender for a man and his main avenue to perfection.

A closer look at 31:14 and 46:15 suggests a profound mystical parallel between the God—man and the mother—child relationships. In our minds, we seldom associate our love and attachment to our mothers with the two great crises recalled in these passages: the act of birth and our

---

[187]*Riyad al Salihin of Imam Nawawi*, trans. Zafrulla Khan, 94, no.421.
[188]Badawi, *Status of Woman in Islam*, 21. Quoted from al Nasa'i, Ibn Majah, and Ahmad.

weaning from the breast. But psychologists maintain that these cataclysms in every individual's life are fundamental to personality growth. The life-long tension—more unconscious then conscious—between the desire to return to the comfort of the womb and breast, and the need to strike out independently on one's own, is a primal catalyst for the development of the self. These two unavoidable upheavals in our lives originate through an irrepressible will to love. Similarly, our earthly separation from God and the inner conflict that creates between our spiritual, often unconscious, desire to return to Him and our innate drive for personal autonomy, fuels the development of our spirituality and total personality. It is in this way that the sacred love of a mother and child is a sign of the supreme mercy that brought us into this world.

As a system, Islam is extremely confident that a mere reminder of the eminence and importance of motherhood is a sufficient encouragement to Muslim women to have and care for children; otherwise it would not grant women an independent economic and legal identity, nor the right to divorce and inherit. And although these days many Muslim families in the West are struggling hard to secure this option for Muslim mothers, the difficulties are continually increasing.

Beyond Husband and Wife

Thus far we have been discussing the relationship of men and women within the family—primarily that of husband and wife. In theory, however, the marriage relationship might involve more than a partnership, since Islamic law allows a man to have up to four wives.

When first proclaimed, this regulation was actually a limitation, for the pre-Islamic Arabs were subject to no restrictions as to the number of spouses a man might have. The reaction of today's Muslims is mixed, ranging from insisting that Islam enjoins monogamy to upholding the notion that men are polygynous by nature and will consequently be compelled to seek illicit ways of satisfying this need if polygyny is banned.

This subject is often discussed by non-Muslims from a purely secular standpoint. Public Television recently aired a program investigating whether or not men were innately polygamous and women innately monogamous. In 1987, the student newspaper at the University of California, Berkeley, polled approximately ten students, asking whether they thought men should be legally permitted to have more than one spouse in response to a perceived shortage of male marriage candidates in California. The poll was not scientific, but it was surprising that almost all of those polled approved of the idea. One of the women even stated that a polygamous marriage would meet her emotional and sexual needs, and at the same time give her greater freedom than a monogamous union. Since Berkeley is well-known for its radicalism, the same reaction would hardly be expected of students on other college campuses. However, the idea of polygyny as a solution to certain social dilemmas accords with the aims of the Qur'an.

And if you fear that you will not be just to the orphans, then marry what is good for you among the women—two, three, or four. But if you fear that you will not be just [to them], then only one, or [a captive] whom your right hands possess. Thus it is more likely that you will not do injustice. (4:3)

There was some disagreement among the Companions of the Prophet as to the exact interpretation and occasion for this verse,[189] but there was unanimity in that it restricts the number of wives a man may have to no more than four. There is also agreement among Qur'anic exegetes that this revelation responded to the steady increase through war in the population of widows and orphans in the Muslim city-state of Madinah. Many commentators believe that this verse is proposing the marriage of the orphaned females as a solution to this crisis.

While there is no doubt that such an action would be within the purpose of the Revelation, its intent is certainly more general, since the concerns of all the orphans, not only female, are addressed, as the masculine plural for "orphans" is employed here (the masculine plural in Arabic includes both male and female, while the feminine plural is used exclusively when only females are designated). Thus it would seem that to solve the problem of fatherless households, the Qur'an is encouraging men to take into their care the destitute families by marrying the eligible widows and female orphans who are victims of such a tragedy.

Common sense would indicate that, under normal circumstances, monogamy is preferable. Barring a crisis of the type mentioned in this verse, and if the population of eligible men and women is nearly equal, monogamous match-making would be the most efficient response to the prescription to "marry the single among you" (24:31-32). It is also expected that there will likely be greater tension in a polygamous family setting. Many modern Muslims argue that monogamy is preferable, citing as their rationale, "You will not be able to be just between women, even if you desire to, but do not turn away [from any of them] altogether so as to leave her hanging in suspense" (4:129). As this verse appears in a differ-

---

[189]Asad, *The Message.*

ent context—that of a marriage on the brink of divorce—it should probably not be taken as a direct comment on 4:2-5; nevertheless, that does not preclude using it to help elucidate the passage. The fact that the verses 4:2-5 voice concern about injustice would in itself argue that the marriage of more than one wife should be undertaken with utmost caution. In Pakistan, for example, in an attempt to lower the level of abuse, the government now requires proof that a husband can meet the needs of all wives equally before it will grant permission for a plural marriage.[190]

Unfortunately, at almost any given time and place, crises of the kind mentioned in the verse on four wives (4:129) are likely to exist. Today in the United States, the population of single Muslim mothers with children is quite large, and frequently one finds in Muslim magazines pleas on their part for another family to take them in. The concern of such mothers is principally for their children, as it is with the Qur'an, for 4:3 begins with the phrase, "And if you fear that you will not be just to the orphans."

The two main barriers to acquiring a second family in the United States are the law and Americans' cultural aversion towards polygyny. In addition, most American males feel that they can barely support one family, much less two. Men wishing to marry for the first time are understandably reluctant to adopt a family that has suffered a tragedy, most men preferring that their first marriage, at least, begin under more favorable conditions. This may explain why the Qur'an says, "Then marry two or three or four" (4:3), for in addition to imposing a ceiling on the number of wives, it may be suggesting that men of means, who already have families, have a greater responsibility to take the destitute families into their care; the wording of this phrase may actually be encouraging them to do so. At any rate, unless and until American Muslims can overcome the obstructions to polygyny, they should at least establish community funds to assist single mothers.[191]

Outside of the marriage relationship, questions about the place of women in business, politics, education, and related topics of dress and segregation are currently generating a great deal of debate. We will conclude this discussion of the position of women in the Muslim community by

---

[190] Hodkinson, *Muslim Family Law*, 95-100.
[191] Occasionally Muslim communities have faced the problem of having more bachelors than potential brides. For example, at the time of the Muslim community's exodus to Madinah and during the Muslim conquests, the conquered territories contained virtually no Muslim women. In cases of temporary need, the Prophet encouraged Muslims to fast as a way of curbing sexual desire. Another option available to Muslim men is that they are permitted to marry women of the People of the Book (i.e., Jews and Christians), although in general marriage to non-Muslims is not encouraged.

briefly touching on these. Since a Muslim woman's inferior status as a witness has often served arguments limiting her access to the civil and civic arenas, we will start by re-examining this topic.

A Woman's Witness

> O you who believe, when you deal with each other, in transactions involving future obligations for a fixed period of time, put them in writing, and let a scribe write down faithfully as between the parties and let not the scribe refuse to write: as God has taught him, let him write. Let him who incurs the liability dictate, but let him fear God, his Lord, and not diminish anything of what he owes. And if the liable party is mentally deficient or weak or unable to dictate, let his guardian dictate faithfully. **And let there witness [it] two witnesses from among your men, and if not two men, then a man and two women, such as you choose for witnesses, so that if one of them errs, the other will remind her.** (2:282)

This verse has been used as an argument for the exclusion of women from political and civil offices, for her intellectual and consequent moral inferiority, and even for the inadmissibility of women's testimony in all cases outside of business transactions.[192] Fortunately, as Badawi demonstrates, such opinions were not universally held by earlier Muslim scholars, and today's scholars seem to be slowly moving in the opposite direction.[193] What one observes immediately is that the principal objective of the passage in question—and I have only quoted half of it—is the protection of business agreements and the avoidance of later contention. Facing widespread illiteracy, Islam set strict standards to guarantee the terms of a business contract and, in so doing, reduced the possibility of deception and misunderstanding that often, at least in the past, would have been settled violently. At that time, and for centuries to come in almost all societies, women were in general less educated and less proficient in financial dealings than men, and consequently the Qur'an required the witness of two men or a man and two women.

In eight places (2:282; 4:6; 4:15; 5:109; 5:110; 24:4; 24:6-9; 65:2), the Qur'an has issued instructions relating to the giving of testimony. Two of these refer only to swearing an oath and not to testifying in general, while

---

[192]Rahman, *Role of Muslim Women in Society*, 260-70, 347-57.
[193]Badawi, *Status of Woman in Islam*, 22-25; Rahman, *Role of Muslim Women in Society*, 260-70.

the other six refer to testifying. In all cases except 2:282, no specification on the sex of the witnesses is made. There are many examples in the hadith collections in which women's testimony is accepted without corroboration and, sometimes, where the testimony of a single female witness overrides the witness of several men.[194] Additionally, many of Muhammad's sayings are accepted in the canonical collections as authentic in spite of the fact that they have only a single woman as their source. From these observations, many modern writers contend that verse 2:282 was never meant to be a general stipulation. Various rationalizations are presented for this requirement in the case of business transactions: woman's greater temperamentality, emotional instability caused by the menstrual cycle and, a man's greater natural aptitude for business and mathematics. If one accepts that 2:282 should not be generalized to non-financial matters, which is the prevailing opinion in the West, then only the last explanation is worth consideration, since the others, if valid, would argue more strongly against a woman's testimony in other situations, such as criminal hearings.

In the United States and Europe, and other societies as well, women are proving that they can compete with men in the financial world. The majority of leaders in big business are still men, but women are making their mark and are gaining influence; thus the claim that men have a greater aptitude for business than women is becoming harder to defend. It has been contended that, in a truly Islamic society, the skills of women would of necessity be channeled into other careers, which would once again cause the world of finance to become an almost exclusively male domain. But utopian arguments depend on one's vision of the "true" society, and there are bound to be many different opinions about what that actually is.

The crux of the matter comes back to the Qur'anic stipulation of "if not two men, then a man and two women." As so often when reading the divine Word, we are forced to match current experience with revelation. Some will insist on a simple submission to the text, while others will advocate interpretation in the light of changed circumstances. As an example, since the Qur'an has set certain standards for the treatment of slaves (i.e., a female slave guilty of adultery receives half the punishment of a free woman), we might ask whether a Muslim government is ever allowed to proscribe slavery. Most will contend that the Qur'an promotes the eventual abolition of slavery and will argue in favor of its end. In a similar way, some will also insist that Islam promotes equal opportunity for men and

---

[194]Rahman, *Role of Muslim Women in Society*, 266-70.

women in education and business. Should this be achieved and differences dissolve, is it any longer necessary to consider the sex of the witnesses in business dealings? Fazlur Rahman answers in the negative:

> Because the case the Qur'an is speaking of is that of a financial transaction and because most women in those days did not deal with finances or with business in general, the Qur'an thought it better to have two women [witnesses] instead of one—**if one had to have women.** This means, of course, that if women should get education equal to men's and also become conversant with business and finance, the law must change accordingly.[195]

The Muslim will almost automatically flinch at such enterprising deliberation, for to him/her the Qur'an is not simply a by-product of holy inspiration. It is pure, direct Revelation. Bold interpretation of this kind departs from conforming to prescriptions, for it presumes the divine intention and, if done carelessly, could be a means of self-indulgence and of evading what God has commanded. Yet all interpretation, even literalist interpretation, involves some speculation, for it presumes that considerations of temporal context were never intended. Therefore, on this point I am inclined to agree with Rahman, because I accept his premise that one goal of Islam is to bring about equal opportunity in learning and business for men and women and that, in the meantime, the Qur'an took fully into account existing disparities in order to protect financial contracts.

Of course, we have to be aware that advances in technology have made possible a greater intersection of male and female roles and have also produced a society whose financial structures are more complex than those of seventh century Arabia. As the business world grows in complexity, more ingenious methods of deception are continually discovered, and financial and legal institutions are forced to impose ever stricter standards to safeguard their dealings. In the United States, if the purchase of a house, long-term loans, or the making of a will are to have legal force, they must almost always pass the review of a number of departments of several institutions and then usually become a matter of public record. Since the Qur'an attaches so much importance to the making and protection of contracts, I contend that existing legal safeguards of financial transactions, which surpass the requirements of the verse in question, are often in the public interest and necessary.

---

[195]Rahman, *Health and Medicine in the Islamic Tradition*, 105-106. Emphasis is the author's.

Leadership

The election of Benazir Bhutto to the post of Pakistan's prime minister has engendered a great deal of discussion as to the possibility of women holding positions of leadership in Muslim society. This also has implications for American Muslims, as so many converts are women who are skilled and trained in organization and leadership, talents that are badly needed in their communities. The Qur'an contains no direct statement against electing female leaders, and the only example given of a woman ruler—that of the Queen of Sheba—is exemplary.[196] The Qur'an shows her to be a wise, thoughtful, democratic leader whose main concern is the well-being of her people and who, through the influence of Solomon, eventually guides her nation to belief in one God. Due to the absence of any Qur'anic prohibition of this possibility, and because the only example provided of female rule is positive, we might expect that the idea of a woman chief of state would be acceptable to Muslims. But, in general, this is not the case.

One argument against it is that a woman is incapable of discharging all the duties that were carried out by Prophet Muhammad and his immediate four political successors. For example, Prophet Muhammad and these four caliphs led the congregational prayer and if men are present, the prayer ritual must be led by a man. Similarly, they were also military leaders who took troops into battle, and it would seem that women would generally be less qualified to fulfill this aspect of leadership. Since the leadership of the Prophet and his immediate four political successors is accepted by Muslims as the norm, a woman would therefore be disqualified from high office.

Today, however, it is unrealistic to insist that a leader should be able to undertake all of the functions performed by the early Muslim rulers. Government is much more complex and, although we would likely favor a candidate thoroughly schooled in Islamic law, military science, economics, and administration, we are satisfied to create various government institutions that specialize in such areas. As a result, the head of state can direct from the periphery. We do not expect our political leaders to go to war, nor need we demand that they have the requisite knowledge and training to qualify them for leading the rituals. Indeed, classical Sunni Islamic law, as contrasted with the Shi'ah view, had lesser expectations of the head of state, whose essential duties were administrative. As long as he could

---

[196]Abbott, *Aishah: The Beloved of Muhammad*, 176.

direct the defense of the state effectively and enforce the Shari'ah (Islamic law), the citizens owed him their allegiance.[197]

A more serious objection might be the statement of the Prophet: "A people who choose a woman as their ruler are unsuccessful." This saying belongs to al Bukhari's compilation,[198] and there are slight variations in other collections, such as the said people being "unfortunate" or "unhappy." The authenticity of this hadith has recently been questioned, but the great majority of Muslim scholars accept it. Technically speaking, there does not seem to be any special reason to suspect this tradition, since the narrator, a man called Abu Bakrah, also known by the name of Nafi ibn Masruh, is believed to have been the freedman of Muhammad and the source of a number of accepted traditions.[199] Also, the close correlation between the details of the narration and the complex political developments of that era add further credibility. If one wanted to disparage female leadership, simpler avenues were available.

About six years into Muhammad's mission, corresponding to 615-16 CE, the thirtieth surah was revealed. Up until that time, a steady stream of Persian conquests against Byzantium had brought the Christian empire to the edge of total defeat, with the loss of Jerusalem signaling the beginning of the end. The pagan Quraysh exulted over this development, since they saw it as a blow to monotheism. The beginning of this surah then predicted an almost inconceivable reversal:

> The Roman empire has been defeated in a land close by, but they, after the defeat of theirs, will soon be victorious within a few years. With God is the decision in the past and in the future. (30:2-4)

History records that the fortunes of the Persians began to turn shortly thereafter. In the interval between 622 and 627, the Roman empire was able to recover its lost territory through a sequence of brilliant victories and penetrate deeply into Persian territories. In 628, the government of the Persian empire collapsed, and Khusrau, the Persian monarch, was imprisoned and then executed. In the chaos of the next three years, at least ten different individuals ascended the throne of the tottering empire, including one of Khusrau's daughters. Her reign lasted little more than a year and represented the first time in the history of Persia that a woman

---

[197]John L. Esposito, *Islam and Politics* (Syracuse: 1987), 26-29.
[198]Abbott, *Aishah: The Beloved of Muhammad*, 175-76.
[199]Ibid. 175.

had assumed the leadership of the empire.[200] When the Muslims, who were carefully watching the political events taking place in Persia to see whether the Qur'anic prophecy would be fulfilled, heard that a woman had become the ruler, they naturally took the news to the Prophet, who then made the above comment.

Whether he meant that as a general principle or as a comment on current political developments is difficult to say. Isolated from its historical context, it may be taken as a permanent injunction against women assuming positions of leadership. On the other hand, he may have been confirming the Qur'anic prediction, assuring his followers that the Persian empire would not recover by such a move and that so radical a departure from its past was further evidence of its impending downfall. The decision as to what the Prophet meant by this saying thus depends on recourse to other evidence. Due to the Qur'an's positive portrayal of the Queen of Sheba, and because the record of woman leaders in the past and present has been rather good, in addition to the fact that this is now a widely accepted idea in Western culture, I would be very surprised if American Muslims were to disqualify women from political leadership.

A Woman's Dress

The invitation of the young, petite Malaysian women was too genuine and kind for Karen to refuse. In the few weeks since she had accepted Islam, the only Muslims she had met were those who, like her, attended the nightly prayers, and with one exception, these were all men. So she looked forward to the opportunity to gather with fellow Muslim women at their meeting.

Karen was somewhat surprised to find that she was the only one present not in traditional Muslim dress, since she had observed other Muslim women on campus wearing Western fashions. But she was even more astonished when she learned that the theme of the lecture that night would be the Islamic dress code, for it was obvious that all of these women met its requirements. Consequently, she felt as if she was on trial, subjected to a holy inquisition.

The women present wore solemn, sanctimonious expressions as the American convert who was giving the lecture spoke of the "dangers," the "sickness," the "cheap and immoral desires" of Western society and especially of its women, who tantalize themselves and others with their "half naked display of flesh." Even fingernail polish was included in her dia-

---

[200]Ehsan Yarshater, *The Cambridge History of Iran* (Cambridge University Press, 1983), 3(1):170-71.

170

tribe as an "evil." Karen wanted to hide her hands behind her back, to slip out of there, to tell them all to get lost, to mind their own business. Her very first lecture on Islam, and it concentrates on—of all things—the essentials of wearing a scarf!

"I wish you had let me know about their invitation in advance," I told her later. "I hate to see you so hurt like this."

Practically all Muslim women at some time or other agonize over the decision to conform to what is usually referred to as the Islamic code of dress. By "Muslim women" I am not referring only to American or Western women, for in my travels to Saudi Arabia I have discovered that many, if not most, Saudi women abide by the standard only in public and because of government enforcement. In their homes, they typically wear Western fashions, even in the presence of unfamiliar men. Yet at the same time, these same women—and this holds true for Muslim women in every culture—will invariably insist that a Muslim female must abide by the code after reaching puberty, while attributing their own remission to a weakness of commitment.[201] Since the Arabian peninsula is by far the most traditional and conservative Muslim culture, a smaller proportion of women should be expected to observe traditional Muslim dress in other places.

Difficulties are intensified for Muslim women in the West, and even more for converts, for several reasons. In addition to joining a system of belief that many of their countrymen see as threatening or strange, the Mus-lim community encourage them to discard their birth names in favor of Arabic ones and to employ several standard Arabic expressions in everyday conversation. Any one of these might seem incidental and in some ways beneficial, but their cumulative effect could result in something of a identity crisis. The issue is aggravated by the fact that although Muslim men technically have a code of dress, it is much more flexible and less obvious than women's, and has lent itself to much freer interpretation. For instance, the 'awrah (the area of the body that must be covered) of a man has always been defined as that part of the body between the navel and knees. Recently, scholars in Saudi Arabia, after reviewing the legal sources, have redefined the male 'awrah as the area between the navel and upper thigh. Hence a Western man can convert to Islam and remain, as far as his faith goes, visually anonymous, while the same does not hold true for a woman who does not wish to compromise a religious requirement.

---

[201]Soraya Altorki, *Women in Saudi Arabia* (Columbia Press: 1986), 35-38.

The Qur'an is undoubtedly unequal in its treatment of men's and women's modesty. It contains no explicit prescriptions on modest dress for men, while it has three direct statements with regard to women.

> And say to the believing women that they should lower their gaze and guard their private parts, and that they should not display of their adornment except what [ordinarily] appears thereof, and that they should draw their head coverings over their breasts and not display their adornment. . . . And that they should not strike their feet in order to make apparent what is hidden of their adornment. (24:31)

> And the elderly among women who have no hope of marriage—there is no blame on them if they lay aside their outer garments without displaying their adornment; but to be modest is better for them. (24:60)

> O Prophet, say to your wives and daughters and the believing women that they should draw over themselves something of their outer garments [*min jalabibihinna*]; that is more conducive to their being known and not molested. (33:59)

In pre-Islamic times, the customary attire of the Arab tribal woman consisted of an ornamental head covering that hung down her back and showed her hair in front, a loosely worn tunic that was cut low in front leaving her breasts in view, and a skirt tied at the waist, together with various pieces of jewelry, such as rings, earrings, arm and ankle bracelets.[202] This style of dress, which was not only alluring but also compensated for the intense desert heat, could still be found among certain bedouin women in Arabia up to the turn of this century and was photographed by certain European travelers.[203] The Qur'an's instruction to the believing women to draw their head coverings (*khimar*; plural, *khumur*) over their bosoms (24:31) and to put on their outer garments when they were in public (33:59), imposed, with the minimum of inconvenience, a modest standard of dress for Muslim women. As 24:31 goes on to say, they can resume the customary attire in their own homes in the presence of their immediate families and household servants. It becomes clear from the Prophetic traditions associated with these verses, in particular those related to (33:59),

---

[202]Yusuf al Qaradawi, *The Lawful and the Prohibited in Islam* (Indianapolis: American Trust Pub., n.d.), 160; Asad, *The Message*, 538-39.

[203]Wilfred Thesiger, *Arabian Sands* (New York: E. P. Dutton & Co., 1959), 192.

that sexual abuse is the concern here. And since society is always more apt to exploit women sexually rather than men, special emphasis is placed on the dress of the former.

Over time, jurists elaborated a strict dress code for Muslim women. However, the wearing of the *khimar* as described in 24:31, when combined with an outer garment of the kind mentioned in 33:59, probably closely approximated later elaborations. The earliest records of juristic discussion on this matter, going back to the generations of the Prophet's Companions and their successors, centered on the debate of whether a woman had to veil her face in public, or if it was appropriate for her hands and face to show.[204]

The latter was the majority opinion and has remained the standard ever since, but this does not mean that all women in the Islamic world recognize a single canonical attire, for there is considerable variation. For example, many Egyptian women cover their hair but allow their necks to show; Malaysian women sometimes wear pants underneath a long bib; Saudi ladies wrap one end of the head-covering loosely around the neck several times; and Iranian women frequently wear their scarves low on their foreheads so that their eyebrows cannot be seen. However, there is a nearly universal acceptance that only a woman's face and hands may be seen. This is not to imply that there are no dissenting opinions, for one can easily imagine the hardships encountered by Muslim ladies traveling and living in non-Muslim societies.

To date, the strongest and most obvious argument for greater flexibility comes from Muhammad Asad:

> Although the traditional exponents of Islamic law have for centuries been inclined to restrict the definition of "what may [decently] be apparent" to a woman's face, hands and feet—and sometimes less than that—we may safely assume that the meaning of *illa ma zahara minha* is much wider, and that the deliberate vagueness of the phrase is meant to allow for all time-bound changes that are necessary for man's moral and social growth. The pivotal clause in the above injunction is the demand, addressed in identical terms to men as well as to women, to "lower their gaze and be mindful of their chastity": and this determines the extent of what, at any given time, may legitimately—i.e., in consonance with Qur'anic principles of social morality—be considered "decent" or "indecent" in a person's outward appearance. . . .

---

[204]al Qaradawi, *The Lawful and the Prohibited in Islam*, 155-59.

Hence, the injunction to cover the bosom with a *khimar* (a term so familiar to the contemporaries of the Prophet) does not necessarily relate to the use of a *khimar* as such but is, rather, meant to make it clear that a woman's breasts are **not** included in the concept of "what may decently be apparent" of her body and should not, therefore be displayed. . . .

The specific time-bound formulation of the above verse [33:59] (evident by the reference to the wives and daughters of the Prophet), as well as the deliberate vagueness of the recommendation that women "should draw upon themselves some of their outer garments (*min jalabibihinna*)" when in public, makes it clear that the verse was not meant to be an injunction (*hukm*) in the general, timeless sense of this term but, rather, a moral guideline to be observed against the ever changing background of time and social environment. This finding is reinforced by the concluding reference to God's forgiveness and grace.[205]

The cogency of Asad's argument is somewhat diminished by his assertion that the restriction against a woman baring her breast is timeless, for if one "covering" has eternal validity, why not the other? The charge of eclecticism will surely be raised, and indeed whenever a new interpretation is advocated in light of changed circumstances, such a charge has to be expected. The vagueness of the verses on certain points definitely provides room for different cultural adaptations and, as already shown, there have been many. But the issue at hand is one of extent.

So far, on matters like these, I and other writers have advocated that those involved try to discern the overall direction of the Qur'an when responding to a given verse. For instance, as remarked previously, Muslims no longer insist upon gathering up horses in preparation for battle, even though that is the explicit dictate of 8:60, because it would not advance the larger objective of making adequate preparations for war. Therefore, in the present case, we might first determine whether or not the Muslim community should observe at least some minimal standard of modesty in dress. Probably all believers, based on 24:31, will concede this much, as does Muhammad Asad in his commentary on the passage. They would also most likely agree that the dress code inherited from the earliest Muslim community and handed down from one generation to the next was certainly appropriate in the past and in conformity with the injunctions of the Qur'an.

---

[205]Asad, *The Message*, 538-539 (notes 37 and 38) and 651 (note 75).

It then might be asked, at what stage did it become advisable or allowable for Muslims to assume Western norms. It would be hard to find a moral or psychological justification for such a change. In fact, in *Islam at the Crossroads*, Asad himself urged Muslims at the early part of this century not to adopt Western standards.[206] In a revised edition that appeared a half of century later, he made no apology for that view and held that it was appropriate in its time. But, he stated, in the years since then, the Muslim people had so absorbed Western cultural values that to attempt to return to earlier norms would be as senseless as the original adoption of Western styles. In his opinion, it would amount to no more than "another act of sterile and undignified imitation: in this case, the imitation of a dead and unreturnable past." In other words, the social mores, for better or worse, have in fact changed as an inevitable consequence of encountering a more powerful civilization. As a result, what was considered as exploitive or indecent dress in the past is simply no longer considered so today.

Many Muslims will not be persuaded by this argument, for it is a main part of the believer's perception that religion sets moral standards for society and not the converse. Furthermore, even though in practice women often do not conform to the traditional dress code, this very code, as an ideal, is upheld almost universally by Muslims of both sexes; recently the global Muslim community has even witnessed the reappearance of traditional women's dress on a large scale. Finally, the traditional dress of women conforms to the spirit of the Qur'an and fourteen centuries of custom, and would deter what Muslims view as the sexual exploitation of women in the West.

I therefore feel that the case for any real revision on this matter is not entirely convincing. On the other hand, there is a desperate need for the community to exercise sympathy and understanding toward those who are grappling with this problem, in particular Muslim women living in the West. The difficulties and hardships—emotional, social, employment-wise—encountered in conforming to this code vary from individual to individual, and the approach of the Muslim should be conciliatory and accommodating rather than accusatory and reproachful. The utmost allowances must be made so that Muslim women are not dissuaded from community participation. Muslim men should also show the greatest sensitivity and propriety in this regard. It was not long ago that I witnessed the absurd spectacle of Muslim women, fully dressed, languishing at a picnic table under the hot summer sun while their spouses frolicked in the sand and waves amidst American sunbathers.

---

[206] Asad, *Islam at the Crossroads*, 78-9.

It will be some time before American and European Muslim women find fashions that harmonize with their culture and religion. But if the demand should grow, then this will surely happen. For now, I would suggest a community attitude on this matter in line with the evocation that concludes 33:59, which reminds the reader of God's forgiveness and compassion. Perhaps this is, as Asad suggests, an acknowledgment of the future difficulties that Muslims will meet in this area and a call for clemency on the part of believers in their efforts to surmount them, for truly "God does not burden any soul beyond its capacity" (2:233).

Education and Segregation

Muslim scholars and jurists have insisted that education is not only a right but also a religious obligation on all Muslim men and women. The Arabic word 'ilm, which means science, knowledge, and/or education, appears in the Qur'an 854 times. It "has never been used to deprive women of education. On the contrary, it has been used to persuade them to educate themselves."[207] Throughout the greater part of Islamic history, Muslim women, much like women in other cultures, contributed little to the development of the natural sciences but exerted considerable influence on the evolution of literature and the legal sciences.[208] The part played by women in the science of hadith is well-documented. Siddiqi states that through the first several Islamic centuries, women were equal partners with men in this field and that:

> This partnership of the women with men in the cultivation of Hadith continued throughout its history. All the important compilers of traditions since its earliest history received many of them from the women *shuyukh*. Every important collection of traditions contains the names of many women as immediate authorities of the author. After the compilation of the various collections of traditions, however, the women traditionists acquired mastery of many of these works and delivered lectures on them which were attended by a large number of students (men as well as women), and many important men traditionists sat at their feet and secured their certificates.[209]

---

[207]Adnan A. Algadi, *Utilization of Human Resources: The Case of Women in Saudi Arabia* (Sacramento: California State University, 1979), p. 56.
[208]Rahman, *Role of Muslim Women in Society*, 56-64; Soha Abdel Kader, *Social Science Research and Women in the Arab World* (Paris: UNESCO, 1984), 140-41.
[209]Siddiqi, *Hadith Literature*, 184.

Later on, he states:

> These fair traditionists of Islam, as one may see from what has been said, did not confine their activities to a personal study of traditions or to the private coaching of a few individuals in it, but they took their seats as students as well as teachers in public educational institutions—side by side with their brethren. They attended general classes which were attended by men as well as women students. The colophons of many manuscripts which are still preserved in many libraries show them both as students attending large lecture classes, and also as teachers delivering regular courses of lectures to them.[210]

Judging from Siddiqi's recounting of the contribution of women in this field, we note a steady decline in women's activity that coincides with the more general cultural decline that had set in by the tenth Islamic century, albeit at a seemingly accelerated rate. It would be interesting to investigate this change and what effects, if any, it has had on modern Muslim viewpoints concerning the ways and means of educating women. This may shed some light on the dilemma facing so many American Muslim communities: on the one hand, women are reminded of their sacred duty to obtain knowledge, especially of their religion, while on the other, they are presented with unequal and grossly inferior opportunities, when these are compared with men's.

This is due mainly to segregation of the sexes, for the main source of learning in Muslim communities in the West is the mosque, just as it was in the earliest days of Islam. But unlike those times, contemporary Muslim women are discouraged from even attending congregational prayers. It is true that they can learn through books and tapes, and hear an occasional lecture that is usually open to the general non-Muslim public, but such resources and opportunities are scarce, require considerable personal initiative and investment, and in no way compensate for the opportunities to learn and observe the implementation of Islam on the community level that are available to men.

I am not saying that segregation by sex is inherently wrong or that it subjugates women, for this, I believe, depends on the cultural context. Cultures in which segregation is still practiced usually have developed very distinct roles for men and women, and different domains over which they have and exercise power. Most often, they give men even less access

---

[210]Ibid., 152-53.

to the women's domain than women have to the men's.[211] Research indicates that the great majority of women in these cultures do not view themselves as oppressed and that they are perhaps more relaxed and confident of themselves than are women in the West.[212] Once, when I told my wife that her culture oppresses women because they do not share in the political process, she retorted, "So what? Men play little or no part in many functions of our society, like arranging marriages and running homes. Besides, Saudi women have no desire to be mayors and governors!"

Without question, an American is in a poor position to decide if segregation by sex is right or wrong in Yemen or Saudi Arabia, because that has to be determined subjectively and within the societies themselves. However, it is my place to argue that the seclusion and exclusion of women is wrong in the West. The history and culture of Western peoples is very different from that of traditional societies, and although segregation by sex can be put into practice in the West, the history, culture, and worldview from which it emerged can not be transferred here. Moreover, the related cultural alternatives that may exist for women in traditional cultures are not found in the West. The subjective reality is that for most American men and women, segregation, be it racial or sexual, is subjugation and oppression, and prevents many Americans—including children from Muslim families—from considering Islam as a viable alternative.

But cannot the same reasoning be used against the Muslim dress code? There are some key differences.

In the first place, there is no explicit prescription in either the Qur'an or the hadith for adopting segregation on the community level. Afzular Rahman states the case clearly:

> Similarly, the custom of seclusion (*harem* or *purdah*) was found to have been in practice in ancient Byzantium and Persia, and from there, it made its way to the court of Baghdad and eventually found common acceptance in most Muslim lands. It cannot, however, be said that these practices are based on Islamic edicts. In fact, there is no religious edict, or at least nothing in the Holy Qur'an which would justify such an inference. The Holy Qur'an only stresses that they (the women) "draw their veils over their bosoms and not display their beauty." The historical origin of the custom of seclu-

[211]Abdel Kader, *Social Science Research and Women in the Arab World*, 147-48; Carka Makhlouf, *Changing Veils* (Austin: University Of Texas Press, 1979), 25-28, 44, 96-97; Amal Rassam, *Social Science Research and Women in the Arab World* (Paris: UNESCO, 1984), 124-28.
[212]Makhlouf, *Changing Veils*, 25-30.

sion of women dates much further back, before the advent of Islam. The restrictions on the scope of the woman's mobility came to gradually superimpose onto the Islamic society through the absorption of local customs and it is this which has made them more and more dependent psychologically, economically and socially on their men-folk, and not the religion itself. The seclusion of women eventually began to be regarded as a status symbol amongst the middle and upper classes, whose economic conditions did not necessitate the employment of women outside the home. Her preoccupation with the family, which by now considerably extended and served as a self-sufficient economic unit in an agrarian economy, tended to enforce her seclusion with the family and to limit her potentiality as a contributor towards the main stream of life.[213]

The hadith literature also indicates that seclusion was at most a limited practice in the first century of the Islamic era—probably, as Rahman mentions, restricted to certain aristocratic families influenced by Persian and Byzantine customs. In the most authoritative hadith compilations, there are accounts of the Prophet and his Companions going to unrelated (non-*mahram*) women to have lice removed from their hair,[214] of a woman from outside Muhammad's family eating from the same dish as the Prophet,[215] of the wife of a Companion serving his male guests,[216] of the Prophet's visiting a married couple in his community and conversing with the woman about a dream from which he had just awakened,[217] of a visit to a female Companion by two male Companions and their mourning over Muhammad's recent death.[218] The evidence leads to Abdel Kadir's and Levy's conclusions that:

Veiling [of the face] and seclusion did not exist in early Arabia. All historical accounts point to the fact that women in the early days of Islam in Arabia and the countries that came under the influence of the Arabs played an active role in the social and political community. A study of the Koran and the Prophet's Hadiths

---

[213]Rahman, *Role of Muslim Women in Society*, 342-33.
[214]*Sahih al Bukhari*, trans. Muhammad Muhsin Khan, vol. 2, "The Book of Hajj" (26), Hadith no. 782, and "The Book of Jihad" (52), Hadith no. 47.
[215]Ibid., 65:10.
[216]Ibid., 62:78.
[217]Ibid., 74:41.
[218]Quoted from *Sahih Muslim* by Imam Nawawi, *Riyad al Salihin*, trans. Muhammad Zafrulla Khan.

shows that there is no particular injunction that indicates that women should be veiled or secluded from participation in public life. . . .[219] And that it was approximately one hundred and fifty years after the death of the Prophet that the system [of seclusion of women] was fully established. . . in which, among richer classes, the women were shut off from the rest of the household under the charge of eunuchs.[220]

The Qur'anic verses 33:33 and 33:53 are often cited as a prescription for the general segregation of men and women. There is reason to doubt that the limits adopted by the Prophet's family in response to these verses were as severe as those adhered to by present-day conservative Muslim families. Going as far back as the third Islamic century, we find al Tabari, in his famous *Tafsir,* interpreting these as a proscription against the type of loose intermixing of the sexes that was common in pre-Islamic times, and not as a prohibition preventing the Prophet's wives from community participation.[221]

When 33:33 was used against Aishah (one of Muhammad's wives) for her leading an army against Ali in the Battle of the Camel, she did not accept her accusers' interpretation.[222] Yet even if the Prophet's family did adopt a severe form of segregation in response to it, one has to remember that the verses direct themselves specifically to the Prophet and his family, and that the same surah contains a number of edicts exclusive for them. For example, the Prophet was allowed to keep more than four wives, was prevented at some stage from ever divorcing them, and his wives were ordered not to remarry after his demise. The very personal nature of these prescripts is emphasized by the surah's statement that the wives of the Prophet "are not like other women" (33:32). Thus, if individuals choose to impose upon themselves a severe form of sexual segregation, the most that they can claim is that they are imitating what is known among Muslims as a Sunnah, a behavior or usage of the Prophet, which, if not related to an explicit prescript, cannot be taken as a general regulation and should not be forced upon the Muslim public at large.[223]

---

[219]Abdel Kader, *Social Science Research and Women in the Arab World,* 145-46.

[220]R. Levy, "The Status of Women in Islam," in *The Social Structure of Islam* (New York: Cambridge University Press, 1965), 91-134.

[221]Rahman, *Role of Muslim Women in Society,* 342.

[222]Abbott, *Aishah: The Beloved of Muhammad,* 128-76.

[223]Mention should be made here of the argument that the separation of men and women in the ritual prayer attests to a general segregation. One simply has to note that in other Muslim rituals, for example, the pilgrimage rites, no separation exists.

It is true that Islam disapproves of the indiscriminate intermixing of the sexes, but the opposite of segregation is not promiscuity. Most converts have personally observed that family participation in lectures and Muslim social gatherings are the most unfavorable breeding grounds for profligacy. Indeed, in both Makkah and Madinah, groups of families sit together between the ritual prayers, separate into male and female groups when the prayer is announced, and resume their places after its conclusion. It would seem that the many moral admonitions found in the Qur'an and the traditions, the adoption of modest dress, and the existence—at least in theory—of severe penalties for adultery, should serve as a sufficient deterrent to moral degeneracy, especially at religious meetings. These will not guarantee prevention, but there are other kinds of sexual perversions that seclusion could engender.

And, more importantly, sexual immorality is not the only nor necessarily the greatest danger to society. The risks of squandering a great and vital resource of knowledge and insight, of providing women with inadequate opportunities for learning and practicing their faith, of women becoming ignorant of their rights and of those rights being abused by male bias, are too grave to be overlooked. As one woman convert told me, "Western women have struggled long and hard to gain some control over their lives, and I am not about to entrust my well-being to the good nature and judgment of men." Which brings us to the second major difference between a dress code and seclusion: modest dress at this point may require a considerable personal adjustment, but, strictly speaking, it should not hinder women from full participation in the religious community. It may even enhance the possibility, for although a Muslim woman's dress is certainly sexual, it is not sexy; it deemphasizes much of her physical or external beauty—as the Qur'an says, "her adornment"—and accentuates her innate strengths. In public interactions, this might place her on a more equal footing with men.

The Woman's Complaint

And they ask you for a judgment concerning women. Say: "God gives you [believers] a judgment concerning them. (4:127)

And they would continue to ask up to the present. Throughout history, religion has not been kind to women, for male-dominated orthodoxies fused cultural biases and aversions with dogma, law, and scriptural commentary. Twentieth-century society was bound to inquire into them, for how can God Himself have rendered such a low judgment concerning the character and place of women? Western Muslims, detached and/or severed from the cultures that have kept and preserved Islam, are discovering in the Qur'an and Islam a different view of women from the one they had harbored in the past. It is true that the "male and female are not the same," and any honest reading has to accept this as a Qur'anic precept. But this is not to say that one is more naturally intelligent or pious than the other. Rather, it means that their personalities profoundly balance and augment each other in ways that are well-suited to all the changes that society will experience.

Equally true—and this accords with the Qur'an and the traditions—is that there is something in the characters of the two sexes that allows men to assume leadership and dominance more readily than women. Yet this reality does not imply that women are not fit to lead, learn, and participate, for I believe that Islam's textual sources are clearly open to this possibility. One thing that it does mean is that society must be alert to the abuse of women, because throughout the Qur'an one finds repeated injunctions and warnings against such mistreatment. A verse such as

> God has indeed heard the words of her who disputed with you concerning her husband and complained [about him] to God, and God hears the conversation between the two of you. Truly God is All-Hearing, All-Seeing (58:1),

which addresses a common injustice committed by men of seventh-century Arabia, must, because of the obvious cultural specificity of the following verse, be read as a universal warning, to be forever heeded by the Muslim community.

A faithful interpretation of Islam by modern Muslims most probably will not agree completely with twentieth-century feminists' platforms, nor will it agree with many of the views about women found in earlier Muslim scholarship. Once again, as on so many issues, the Muslim community finds itself forced into being "a people of the middle way" (2:143) in its struggle to work out what it means to be a Muslim man or woman in the modern world.

LAW AND STATE

Unity, brotherhood, the elderly, the family, marriage, and the roles of men and women are the main topics of discussion right now among the American Muslim community. A survey of American and Canadian Muslim newsletters and magazines would confirm this. Since American Muslims are not in a strong position to influence legislation, the current discussion on civil, criminal, and international law remains limited and hypothetical.

There has been some effort at devising an alternative to Western banking in accord with Islam's ban on usury (*riba*),[224] but, as can readily be imagined, both the theoretical and practical problems are immense. Nearly all Muslim economists agree that a truly suitable alternative has not yet been implemented.[225]

The attention of Muslims in the West has been drawn to a few issues of no immediate bearing on their lives. The founding of the Islamic Republic of Iran, the numerous and multifarious calls for jihad, the death sentence by Imam Khomeini against Salman Rushdie, and other incidents have reopened in the West questions about Islam's positions on government, non-Muslim minorities, war, and apostasy. Frequently, the Western Muslim is shocked to find himself or herself in the uneasy role of Islam's spokesperson to a non-Muslim culture, as microphones and television cameras zoom in on an ordinary believer to extract his or her spontaneous sorting-out and explication of world events.

JIHAD

Then, when the sacred months are over, kill those who ascribe divinity to other than God [mushrikeen]wherever you find them, and take them captive and besiege them and wait for them in every place of ambush. But if they repent and establish the *salah* and give the zakah, then leave their way free. Truly, God is Most Forgiving, Most Merciful. (9:5)

"An Islamic state," proclaimed the Muslim speaker, "does not simply wage war on non-Muslim political systems. It must follow very strict guidelines. Before it may attack a non-Muslim country, it must make every effort to send emissaries to invite the regime and its people to accept either Islam or Islamic rule. If the invitation is ultimately rejected, then and only then may the Islamic government declare war against the non-Muslim government."

"But that's like saying that I have to listen to your preaching or your going to punch me in the mouth," a member of the university audience exclaimed. "I'd like to know," she continued sharply, "if Muslim governments are equally obliged, under Islamic law, to accept missionaries from other religions."

[224]Muhammad N. Siddiqi, *Muslim Economic Thinking* (Leicester, UK: The Islamic Foundation, 1981).
[225]Ibid.

Theists cannot but apprehend God's control over the human drama, be it through God's ordained laws built into the total system, or through direct and subtle manipulation, or some combination of these two. Religious communities will often interpret prosperity as divine favor and misfortune as divine disapproval: the latter must be on account of the nation's collective sinfulness and demands a return to the pure sources of faith.

The Qur'an contains persistent reminders that such a formulation is inaccurate and oversimplified. Worldly achievement involves important tests, and patient suffering brings great reward. Yet during the lifetime of the Prophet, ultimate victory was heavenly confirmation of the truth of his mission and the fidelity and sincerity of his followers.

Immediately after his death, the Muslim community found itself locked in war, first with apostate tribes and then with the Roman and Persian empires. Its remarkable and rapid successes, under the pious leadership of Abu Bakr and afterwards 'Umar, could only have further reinforced the conviction that God was always with the Ummah and that it was to be His instrument in establishing the universal kingdom of God on earth. However, not all Muslims who had a part in the great conquests— almost surely, not even most—had purely pious and non-material motives. The spoils of war were always a strong enticement which, on many occasions, the Qur'an and the Prophet played down in favor of the spiritual reward for self-sacrifice in a just cause.

> Let those fight in the cause of God who sell the life of this world for the Hereafter. And the one who fights in the cause of God, and then is [either] slain or attains victory, We shall give to him a mighty reward. (4:74)

> God has purchased of the believers their lives and themselves for [the price that] theirs is paradise. So they fight in His cause and slay and are slain. A promise binding on Him in truth, through the Torah, the Gospel, and the Quran. And who is more faithful to his covenant than God? Then rejoice in the bargain you have made: That is the triumph supreme.(9:111)

Within a few generations after the death of Muhammad, the Muslim empire stretched westward across North Africa to the Atlantic and eastward through Persia and into China. Later there would be major setbacks at the hands of the Moguls, Turks, and Crusaders. Yet the first two of these were eventually to adopt Islam, and the Ottomans would counteract much of the Christian conquest and, in the seventeenth century, reach as far westward as to besiege Vienna.

The recurrence through a millennium of inevitable triumph going back to the lifetime of the Prophet helps to explain the supreme confidence and one-sidedness of classic Muslim religio-political thought. Muslim scholars of the past divided the world into two mutually exclusive domains: *dar al Islam* (the abode of Islam), which was the territory ruled by Muslims, and *dar al harb* (the abode of war), which was to be subjected, through conquest if necessary, to Muslim rule. Although, at least in theory, a constant state of conflict was to exist with non-Muslim powers, long intervals of peace and commercial and cultural exchange did in fact transpire between the Islamic and other systems. Conversion was not a primary objective; only subjugation to God's law as they understood it. As a matter of fact, Muslim rulers were usually in no hurry to have conquered peoples convert, not only because they were constrained by Islamic law from forcing conversions but because of the economic benefit they often reaped from taxing non-Muslim citizens at a higher rate than Muslim subjects.

On the whole, conversion occurred continuously but gradually. And in many parts of the Islamic empire, Muslims remained in the minority for hundreds of years. Western scholarship has finally dispelled the stereotypical depiction of the fanatical Arab horseman, wielding a sword in one hand and a Qur'an in the other, offering conversion or death.[226] As must be expected, religious discrimination did exist, but in the pre-Enlightenment period, Muslim civilization compared very favorably with most others—in particular, with Christian Europe—on this score, and intolerance very rarely took the form of forced conversion.

The Muslim world is still struggling to make sense of and recover from its unexpected humiliation and exploitation under European colonialization, its steady decline to Third World status, and the return of a Jewish state to Palestine, the Muslim possession of which had so long been a living proof of the superiority of Islam over its two major predecessors, Judaism and Christianity. Frustration erupts as depicted on the newscasts in the seemingly perpetual calls from multifarious sources for jihad. These calls are almost always directed against the West or against governments—and sometimes individuals—believed to be "puppets" of the West; occasionally, Muslims on both sides of a conflict will even call for jihad against each other. The Western audience watches in horror, reminded of its own atrocities committed in the past and, in some places, still being committed in the name of God. As a

---

[226]Bernard Lewis, *The Jews of Islam* (Princeton: Princeton University Press, 1984), 3-4.

result, it fervently hopes that the separation of church and state in its own domains is never eroded.

The deeply felt threat of religious militancy and fanaticism draws the Western listener into a strange kind of "holy" conflict, waged to the background of enraged cries of "Death to America!"—"Death to Israel"—"Death to England!"—"Death to Bush!"—"Death!"—"Death!"—"Death!" It does not matter to the listeners that the shouts are coming from peoples who have suffered miserably under past Western imperialism and manipulation, colonialism and neocolonialism. Most are unaware of this, but, even if they were aware, the deep-seated paranoia that it arouses might justify the past anyway. "The fact of the matter is that they hate us and we hate them, and they want to kill us or destroy and subjugate us in the name of God!" The Islam seen by the West as it "unfolds" on the television screen has little to do with peace and mercy. To the viewer, it looks and sounds like hatred and death.

Thanks in part to the Western media, and even more to the way the term is presently used by the Muslim masses, jihad is almost exclusively translated into English as "holy war" or "religious war." However, the primary meaning of jihad to the ancient Arabs, and also the one found in modern dictionaries is, surprisingly enough, not fighting or killing; rather, the Arabic qital conveys this meaning. The verb *jahada* (*jihad* being the associated verbal noun) means "to toil," to become weary, to struggle, to strive after, to exert oneself. For example, the derivative *ijtihad* means effort or diligence. A survey of the Qur'an's usage of the verb *jahada*, particularly in passages revealed in Makkah before warfare began, demonstrates its more general connotation:

And those who strive hard [*jahadu*] for Us, We shall certainly guide them in Our ways, and God is surely with the doers of good. (29:69)

And whoever strives [*jahada*], he strives [*yujahidu*] only on behalf of himself. Surely God is independent of all beings. (29:6)

And We have enjoined on man goodness to parents, but if they contend [*jahada*] with you to associate with Me that of which you have no knowledge, do not obey them. (29:8)

And strive hard [*jahidu*] for God with due striving [*jihadihi*]. (22:78)

Then do not obey the unbelievers, and strive a great striving [*jihadan*] against them [*jahidhum*] by it [the Qur'an].[227] (25:52)

The last verse occurs in a passage telling the Muslims to make use of the Qur'an when they dispute with disbelievers.

A number of traditions convey the wider significance of jihad. In general, they describe various substitutes to fighting. The hadith stating that "the hajj (pilgrimage to Makkah) is the most excellent of all jihads" is of another genre.[228] A saying attributed to one of Muhammad's Companions may best illustrate the breadth of the concept. After leading the troops back from battle, he called to those near him, "We go now from the lesser jihad to the greater jihad." When they asked if a more difficult military assignment was intended, he explained that by the greater jihad he had meant the *jihad al nafs* (the struggle within oneself).[229] This is an eloquent summary of the view that an individual's earthly life is essentially an unremitting personal struggle.

The emigration (hijrah) to Yathrib (pre-Islamic Madinah) represented a critical transition in Muslim–pagan relations. Patient suffering would now give way to military action. Tradition records that both sides were conscious of its deadly implications. Hence we have the pagans' attempt to track and kill Muhammad before he reaches Madinah.[230] Subsequently the crucial jihad for the Muslim community would be realized in battle (*qital*). The immediate problem was how to motivate the less-committed Mulsims to risk their lives for a new ideal, when the odds seemed against them and the promise of booty was in doubt, for the pre-Islamic Arabs were normally much too pragmatic to fight when personal honor or wealth was not at stake.

Fighting [*qital*] is prescribed for you, and you dislike it. But it is possible that you dislike a thing which is good for you, and you love a thing which is bad for you. (2:216)

What ails you that you do not fight [*tuqatiluna*, from the verb *qatala*, "to fight"] in the cause of God and the helpless men, women, and children who say, "O our Lord, bring us out of this land whose people are oppressors, and appoint for us from

[227]See also Qur'an 61:11-12.
[228]*Sahih al Bukhari*, trans. Muhammad Muhsin Khan, vol. 2, "The Book of Hajj" (26), Hadith no. 40.
[229]Sayyid H. Nasr, *Traditional Islam in the Modern World* (KPI Limited, 1987), 27-33. This hadith is attributed to Ibrahim ibn 'Aylah and is considered weak by hadith scholars.
[230]Al Tabari, *Tarikh al Rusul wa al Muluk*, vol. 6, trans. W. Montgomery Watt and M. V. McDonald (Albany, NY: SUNY Press, 1985), 140-52.

Yourself a protec-tor, and appoint for us from Yourself a helper."
(4:75)

O Prophet, arouse the believers to the fight [*qital*]. If there are
twenty among you who are steadfast, they will vanquish two hundred; if a hundred, they will vanquish a thousand of the unbelievers, for these are people without understanding. (8:65)

Those who were left behind rejoiced in their inaction behind the
back of the Messenger of God; they hated to strive [*yujahidu*,
from *jahada*]with their goods and persons in the cause of God.
They said: "Do not go not forth in the heat." Say: "The fire of Hell
is fiercer in heat," if only they could understand. (9:81)

But when a surah of basic meaning is revealed and fighting [*qital*]
is mentioned therein, you will see those in whose hearts is a dis-
ease looking at you [Muhammad] with a look of one fainting at
the approach of death. (47:20)[231]

As the Qur'an now urges the believers to battle, we note the parallel
emergence of restrictions in warfare.

Fight [*qatilu*] in God's cause against those who fight against you
[*yuqatilunakum*]; **but do not commit aggression, for truly, God
does not love aggressors.** And slay them [*wa aqtiluhum*] wherever you catch them, and turn them out from wherever they have
turned you out, for sedition is worse then killing [*qatl*]. . . . **But if
they cease, God is Most Forgiving, Most Merciful.** (2:190-192)

And fight them [qatiluhum] until there is no more sedition and
religion is for God alone; **but if they cease, let there be no hostility except toward the wrong-doers.** (2:193)

There is no compulsion in religion. (2:256).

You will find others who desire to gain your confidence as well as
that of their people. Each time they are sent back to temptation,
they succumb to it. **If they do not let you be and do not offer you
peace and do not stay their hands, seize them and slay them
[*aqtuluhum*] wherever you come upon them: and it is against
these that We have empowered you.** (4:91)

---

[231]See also Qur'an 48:11-6.

But if the enemy inclines towards peace, then you [too] incline towards peace, and trust in God. Truly, He is the All-Hearing, All-Knowing. (8:61)

To those against whom war is made [*yuqataluna*] wrongfully, permission is given [to fight], and truly, God has the power to defend them—those who have been driven from their homelands against all right for no other reason than their saying, "Our Lord is God." For if God had not enabled people to defend themselves against one another, all monasteries and churches and synagogues and mosques, in which God's name is abundantly extolled, would surely have been destroyed. (22:39-40)

These passages (emphasis mine) make it quite clear that fighting is allowed in self-defense or in defense of victims of tyranny or oppression who are too weak to defend themselves. It is significant that three of these occur in the second surah, which is believed by many scholars to be a recapitulation of the Qur'an's major themes. The last reference may best describe the Qur'an's attitude toward war: it is cautionary, circumspect, and realistic. But one finds little Qur'anic support for the use of aggression to force non-Muslim states to accept Islamic rule. The verse that heads this section is sometimes cited, but a quick glance at the context shows that this passage is directed against those who, through treachery, break their treaties with the believers. The preceding verse reads:

[But treaties] are not dissolved with those pagans with whom you have entered an alliance and who have not subsequently failed you in anything, nor aided any one against you. So fulfill your engagements with them to the end of their term, Truly, God loves the God-conscious. (9:4)

And later,

As long as they remain true to you, remain true to them. Truly, God loves the God-conscious. (9:7)[232]

---

[232] Ibid. Verses from the ninth surah, such as 9:123 and 9:29, are often employed to justify the conquest of non-aggressive states in order to subjugate them to Islamic rule. Not only does such usage imply a blatant contradiction of the verses just cited, and thus the need for a hypothetical large-scale abrogation, but, as Ali argues exhaustively in his *The Religion of Islam*, it ignores both the historical and revelational contexts.

The division of the world by past Muslim scholars into "the abode of Islam" and "the abode of war" reflected existing realities. Any significant power of their day was essentially in a conquer-or-be-conquered situation.[233] Today we would like to believe that that is changing, but perhaps the best we can do is replace the word "conquer" by the words "dominate" or "control." I believe we have reached a state of awareness, however, that is uncomfortable with either notion and that accords more easily with the Qur'anic ethics of warfare.

FAITH AND POWER

"I'm sure you know that it's incumbent on Muslims living in the United States to work and struggle and, if necessary, to fight to establish an Islamic state here," said the dean of the Middle Eastern University, aware that tradition and scholarship were on his side.

"My idea of what makes a state Islamic might be very different from yours," I answered. "Do you, for example, feel that your country is an Islamic state?"

"Of course it's not perfect," he offered. 'But we're free to practice our faith and most of the Shari'ah is enforced."

"But what if we're already free to practice our rituals here and to influence the laws and government through democracy?"

"But democracy recognizes the will of the majority, while an Islamic state gives final authority to God as revealed in the Qur'an and teachings of the Prophet!"

"Might not the two converge in a society where the majority are committed to the viewpoint that God is the supreme authority and Muhammad is His Prophet? If the majority is not so committed, then what purpose is served by declaring an Islamic state or a state religion?"

"What you're advocating is secularism!"

Our conversation had ricocheted off a number of issues that vex contemporary Muslim political discussion: the duty to establish an Islamic state, the problem of defining what an Islamic state actually is, and the re-

---

[233]This is typified by the conquests of 'Umar. *In The Religion of Islam*, Ali points out that after Muhammad's death, a number of Arab tribes rebelled and presented a military challenge to the political authority of the Muslim state. The focal point of this activity was, roughly, the western border lands with Syria and in the east (i.e., Bahrain). These rebellions were supported with equipment and manpower by the Roman and Persian empires, respectively. The newly emerging Muslim nation thus found itself thrust into conflicts with these two empires. In the case of Persia, for example, even Muir admits in his *History of the Caliphate* that the situation "left Umar no choice but to conquer it in self-defense."

lationship between Islam, democracy, and secularism. It might be best to consider these in reverse order.

Islam and secularism are irreconcilable. By definition, secularism implies indifference to or exclusion of religion. It embraces the doctrine that the basis of morality should be nonreligious, a doctrine that a Muslim cannot accept. But secularism and democracy are not synonyms, and the latter does not appear to be inconsonant with Islam, for democracy is government by the people or rule by the majority. Many Muslim thinkers have seen close parallels between the principles of democracy and the Islamic concept of *shura* (mutual consultation). Democracy does not mean the exclusion of religious convictions from government policy making; indeed, the legal and political systems of modern democratic nations are grounded in moral convictions that have a predominantly religious basis. And democracy does not prevent religious groups from lobbying for their causes: the American anti-abortion movement, the presidential candidacy of Pat Robertson, and the recent protest of the Gulf War by the American Roman Catholic Church, to name only a few. Thus, the word "secular," when applied to most Western democracies, is something of a misnomer.

A democratic system attempts to insure that every individual's political opinion weighs equally and that all citizens cannot be subjected to a minority viewpoint. In a society that is homogeneously Muslim, democracy should no more challenge the supreme authority of God than any other system of rule. Whether or not the collective will coincides with the divine Will would depend on the commitment and understanding of the masses and their elected representatives.

In a pluralistic society, democracy helps to protect religious and political freedom; it helps, but does not **guarantee**, for the dominant viewpoint will naturally have greater influence. Muslims living in the United States, for instance, are subject to marriage laws predisposed to Christianity that conflict with their beliefs. However, the opportunity is also open to Muslims to argue their case and to bring about a change in government policy.

Similarly, history records a fair degree of religious tolerance by Muslim governments, especially when compared to other systems. Nevertheless, in accordance with Islamic law, non-Muslim communities were sometimes forbidden to proselytize their religion or to construct new places of worship.[234] For Christians, both of these are considered religious duties. While the danger exists of offending what a minority feels to be its right, it is the modern democratic republics that now seem to do the best job of protecting individual rights; in fact, it is difficult to conceive of a

---

[234]Lewis, *Jews of Islam*, 25-26.

preferable alternative. Indeed, Muslims themselves often testify that in many ways they are freer to practice their faith in the West than in the countries from which they came.

I am not going to venture as far as to say that the Western democratic republic suffices as a model of an Islamic state or that if the Muslim community continues to grow in the West such a transmutation will naturally occur. In the first place, I do not know of any existing practical model, nor even a definition, of an Islamic state that is acceptable to a majority of Muslims. Saudi citizens generally believe that their government is Islamic, or at least legitimate from the standpoint of Islamic law, but practically no Muslims outside the Arabian peninsula agree. The initial goal of the Islamic Republic of Iran was to conform to Imam Khomeini's blueprint of "government by the juriconsult (*faqih*),"[235] but supporters acknowledge that this has not yet been achieved and that the Iranian system is still in a state of transition. Be that as it may, the Iranian attempt will not suit the Muslim world's Sunni majority, for it is seen as an essentially Shi'ite construction. The next and least possible candidate would have to be Pakistan, which became an independent state in August 1947. However, Pakistan, which has been under different types of military dictatorships for much of its history, lays no claim to being an Islamic state. And the part that Islam should play in the political process has been a long-enduring controversy among Pakistani leaders and intellectuals.[236]

In contrast to the dearth of modern models, numerous theories on Islamic statehood have been put forth recently by Muslim writers, ranging from theocracies on one end of the ideological spectrum to democracies on the other.[237] Almost all agree that an Islamic state must conform to the will of God, but beyond that there are diverse interpretations and major theoretical differences. Two areas in which there is considerable discrepancy are the role that should be assigned to the religious scholar in an "Islamic" state and the status of non-Muslim citizens.

---

[235]Ayatollah Ruhollah Khomeini, *Wilayat-i Faqih* (Tehran: 1978).

[236]Ishtiaq Ahmed, *The Concept of an Islamic State* (London: Frances Pinter, 1987).

[237]Ibid., 187-94. See also: Muhammad Asad, *The Principles of State and Government in Islam* (California: University of California, 1961); David D. Commins, *Islamic Reform* (London: Oxford University, 1990); Asghar Khan, *Islam, Politics and State* (London: Zed Books, 1985); Metin Heper and Raphael Israeli, *Islam and Politics in the Middle East* (Sydney: Croom Helm, 1984); Tareq Y. Ismael and Jacqueline S. Ismael, *Government and Politics in Islam* (London: Frances Pinter, 1985); S. Abul A'la Maududi, *The Islamic Law and Constitution* (Lahore: Islamic Publications Ltd., 1980).

As regards the latter question, while nearly all Muslim authorities agree that every citizen is guaranteed the right to life, liberty, and property, restrictions on political liberty and religious belief and practices are often imposed. In some theories, non-Muslims are allowed to propagate their faith only among non-Muslims. Each community has its own religious courts, but non-Muslims may be inferior before the general law (for example, they could be disqualified as witnesses and the penalty for the murder of a Muslim by a non-Muslim may be harsher than the punishment of a Muslim who kills a non-Muslim), and non-Muslim citizens may be disqualified from any substantial and meaningful participation in the political process.[238]

In consideration of the widely-held view among Muslims that all the present governments of Muslim countries are not Islamic, as well as the great diversity of theoretical programs for Islamic rule, it is something of a surprise to hear Muslims speak of an Islamic state as if it were a firmly established and agreed-upon concept. It seems that the average Muslim's use of the term involves both a rejection and a dream: a rejection of Western domination and the oppressive rulers who now govern Muslim lands, and a vague vision of a utopian solution. The model of the Prophet's city state of Madinah is always in the back of the believer's mind, but little thought has been given to how that model can be adapted to meet the needs of twentieth century society. Of course, no more than this should be expected of the man in the street, since he is hardly ever a political scientist. And an expert talking about an Islamic state would have to be pressed for details before obtaining a clear idea of what he or she has in view. One high-ranking member of ISNA (the Islamic Society of North America) admitted to me recently that if the American people were to accept Islam tomorrow, he would have no idea what the new converts would do in the way of governing themselves as an Islamic society.

Despite prevailing differences of opinion and uncertainty, almost all Muslim theorists agree that an Islamic state must have a religious basis. An assumption that obviously follows is that its major political and legal institutions should be led by Muslims. This much, I feel, must be conceded, or why use the adjective "Islamic" at all? There are a few Muslim theorists who see no problem with the democratic model, but the closer their programs approximate Western democracies, the more the word "Islamic government" is stripped of any real significance.[239] And this is the second cause for my reluctance to offer the modern democratic republic as a pos-

---

[238] Ahmed, *Concept of an Islamic State*,87-116; Lewis, *Jews of Islam*, 27-40.
[239] Ahmed, *Concept of an Islamic State*, 121-62.

sible "Islamic" model, because it does not limit political office to a particular religious affiliation.

The European or American Muslim is then caught in yet another quandary: Should he/she wish for the end of his/her present form of government, which possesses many apparent advantages and features that seem to agree with his/her understanding of Islam, in order to replace it with a system that remains poorly defined even now? Such discomfiture may indicate the need for circumspection.

Muslim scholars have seen a divine blessing in the different phases of the Prophet's career, for it helps believers who are facing a variety of ordeals. It is therefore natural for them to look for parallels to their own trials in his, as well as the early Muslim community's life experience. But this can be exaggerated to the point at which Muslims force analogies where there are, in reality, only superficial resemblances.

The Qur'an and the traditions testify to the fact that Muhammad and his followers displayed tremendous patience and fortitude in their effort to practice and propagate Islam in the hostile milieu of Makkah. It was only after all avenues were exhausted that the community, then under severe persecution, took the necessary action of seeking political autonomy and retaliation. It would be fruitless to speculate what direction would have been taken if they lived in a polity where their freedom to propagate and practice were protected by law, for their situation was vastly different. But it seems safe to say, along with Bernard Lewis, that "Muhammad became a statesman in order to accomplish his mission as a prophet, not vice versa."[240]

Muslims in the West—women more than men—have faced some prejudice and inconvenience, but in no way have they encountered persecution and intolerance on the same scale as did the early Muslims. As long as they are able to share equally, according to their religious convictions, in the social and political evolution of their societies, I see no mandate to dismantle the existing democratic systems of government. Muslim writers assert with great confidence that Islam has always fared better in its calling in a peaceful rather than a coercive environment, and there are already signs that Western lands may turn out to be extremely fertile soil for its growth. A Muslim must strive to "enjoin the right and oppose wrong" (3:110), to "obey God and His Messenger" (3:32), and to be among the best of people "brought forth for mankind" (3:110). And at present that opportunity exists for them more in Western lands than it does in Muslim countries. Frankly, my greatest concern is that, should the tables be turned, Muslims would deny others similar privileges.

---

[240]Lewis, *Jews of Islam*, 12.

APOSTASY[241]

"Do you or do you not agree that Salman Rushdie deserves the Qur'anic punishment for apostasy?"

There was no way to sidestep her question, for this was already her second attack. Almost half of the audience was non-Muslim, and the BBC cameras were catching every word. Didn't she consider the impact of her words? How do you answer such a challenge without confirming others' worst suspicions about Islam?

"I already stated that he's a murtad (apostate)."

Please go away! What are you trying to accomplish? Didn't you see the media's reaction to Yusuf Islam? It was news in every Western country! "RIDE ON THE DEATH TRAIN," "SONG OF THE KILLER MAN," "FROM FLOWER CHILD TO TERRORIST," ran the headlines. They talked to old girlfriends, who said that he had always had it in him.

"Does he or does he not deserve the Qur'anic punishment of execution?" she demanded.

The scarf forced him to concentrate on the wrath in her eyes, eyes that were sure to exact revenge for two centuries of anguish and humiliation at the hands of disbelieving imperialists. There was no stopping them. With a heavy heart, he sighed, "Yes. He deserves the Qur'anic punishment for apostasy."

"Assalamu alaikum," she said. Then she turned from the microphone and headed down the aisle towards her seat.

"Allahu akbar!" they shouted. "Allahu akbar!"

Conversion to Islam has almost always had serious political consequences. More than a mere statement of belief, it has meant communal and political identification with the Muslim community and its causes. One's public testimony of faith theoretically provided instant access to all the Muslim community's institutions and the privileges of equal partnership. A person's life, property, and honor became immediately sacred by pronouncing the terse declaration, "I bear witness there is no deity but God, and that I bear witness that Muhammad is God's Messenger."

It is easy to imagine how conveniently this formula could be manipulated: to save one's life on the battlefield, to acquire a material or political advantage, or to deceitfully infiltrate the Muslim community. Records of such abuses are frequent in Muslim annals. The chief means available to

---

[241]This subject is given a more thorough treatment in two modern works that challenge the traditional ruling: Mohamed S. El-Awa, *Punishment in Islamic Law* (Indianapolis: American Trust Pub., n.d.), 49-68, and Ali, *Religion of Islam*, 591-99.

the early jurists to counter this danger was to threaten the defector with execution. Non-Muslim citizens were allowed to switch religions as they chose, provided they did not accept Islam. However, once a Muslim, always a Muslim. Thereafter, the only alternative was death. Of course, this did not augment the rate of conversion to Islam. The primary concern of jurists was not to retain community membership, but rather to prevent surreptitious ingression.

A crisis of belief is not always a political crisis. Many who experience the agony of uncertainty have no worldly motivation and often admit to envy of those who are capable of blind acceptance. Doubt can lead to rejection of faith, the more if it is prohibited, but it can also lead to deeper and richer faith, especially if it is given room to do battle with itself. Some Muslim theologians, such as al Ghazali, maintained that doubt was the first step on the road to true faith.[242] Some early jurists distinguished between doubt and deceit. The Hanafi school, for example, held that a female apostate should not be executed, since "she is not in any position to fight against Islam, which is the ostensible reason for putting to death an apostate."[243] The majority view, however, was and still is that apostasy from Islam under any circumstances demands the death penalty.

Contrary to the assertion of the speaker in the foregoing dialogue, the Qur'an never specifies execution or any other punitive action vis-à-vis the apostate. It mentions apostasy a total of thirteen times, but "all that these verses contain is the assurance that the apostate will be punished in the hereafter."[244]

And if any of you turns away from his faith and dies as an unbeliever—then the works of those will go for naught in this world and the Hereafter. (2:217)

Indeed, those who deny the truth[245] after having professed their faith and then increase in their denial of the truth, their repentance

---

[242] Ignaz Goldziher, *Introduction to Islamic Theology and Law* (Princeton: Princeton University, 1981), 87-8.

[243] El-Awa, *Punishment in Islamic Law*, 53.

[244] Ibid., 50.

[245] I prefer here Muhammad Asad's translation of the verb *kafara* as meaning "to deny the truth" or "to reject the truth," rather than the usual rendition, "to disbelieve." Its primary meaning is "to cover" or "to hide," and in pre-Islamic times it was often used in the sense of "to show ingratitude" or "to deny or reject something" (i.e., a favor or a gift). I feel that Asad's interpretation comes closer to the more general connotation of the term and its use in the Qur'an. Unfortunately, as with so many terms and phrases in the Qur'an, no immediate English equivalent exists. Toshihiko Izutsu has an interesting analysis of this verb in his *God and Man in the Koran*.

will not be accepted; and those are the ones who have gone astray. (3:90)

Indeed, those who believe, then deny the truth, then believe, then deny the truth, and thereafter increase in denial of the truth—God will not forgive them nor will He guide them in any way. (4:137)

O you who believe, if any of you turns back from his religion, then God will bring a people whom He will love and they will love Him. (5:54)

Whoever disbelives in God after accepting faith—excepting the one who is compelled, while his heart remains firm in faith—but whoever opens their breast to unbelief, on them is wrath from God, and theirs will be a dreadful punishment. (16:106)

The Qur'an refers to two historic—and unpunished—cases of apostasy during the Madinan period. One involved an attempt by the Prophet's Jewish adversaries to encourage others to leave the faith by setting an open precedent. The other involved six Muslim wives who, after the treaty of Hudaibiyah chose to rejoin the pagan community:

And a party among the People of the Book say: "Believe in what has been revealed to the believers at the opening of the day but reject it at the other [end of the day], in order that they may turn back." (3:72)

And if any of your wives should go over to the deniers of the truth, and you are thus afflicted in turn, then give to those whose wives have gone away the equivalent of what was spent. (60:11)

The command, "There is no compulsion in religion: truth stands out clearly from error" (2:256), would seem to argue against a penalty for apostasy outside of a manifest act of political treason. The majority trend of those traditions of the Prophet related to incidents of apostasy also point to this conclusion. In the first place, there are authenticated traditions in which no action was taken against apostates. An incident is related by al Bukhari that concerns a man who took back his pledge of allegiance to the Prophet and then left unharmed.[246] Similarly, there is the case of a Christian who became a Muslim, served for a short time as one of the Prophet's scribes in Madinah, and then went back over to Christianity. He was fre-

---

[246]*Sahih al Bukhari*, trans. Muhammad Muhsin Khan, "The Book on the Virtue of al Madinah" (30), Hadith no. 107.

quently heard making the blasphemous claim, "Muhammad knew nothing except what I wrote for him." Anas, the narrator, goes on to mention that he later on died of natural causes.[247]

Secondly, there is the group of traditions that associate apostasy with high treason. These include the only authenticated case of the punishment of apostates, the case of a party of the tribe of 'Ukul, who accepted Islam, then apostatized and subsequently committed murder. The saying of the Prophet, "The life of a Muslim may be taken only in three cases: the case of a married adulterer, one who has killed a human being, and one who forsakes his religion and separates himself from his community" is given further elaboration in the version in Abu Dawud, where the Prophet explains that the last category refers to "a man who went out (of the community) to fight against God and His Prophet."[248]

In classical legal texts, the hadith saying, "Whoever changes his religion, kill him," is used to argue for the death penalty in general cases of apostasy.[249] However, Muhammad Ali argues that this statement demands interpretation, for, if taken literally, it implies that all converts to any religion should be killed. He opines that the only way this statement can be reconciled with other evidence, much of which is presented above, is to assume that high treason is the point at issue here.[250] Mohamed el-Awa objects that Ali's position is apologetic and goes on to present a grammatical argument that shows that the statement could be interpreted in any one of sixteen ways (among which are a recommendation or permission), but not necessarily as a command.[251]

Regardless of what ideals have influenced Ali, I personally find his reasoning to be sound and appropriate. Giving precedence to the Qur'an, and in consideration of other authenticated traditions, he concludes that one apparently incomplete fragment of a saying should not be allowed to overrule what conscience dictates as just. El-Awa only enhances Ali's claim regarding the insufficiency of the particular hadith. We must allow that cases may arise in which not all the pertinent data can be reconciled. In such instances, I believe, one should yield to the perceived weight of the evidence without necessarily having to reconcile every minute detail.

---

[247]Ali cites and translates this hadith from *Sahih al Bukhari* in his *Religion of Islam*, 579.
[248]Abu Dawud, *Al Sunan*, 4:223. El-Awa cites and translates this tradition from *Sahih al Bukhari* in his *Punishment*, 52. He states that it appears in *Sahih al Bukhari* (Cairo: 1934), 12:169.
[249]*Sahih al Bukhari*, trans. Muhammad Muhsin Khan, vol. 4, "The Book of Jihad" (52), Hadith no. 260.
[250]Ali, *Religion of Islam*, 596.
[251]El-Awa, *Punishment in Islamic Law*, 52-53.

In the case of the Prophet's sayings, for example, it must be remembered that scholars of traditions knew very well that the narrators, especially in the first few stages, were not always reporting what they had heard verbatim, but rather what they understood to be the sense of the saying. This explains the variety of versions encountered in the standard collections. Thus, while we may justifiably respect the traditions as an essential source of information, we must be ready to approach discrepancies analytically and realistically, to compare them with other relevant data, and to allow for the possibility of imperfection.

While the death penalty for apostasy still has important implications for Muslims in countries such as Iran, Saudi Arabia, and perhaps Pak-istan, it is of little immediate consequence to Muslims now living in Western countries, where the idea of killing a person for having second thoughts about his or her faith is highly repugnant. The evidence resorted to in classical texts to justify execution for a mere change of faith might better suggest limiting such a punishment only to cases of aiding and abetting an enemy of the state. The Qur'an, with supreme confidence, announces that "Evidences have come to you from your Lord. Then the one who sees, does so for his own soul, and the one who is blind, it is upon himself (6:104)." Muslims should, in turn, be assured that their religion will prevail in an environment where there is truly "no compulsion in religion."

CHAPTER 5

Ahl al Kitab

Revelation and History: An Interpretation

In the second chapter, I mentioned that one is struck instantly by the many Qur'anic references to Biblical prophets. In a debate I witnessed between Gamal Badawi and Anise Shouroush, the latter remarked that seventy percent of the verses in the Qur'an are related to Judeo-Christian concepts. Although this is an exaggeration, unless by this Shouroush includes the concepts that all monotheistic faiths have in common, his statement contains a substantial degree of truth. Certainly the stories of Biblical prophets, accounts related to the Judeo-Christian tradition, and criticism of Jewish and Christian understandings and behavior dominate the Qur'an's discussions of other religions.

Orientalists are naturally skeptical concerning this and have charged Muhammad with borrowing from Jewish and Christian sources, citing parallels to the Qur'an in the Bible, the Talmud, Talmudic commentaries, Gnostic Christian apocrypha, and ancient Christian and Jewish letters and poetry.[252] Many of these parallels are nothing more than superficial similarities that can be found between any two religions. But even where substantial resemblances exist, the diversity and obscurity of the sources suggest to skeptics that Muhammad must have taken much more than just a passing interest in Judaism and Christianity—that he had mastered, or at least been exposed to, large amounts of information, apparently unbeknownst to his followers, that would normally be accessible only to experts.

There is, of course, another possibility: that there was a much larger and more significant Jewish and Christian scholarly presence in the Hijaz then has heretofore been supposed, which led to the appropriation of Judeo-Christian traditions by the larger Arab culture. The Qur'an does assume that the Arabs had at least a small degree of familiarity with the Biblical accounts, but it does not indicate a shared heritage. The Makkans may have taken a fleeting interest in the stories told by Jewish and Christian merchants during the annual trade fairs, but no more than

---

[252]Abraham I. Katz, *Judaism in Islam* (New York: Sepler-Hermon Press, 1980).

that, for pre-Islamic poetry contains virtually no mention of Biblical personalities.

For two centuries after the Prophet's death, Muslim exegetes were forced to look beyond the Arabian peninsula for Judeo-Christian sources (designated as *Isra'iliyat*) in order to explain parallel Qur'anic passages. This proves not only that the Arabs of the Hijaz were largely ignorant of the Jewish and Christian traditions, but also that Muhammad left little commentary on the subject. This observation only adds to the puzzle surrounding the profusion of Biblical allusions in the Qur'an, for skeptics have yet to provide a satisfactory accounting for the source(s) of Muhammad's knowledge of Jewish and Christian tradition or of its ubiquitous use in the Qur'an.

It is accepted universally that the Prophet's principal objective was to rid Arabia of idolatry and, with the exception of a few references to the Jews and Christians, all verses related to actual combat are directed against the pagans. Yet the Qur'an itself contains very few explicit references to actual pagan beliefs and practices. For example, the gods of the polytheists are mentioned by name only once (53:19). It would seem more natural that one engaged in a life-and-death struggle with an enemy would direct all of his resources against the immediate danger. But from the early years in Makkah, long before the six-year-long confrontation with the Jews of Madinah, and in the years succeeding the removal of that threat, the Judeo-Christian religious tradition was the main target of the Qur'an's attack on other faiths.

One should realize that there were other major religious influences in the region. During Muhammad's lifetime, Persia had the strongest political presence in Arabia, and the Hijaz had close economic ties with India; thus, Zoroastrianism, Hinduism, and Buddhism might have been eligible for a little criticism in the Qur'an. Of course, it would be much easier to build a strict monotheism on the Jewish precedent, but the same does not apply to Christianity.

From the political perspective, who could have foreseen, especially in the early years of Muhammad's mission, that Rome and not Persia would be the ultimate nemesis of the Islamic world? Much of the perceived relevance of the Qur'an would have been lost if Persia or India had turned out to be the more formidable enemy; but, as history demonstrates, only the Christian West would pose a continued threat to Muslim world dominance.

The Muslims' lightning conquest of Persia and North Africa immediately after Muhammad's death provided the Islamic empire with vital material and intellectual wealth, and it would soon penetrate eastward through India and into China. Although Muslim armies came close to defeating

Europe a number of times, it never actually happened, and ultimately Europe rose from near total defeat to challenge the Muslim world, as it still does today in a pivotal confrontation between the Islamic and Western cultures. Whether one attributes it to coincidence, Muhammad's genius, or divine wisdom, the importance the Qur'an gives to Judaism and Chris-tianity fits well with history's unfolding.

Had Muslims conquered Europe, it is very possible that they might have achieved total world domination and might never have felt the same urgency to recapture their faith's original power and to purge it of cultural accretions as they do now. For example, the need to reexamine the status and social position of women or the institution of slavery was provoked, in large measure, by the Islamic world's encounter with a West that had itself recently undergone such reforms. This is not to say that reform on these matters would have been inconceivable without this convergence of cultures, for the Western experience argues otherwise, but it has acted as a catalyst for rapid change. On the other hand, it is interesting that some eminent Western Islamists, such as Gibb and Watt, have seen in the encounter an opportunity for the Western world to recover a lost spirituality, an opportunity that would have diminished had Muslim society completely embraced Western culture and values that came with colonialization.[253] What such scholars have in mind is not a wholesale conversion to Islam in the West, but a chance for a new stage of reform and rebirth within their own faith communities by means of an interfaith dialogue.

Almost all "experts," for various reasons, agree that humanity has reached a critical juncture: the current confrontation between Muslim society and the West. On both sides, there are those who believe that the future salvation or ruin of humanity may hang in the balance. Until now, the confrontation has not been principally religious in character, but religion does and will continue to play an integral part, and probably an even greater one in the future. For many Mulsims, it is a meeting envisaged in the Qur'an: between Muslims and the People of the Book (i.e., Jews and Christians), with the Biblical prophets, and, hence, Judaism being the acknowledged common ground.

Ahl al Kitab (People of the Book)

You will find the strongest among men in hostility to the believers to be the Jews and the pagans. And you will find the nearest

---

[253]Gibb, *Wither Islam*, 376-79; W. Montgomery Watt, *Islamic Revelation in the Modern World* (Edinburgh: 1969), 126-29.

among them in love to the believers to be those who say, "We are Christians." That is because among them there are priests and monks, and they are not proud . And when they listen to what has been revealed to the Messenger, you will see their eyes overflowing with tears because what they recognize as the truth. They say: "Our Lord, we believe. Then inscribe us among the witnesses. And it is not for us not to believe in God and what has come to us of the truth, and we long for our Lord to admit us among the righteous people." And their Lord confirmed them for what they said with gardens with rivers flowing underneath, to remain therein; and that is the recompense of the doers of good. But for those who reject the truth and deny Our signs, they shall be the people of Fire. (5:82-86)

In the Qur'an, the Jews and Christians are referred to collectively as *Ahl al Kitab* (literally, the People of the Book), which points to the fact that both communities are founded upon an originally divinely revealed scripture. The appellation attests to their exceptional and, at the same time, peculiar status in Islam, for they occupy an ambiguous position between the Muslim and the idol-worshiper. For instance, certain marital and dietary restrictions which Islam establishes vis-à-vis non-Muslims do not apply to Jews and Christians (5:6). In a number of verses of the Qur'an (2:62; 3:113-15; 5:72; 22:17), Judaism and Christianity are granted a degree of legitimacy, and Muslims are told to invite the People of the Book to a dialogue in which they are to display the utmost courtesy (16:125; 29:46).

The Qur'an contains numerous references to Old and New Testament personalities, and parallels to many of its stories can be found in the Bible as well as other ancient Judeo-Christian sources.[254] Furthermore, the Qur'an mentions that it confirms the fundamental message of the two previous scriptures (2:89; 3:81), invites their investigation in order to cor-roborate specific details (3:93; 10:94), and that it corrects some points (5:16-17, 21) and elaborates on others (3:44; 5:30-34; 28:44). The Qur'an states that all previous prophets, in particular those mentioned from the Judeo-Christian tradition, taught the same essential truths. Therefore, it does not discount Judaism or Christianity, but maintains that the pure teachings of these prophets have been distorted over the years via their contact with earlier and other religions. Hence, the Qur'an had to be sent to restore their original purity.

---

[254]Firestone, *Journeys in the Holy Land.*

Yet the Qur'an's attitude towards Jews and Christians is not always congenial. For one thing, as is to be expected, there was opposition from both communities living in and around Arabia, although much more from the Jews than the Christians. This conflict can be discerned in many passages. The Qur'an states that the People of the Book will never be happy with the Muslims until they follow their religion (2:120). The Jews and Christians frequently side with the pagans against the Muslims (2:105; 5:83; 33:26), and the believers are cautioned not to take them as allies (5:54, 60). Many of them are *kafirun* (deniers of the truth) (98:1, 6), although others are entirely sincere and trustworthy (3:75, 113-114); many are among the worst of creatures (98:6), yet others are among the best (98:7). Before the campaign of Tabuk, Muslims are instructed to fight against the People of the Book until they are humbled and pay the *jizyah* (poll tax) (9:29).

Another factor to bear in mind is that although the Qur'an emphasizes the relationship of Islam to the former religious tradition, it would soon become absolutely necessary to distance the Muslim community from the People of the Book so that Islam would not be mistaken for a Jewish or Christian offshoot or heresy. Thus we have reports of Mu-hammad stressing his community's difference from the earlier communities in matters of appearance, behavior, and practice. The Qur'anic verses that deny the crucifixion of Jesus (4:157) and change the direction of prayer (*qiblah*) from Jerusalem to Makkah (2:142) are decisive demarcations. Curiously, in an attempt to counter previous orientalist claims that these passages were devised by Muhammad after he failed to convince the Jews and Christians of Madinah of his prophethood, many Muslim apologists claim that these two passages were not associated with major breaks with the People of the Book. But this claim can be rejected without having to deny that both events were key steps toward establishing Islam as an independent reformative and definitive religious movement. The Qur'an itself, in 2:143-45, attests to this. Such unequivocal departures were of the utmost necessity, considering the microscopic size of the new community in comparison to its two predecessors.

The Qur'an also opposes certain dogmatic and practical features of Judaism and Christianity. Both religions are censured for giving too much authority to their clergy (9:31), for their claims to exclusivity (2:111, 135), for committing excesses in their religion (4:171; 5:80) such as Christian monasticism (57:27), and, as Muhammad explained, for "making lawful things unlawful and unlawful things lawful."[255]

---

[255]Ibn Kathir, *Tafsir al Qur'an al 'Azim*, 1:137.

The Qur'an strongly denounces certain doctrines prevalent among the earlier scriptural communities. Among these, is the use by Jews and Christians of the phrase, "son of God." For example, we read:

The Jews say 'Uzair is a son of God, and the Christians say the Messiah is the son of God. That is a saying of their mouths. They imitate what the deniers of truth of old used to say. (9:30)

It singles out Christianity in particular for formulating the concept of the Trinity:

Do not say, "Three" Cease! That is better for you. God is one God. Glory be to Him, [high exalted is He] above having a son (4:171),

and for the widespread practice among several major sects of worshipping Jesus and his mother Mary:

And when God will say: "O Jesus, son of Mary, did you say to the people, 'Take me and my mother as gods besides God?'" he will say, "Glory be to You, it was not for me to say what I had no right [to say]! If I had said it, You would have known it." (5:116)

Most contemporary Christian theologians agree that the expression, "son of God," is symbolic and that the concept of the Trinity says something about three means by which God reveals Himself to man and about His involvement in our earthly lives. It is therefore now a common practice among Christian critics of Islam to trivialize the above-mentioned passages by stating that Muhammad did not understand the subtlety of the concepts of the son of God and the Trinity. They maintain that he must have been unaware of the intricate theological concept of the three hypostases, the complexities inherent in the mystical doctrine of the son of God, and that he must have mistakenly included Mary as one of the persons of the Trinity. It very well may be the case that the Prophet had little personal knowledge of these enigmatic tenets, but these conclusions are no more than interpretative conjectures that are very difficult to prove based on the Qur'an.

It is quite obvious from the text that the issue for the Qur'an is the use of dogmatic statements that are easily misunderstood and misleading, not anyone's particular Christology. As the Qur'an's main problem is with the wording of these tenets, it stresses that "the Jews say," "the Christians say," and "Do not say" in the above verses, for these expressions "imitate" and could lead to idol-worship and it would be better to avoid such language. Even though Judaism and Christianity each uses the expression "son of God" in different senses, they are warned of the inherent danger in the **words** themselves. The fact that the Qur'an does not substitute "they believe" for "they say" in these references argues for an awareness that the symbols are open to a range of theological interpretations. Thus we find other passages that include some Christians and Jews among the true believers in God.

But the Qur'an is here not so much concerned with theological postulates as it is with the effect of these formulations on the common man. As a result of these phrases, the average Jew may come to believe that Jews alone are God's beloved people (5:20), and the average Christian could very easily misread these doctrinal statements and understand, incorrectly, that Jesus is God or the "begotten" son of God, and that he and even his mother should be objects of supplication and worship. Even today, if you ask any Christian if Jesus is literally God's son and if he should be worshipped, he or she is more than likely to respond in the affirmative, while Catholics are likely to say that Mary, the mother of Jesus, should also be worshipped. Thus 5:119 is not a reference to the Trinity but to this very real hazard. That the Qur'an's concern is with the misleading character of the above-mentioned doctrinal phrases is evidenced further by its own references to Jesus as "a messiah," "a spirit," and "a word" from God, in effect indicating that these Christian descriptions are acceptable and not exclusive to Jesus.

The function of the Qur'an's account of the Jews and the Christians is not simply to chide them or to relay information. It also includes a portrayal of those human tendencies and weaknesses that are always there to undermine the purity of any community's worship and a partial explanation of why the prophetic office was terminated. Concerning the first matter, it is sufficient to say that Muslim scholars have repeatedly criticized the faithful for having committed the same errors as their predecessors. Ibn Hazm of Barcelona complained that the practice of *taqlid* (blind acceptance of scholarly decisions arrived at during the first three Islamic centuries) is in blatant imitation of "they have taken their rabbis and priests as Lords beside God" (9:31). There are still Muslims who pray to saints at gravesites and beg them for their intercession, and many Muslims continue to repeat the same claim of a Muslim monopoly on God's mercy and forgiveness.

On the second point, the question is often asked: Why was there a final prophet? For the early Muslims, this question stretched across the chasm separating Muhammad's leadership from the corrupt order that was currently ruling them. Not surprisingly, it was soon tied to the question of divine justice and mercy, for why would God so directly guide man throughout history and then suddenly leave him to himself until the end of creation? Two responses—and there were many others—that were formulated survive today as the two major factions of the Muslim community: the Sunni and Shi'ah. Rather than review these, we present another, although not opposing, point of view.

True faith, from the standpoint of Islam, is based on belief in the unity of God (*tawhid*). A natural corollary to this, which is also a major Islamic belief, is the essential oneness of man. Every monotheistic faith must come to terms with both of these strains, which are by no means always harmonious in earthly practice. The story of the Children of Israel is about a people who are uniquely receptive throughout much of their history to monotheism, yet who live in a predominantly pagan milieu. Outside influences, which penetrate their community with great frequency, cause them to waver at times from the teachings of their prophets. In the Qur'an, they appear as a nation involved in a constant struggle between pure monotheism and heathen pressures, which, in part, explains their need to insulate themselves from their social surroundings and their attempt to preserve and protect their racial and cultural purity. But they came to see themselves as God's chosen people, to the exclusion of all others, and as sons of God in the Old Testament sense of the term. As a result, because of Muhammad's non-Jewish origins, they could never accept the final Messenger of God, even though he confirmed the essential message of the revelation in their possession. The Qur'an blames them repeatedly for their refusal in this regard. In short, Judaism, although successful in preserving the belief in one God, was unable to accept the oneness of man under God.

While Christianity goes back to the same Biblical roots, unlike Judaism, it is a universal religion. Its coherence derives from an intense spiritual yearning to know and to be loved by God. Thus, while the Jews and the pagans of the Arabian peninsula were stubbornly closed to a message that departed from their traditions, the Christians are shown to be more easily affected by its spiritual force (4:85-89).

The difficulty that universal faiths encounter is the great diversity of the peoples they absorb, for they bring languages, ideas, symbols and cultural practices that could potentially distort the original faith. From the Muslim view, such was the case with Christianity. Although it embraces all mankind, its tenets compromise pure monotheism and it lends itself too easily to associating others with God. In this way, the Judeo-Christian experience exemplifies the dilemma faced by all the great world religions:

monotheism or universalism were invariably compromised in attempting to preserve one or the other.

Islam also struggled, and still does, with these internal tensions, and extreme measures would be taken by the mainstream to protect both implications of *tawhid*. Philosophical and mystical speculation were discouraged, all aspects of life were systematized into religious law, and all innovative thought was forbidden through the adoption of *taqlid*. Of course pressures continued to arise, but, for the most part, Islamic orthodoxy succeeded in placing the major sources and principles of early mainstream Islam on ice, so to speak, preserved in a type of suspended animation that would eventually be transferred intact to the present time. Whatever the cost to Muslim civilization of the rigorous steps taken by these earlier Muslim scholars, the two major features of *tawhid*, the oneness of God and the oneness of humanity, were successfully united in Islam and passed on to future generations. For Muslims, this is one example of how God, through Islam, completed His favor to mankind (5:3).

Muslim-Christian Dialogue

> And do not dispute with the People of the Book except with what is better, unless it be with those of them who do wrong, and say: "We believe in what was revealed to us and revealed to you; and our God and your God is One, and we have surrendered to Him." (29:46)

> Invite to the way of your Lord with wisdom and beautiful preaching; and argue with them in ways that are best and most gracious. (16:125)

> Woe to you scribes and pharisees, hypocrites that you are! You traverse mountains and valleys in search of a single convert, and when you make a convert, he becomes twice the child of Hell that you are! (Matthew 23:15)[256]

It would seem more likely that Muslims would engage in dialogue with Jews rather than with Christians, for, at least in matters of dogma, Judaism and Islam are quite close. But, surprisingly, almost all of the current interfaith conversation is between Muslims and Christians. One possible reason might be that the Arab-Israeli conflict and the antagonism of

---

[256]May and Metzger, *The New Oxford Annotated Bible.*

the Qur'an towards the Jews of Madinah may incline Muslims more towards Christians. However, the fact that Christianity and Islam compete for converts probably has more to do with it, as each community views the other and not Judaism as its main religious threat.

In the past, Jewish scholars played an important mediating role between the competing communities. There have also been notable Jewish converts to Islam, such as Muhammad Asad and Maryam Jameelah, both of whom have made significant contributions to Muslim thought.[257] But the political climate has limited current Muslim dialogue with Jews mostly to the issue of Palestine, and even here there has not been much direct communication. The titles of this section and the next reflects this unfortunate situation.

It is quite easy for meetings between members of different faiths to degenerate into a kind of religious warfare. Propaganda and tactics of promoting and defending something in which we are so personally involved is unavoidable, but it leads often to deceit and mistrust and the subsequent blocking of truthful communication. The goal of collectively moving closer to the truth is obscured by other ambitions.

In colonial times, Christian evangelism was supported by various European states as one wing of a program for world domination; accounts of coercion and fraud abound and are not easily forgotten. Muslims may have been comparatively better, but they were also guilty, as evidenced by the so-called *Gospel of Barnabas*, a blatant forgery surfacing in Muslim Spain in the twelfth century and which is still in wide circulation in the Islamic world today. Things have improved considerably, for we live in a period of greater tolerance and Western research into Islam has grown more independent of church and state. Even clerics like Montgomery Watt and Kenneth Cragg have shown commendable objectivity, fairness, and insight—more, it has to be admitted, than Muslim writers have demonstrated toward Christianity.

An accurate appraisal of how far apart you are involves a true assessment of how close you are as well. In this respect, the Christian side in the dialogue is much further along, for Christian understanding of Islamic thought is much greater than Muslim knowledge of Christianity. Regardless of past motivations, the acquisition of this knowledge is a great help when it comes to sharing perspectives. Muslims who wish to engage in fruitful dialogue should become students of Christian thought. What is required is more than merely reading the Bible and borrowing from ancient polemics; Muslims need to study the development of Chris-

---

[257] Asad, *The Message*; Jameelah, *Western Civilization Condemned by Itself*.

tianity from the Christian point of view, and both sides must bear in mind that religious perspectives within each tradition are varied and changing.

There also needs to be a mutual willingness to learn as well as to teach, for each can gain from the other's experience. Christians have wrestled with modern rationalism and secularism much longer than Muslims and have had to differentiate between scientific-historic data and the use of legends and traditions in the growth of their religion. Their findings are bound to affect Muslim thought, for there are many parallels in Muslim and Christian sources. It is therefore necessary for Muslims to study these developments both critically and cautiously. And, in spite of its abrupt collision with this secular age, Islam has thus far been able to maintain its hold on the Muslim masses, including the great majority of the Islamic world's intellectual leaders. It continues to provide a spiritual haven to the faithful in an increasingly mechanistic and impersonal world, and is gaining many adherents in the leading industrial countries. In the continued resilience of Islam, there are important lessons for Christians.

Another volume and much greater expertise would be needed to do some justice to this subject. However, I would like to share a few impressions I had after attending a recent dialogue. Actually, it was a two-part discussion. The title of the first program was "Jesus: God or Man?" and the second was entitled "Is the Bible or the Qur'an the Word of God?" The titles indicate that the programs were sponsored by Muslim organizations.

Judging from announcements in Muslim newsletters and magazines, these are very popular themes for Muslims in the United States, yet from the start they obscure some of the most basic issues. For example, Christian theology maintains that Jesus is neither God nor man but that he is uniquely possessed of both natures. Also, for Christians, the definitive revelation is not the Old nor the New Testament but Jesus Christ himself. The Bible is no longer seen by most Christian theologians as pure revelation (that role belongs to Christ), but as a synthesis of inspiration, interpretation, commentary, and witness. The Old Testa-ment is believed to herald Jesus' coming, and the New Testament serves to witness and explain it. From the Christian perspective, a more appropriate contrast than the Bible and the Qur'an might be a Jesus—Qur'an and New Testament—hadith analogy. A title such as "Revelation in Christianity and Islam" might better accommodate the viewpoint of Christians.

A Christian might argue that whereas the Qur'an, at least for Muslims, is the eternal and uncreated word of God revealed as a book or as script, for Christians Jesus is the eternal and uncreated divine word revealed in the person of Christ. In their belief system, Jesus not only verbally communicated a revelation, but his every action, emotion, word, and impulse revealed the eternal word of God. Inasmuch as the revelation was authentically human, Christians view Jesus as fully and truly man, and, inasmuch as the word of God was made manifest by his humanity, he is also truly divine.

At times, Muslim speculation about the mystery of Muhammad's prophethood shows similar tendencies. Supported by the Qur'anic verse that states that Muhammad, "does not speak of his own desire" (53:3)—even though the context shows that this refers to the revelation of the Qur'an—the notion arose that every utterance of Muhammad and, by extension his every deed, no matter how mundane, was revealed to guide mankind. This is despite the fact that the Qur'an emphasizes repeatedly his humanity and confines his role to that of messenger, warner, and teacher (25:56; 27:91-93). In consequence, the imitation of any of Muhammad's most mundane habits is believed by many to possess immense spiritual reward. Orthodoxy would avoid deeper theorizing on the connection between the Revelation and its recipient, but, in some aspects, Muslim veneration and emulation of Muhammad outstrips that accorded to Jesus by Christians.

Both Christians and Muslims will find this Jesus—Qur'an and New Testament—hadith analogy wanting in many respects. For one thing, its brevity cannot possibly do justice to the development of Christian theology, as it cannot bring to light the philosophical difficulties discussed nor the grave consequences perceived, that were behind the formulation of Christian dogma. It also does not convey adequately the Christian perception of God's very personal entry into mankind's struggle by His revelation in Jesus. The Muslim's objections might be more pragmatic. He would maintain that while Muslims admit a close connection between God, His word, and prophethood, they represent different levels of existence. Just as he does not worship creation, which indeed manifests God, he neither worships the Qur'an nor prays to Muhammad, even though God is made known to man through both. In addition, he would counter that the definitive revelation of Muslims is for all to examine and judge, but that in the case of Christianity, one must rely on secondary sources. We can no longer experience directly the person of Jesus, but we can still experience the Qur'an and either accept or reject it. From the Muslim perspective, it would be as if the Qur'an no longer exists, yet one was to believe that it was a divine revelation based on the Prophetic traditions and later communications.

The doctrines of the Trinity and the divine sonship of Jesus are not revelations, for all dogmas are nothing more than proclamations worked out and agreed upon by religious authorities over the course of time. A dogmatic statement is something that, when arrived at, represents a formula acceptable to those who frame it, that allows for their individual understandings. Even though a dogma sets boundaries **for** the community, it is open to different interpretations **within** the community. To appreciate it correctly, one has to go back to the intellectual and social atmosphere that gave rise to it.

In the case of Christianity, this means returning to the Palestine, Rome, Alexandria, and Antioch of the early centuries after Christ. It means studying the Hellenic and Judaic cultures that influenced it, learning the ideas of the Greek philosophers and their modes of expression, and reentering the debates at Nicea, Ephesus, and Chalcedon.

The environment into which Christianity was born was markedly different from that which nurtured nascent Islam. The early Church fathers were inheritors of a rich merging of advanced cultures. Unlike the early Muslims, their first concern was not state government and legislation, but establishing the philosophical integrity of the emerging faith in an atmosphere charged with competing religious and ideological currents. Whereas for the Muslims religious scholarship principally meant law, for the Christians it meant theology.

Philosophy and metaphysical inquiry, while never stifled completely, were discouraged by Muslim orthodoxy because of the risks they posed to monotheism, especially at the level of the common believer, who was considered unequipped to wrestle with the subtleties of logic and symbolism. To a large extent, Islam was willing to sacrifice speculation to preserve correct worship and practice. The history of Christianity, on the other hand, is dominated by church councils in which the most profound theological mysteries were expounded upon and debated. Whereas the Muslim scholar kept close to the man in the street, elaborating a comprehensive system of conduct for the faithful, the Christian theologian soared to philosophical heights that were far beyond the reach of laymen. To this day, the theologies of the Muslim scholar and layman are not very different, while the Christian theologian and layman appear, from the outside, to be very far apart.

Muslim schools of thought did debate theological issues, not under ecclesiastical authority and not in synods but on a scale large enough to generate inquisitions and persecution. And unavoidably, some dogmas were formed and preserved: the uncreatedness of the Qur'an, the createdness of the world, the doctrine of *qadr* (predestination), the theory of the abrogation of Qur'anic verses, and al Ash'ari's anti-dogmatic dogma of *bi la kayf.*[258] The great concern of the Muslim scholars engaged in these disputes was to safeguard monotheism at almost any cost.

By contrast, Christian theologians were determined to preserve not only monotheism but also the conviction that God, in Jesus, had entered history in order to save mankind. They elaborated a complex and subtle theology that is by no means logically absurd or ridiculous. Such an opinion underestimates the genius that went into centuries of near continuous philosophical refinement. But the question is not whether a fully consistent theoretical system has been or will be reached at some point in time, for a logically consistent system may be unrelated to reality, but how close it is to the Message originally preached and how effective is it in guiding the believers to submission to God. The same should be asked of every dogmatic formulation of any religion, Islam's included.

We often reach a point at which a dogma becomes so far removed from its beginnings that it either loses its relevance or, far worse, becomes misleading. In our efforts to hold fast to it, we begin to sound like a person who makes an erroneous statement and then, rather than admit his error, insists on his original dictum and thus interprets it in a way contrary to the generally accepted sense of the words. When this is the case, might it not be better to discard it altogether, or at least replace it with a new formulation?

Within the Muslim community, this and related questions about the integrity and authority of certain textual sources are sometimes asked, but not with the same frequency and urgency as they are in modern-day Christianity, which now appears to be nearing a state of crisis. In the dialogues I have seen so far, each side tends to gloss over or deny the existence any hint of internal controversy. But this is sure to change as the two communities become better acquainted.

The Israeli-Palestinian Problem

Racism is one of the darkest inculcations of childhood. Bridgeport, Connecticut, when I was growing up there, was made up of many unassimilated cultures. It was a melting pot that had not yet begun to simmer. Bigotry was much more evident there than in the Midwest where I now

---

[258]The phrase *bi la kayf* has the literal meaning of "without [asking] how." This doctrine holds that the anthropomorphic references to God in the Qur'an reveal truths but should not necessarily be taken literally. Thus it states that a Muslim should accept the truth of such statements without insisting on knowing exactly how they are true. Watt might say that such statements "diagram" certain truths. See Watt, *Islamic Revelation in the Modern World*, 80-90.

live, for you were in daily contact with the objects of your prejudice. Of the racial slurs we hurled against each other, the word "Jew" is unique in that it was not a corruption of or departure from a word that defines an ancestry and because it is a dictionary term. Another distinction is that it was not only used to deride Jews, but would be used, sometimes alone or in combination, against persons of any race. For the gentiles, it had different shades of meaning, including miserliness, cowardice, and dirtiness.

I remember how the young kids from our neighborhood would ambush little Jewish boys on their way home from the synagogue, yelling, "Get the Jew!" or "Kill the Jew!," chasing them down the street. And unlike others, their parents rarely if ever complained to ours. Was it a part of their upbringing? I wondered. Did they come from a long line of publicly humiliated laughingstocks? How utterly weird to be chastised by the word that merely describes your descent! How often in later years I listened to adult friends of mine, who, after knowing me for some length of time, would privately confess their Jewishness, as if they were confiding that they were ex-convicts. Some would go as far as to divest themselves of Jewishness altogether by adding, "It's only a religion that I don't believe in any more."

Through my first marriage, I obtained an inside look into Jewish family life, which turned out not to be as unusual as I had presumed. The only thing that struck me as definitely peculiar was how uncertain they saw their existence, how convinced they were—and their relations and friends as well—that what had happened in the past could happen again, and that even in the United States the political climate could change quickly. Although some Jewish organizations make it their onus never to allow the Nazi Holocaust to be forgotten, I can hardly recall anyone in my first wife's family mentioning it by name, although it was alluded to frequently. True enough, this unspeakable tragedy is exploited for propaganda purposes by Zionists, but that does not detract from the fact that the Nazi death camps have sunk deep into the Jewish soul and have been added to the centuries of persecutions that are relived cyclically in their religious rituals, where even humor is some times called upon to relieve the sadness of their history.

I recall a conversation with my ex-wife more than three years after our divorce, in which she told me that she had lately resumed using her maiden name. When I asked her why she had not done that long ago, especially since the divorce was her idea and there had been no hard feelings on either side, she explained that she had received much better treatment when her last name was Lang: "They assumed I was German." No bitterness nor sorrow was implied, for she said it half-jokingly, yet what should

215

have passed as insignificant was for me an eye-opener that fit together many bits and pieces.

Until then I had thought that American Jews worried most about the future—that the horrors of their past might someday return. But her statement made me perceive a more pervasive anxiety and realize that, for Jews, there are probably times when many feel it advantageous to conceal their identity, when they hope that certain strangers do not discover their secret. And I wondered how, under such circumstances, one avoids feelings of guilt and self-reproach. Perhaps this is an exaggeration on my part, but if such anxieties are prevalent among American Jews, the long chronicle of atrocities suffered by Jews in Europe and Russia would certainly justify them.

Muslim readers may protest that the situation of Jews in Muslim lands was much better than in the Christianized countries. This opinion finds support in Bernard Lewis's recent study.[259] He points out that before the Age of Enlightenment in Europe, the best chance for Jews to find a tolerant environment and one in which they could advance was to be found in Muslim lands. But the author also shows that Jews in the Muslim world did not enjoy complete equality of rights and opportunities. In Islamic law for example, evidence given by Jewish and Christian subjects (collectively classified as *dhimmis*) was not admissible before a Muslim court. In addition, their lives had a lower value than that of Muslims when it came to the bloodwit compensation that had to be paid for an injury.[260] Also, many Muslim law manuals insisted that Jews and Christians should be subjected to a number of petty humiliations: a *dhimmi* must ride an ass, not a horse; he must not sit astride his animal, but ride sidesaddle, like a woman; he must not carry a weapon; he must be distinguished from Muslims by his dress; and restrictions on housing are frequently mentioned.[261]

In spite of various expressions of inferiority, Islamic law guaranteed Jewish and Christian communities a large degree of autonomy and "in most respects the position of non-Muslims under traditional Islamic rule was very much easier than that of non-Christians or even of heretical Christians in medieval Europe, not to speak of some events in modern Europe."[262] Lewis describes their legal status as one of second-class citizenship, but he cautions that the phrase deserves a closer look.

---

[259]Lewis, *Jews of Islam.*
[260]Ibid., 27.
[261]Ibid., 35.
[262]Ibid., 62.

Second class citizenship, though second class, is a kind of citizenship. It involves some rights, though not all, and is surely better than no rights at all. It is certainly preferable to the kind of situation that prevails in many states at the present time, where the minorities, and for that matter even the majority, enjoy no civil or human rights in spite of all the resplendent principles enshrined in the constitutions, but utterly without effect. A recognized status, albeit one of inferiority to the dominant group, which is established by law, recognized by tradition, and confirmed by popular assent, is not to be despised.[263]

We should also note that Jewish and Christian citizens were treated more or less the same under Islamic law, and that persecutions of either minority were rarely condoned by the government.

Even though Jews living under Muslim rule generally had it better than those living under Christian rule, from a twentieth-century point of view their existence was precarious in either case. Their well-being and survival depended on the goodwill and mercy of the majority, as they had no outside political power to represent them or to exert pressure on their behalf. I feel that political Zionism was inspired and impelled by this perception, and that it also accounts for the practically unconditional support given by many American Jews to the State of Israel. I do not believe that that support from the Jewish masses is based primarily on greed or racial pride or chauvinism; rather, I believe it derives from very deep-seated fear and tribulation. Ironically, the creation of the State of Israel may eventually lead to the very catastrophe that it is supposed to avert.

A full account of the histories of the Palestinians, Zionism, and the modern state of Israel is needed to appreciate the passions involved in the current Palestinian-Israeli conflict. I only provide here a very brief sketch and refer the reader to fuller treatments in the notes.[264]

Historians agree that the ancestors of the great majority of the Arabs of Palestine did not come to Palestine with the Muslim conquest, but that they are primarily descendants of Semites whose tenure of Pales-

---

[263]Ibid., 62.
[264]William W. Baker, *Theft of a Nation* (Las Vegas: Defenders Publications, 1982); Beatrice Erskine, *Palestine of the Arabs* (Westport, CT: Hyperion Press, 1976); J. M. N. Jeffries, *Palestine: The Reality* (Westport, CT: Hyperion Press, 1976); Edward W. Said, *The Question of Palestine* (New York: Times Books, 1979); Frank C. Sakran, *Palestine: Still a Dilemma* (Pennsylvania: Whitmore Publ., 1976); Clifford A. Wright, *Facts and Fables: The Arab-Israeli Conflict* (London: Kegan Paul International, 1989).

tine goes back at least three millennia before Christ and is "probably one of the simplest and longest in the world."[265] The ancient Hebrews arrived in Palestine much later, approximately fourteen hundred years before Christ. At first they established small settlements in the hills and lived in peace with their neighbors. At a later date they took up arms, and a great deal of their ensuing warfare is recounted in the Old Testament. The state or states established by the Israelites in Palestine were destroyed by the Assyrians in 700 BC and by the Babylonians in 550 BC.

The duration of ancient Jewish territorial possession of Palestine was ephemeral. Before the time of David, the settlement of the twelve tribes of Joshua was purely nominal;[266] only during the reign of David and Solomon did anything like Jewish possession of what we call Palestine exist. Eight hundred years afterwards, the Maccabees re-established the Jewish power that had faded with Solomon, but only for a very short span did it perhaps reach again the dimensions of David's and Solomon's days. Baker states that Palestine is:

the country where Jews had once upon a time (over 2000 years ago) established a state for a relatively short period of historical time. The same "state" eventually broke into smaller states.[267]

The argument for a Jewish historical claim to Palestine is therefore untenable. The possession by force of scattered parts of a territory for a few centuries more than two thousand years ago no more entitles today's Jews to that land than it would entitle today's Arabs to Spain, which they possessed for several centuries. In addition, Baker points out that:

the present day Jews now occupying Palestine are but mere fragments and in no way traceable to the former Hebrews or Habiru who once conquered the land of Canaan. . . . Those Palestinian Arabs still living in Palestine are true descendants of the original semitical inhabitants. Their roots do not lie in Syria or Lebanon, Jordan or Egypt, but rather the only country they have ever known as their homeland, the land of Palestine.[268]

---

[265]Jeffries, *Palestine: The Reality*, 6; Baker, *Theft of a Nation*, 5-6.
[266]Jeffries, *Palestine: The Reality*, 8.
[267]Baker, *Theft of a Nation*, 7.
[268]Ibid., 6.

He adds:

> Those Jews in 1897 who desired to once again possess Palestine as their homeland were in no way connected with the Semitic Jews of some 2500 years previous. This is attributable to the admixture of blood through marriage; but it is also due to the large number of non-semites who were converted to Judaism. The classic example of this occurrence is the Khazzar tribe living in present day Russia. Their wholesale conversion took place in the 8th century A.D., and many of the present Jews are descendents of this tribe.[269]

Nonetheless, it was upon the "historic connection" argument that Zionists in the early part of the twentieth century pressed their claim to establish a national Jewish homeland in, and eventually encompassing, the land of Palestine.

Zionism, which had its beginnings in the nineteenth century, was a Jewish movement to re-establish a Jewish nation. For some, this meant a spiritual restoration and a return to their religion, neither of which entailed a desire for territory. Many others, however, envisioned turning the Syrian province of Palestine into a Jewish nation. The two approaches are differentiated by referring to the former as spiritual Zionism and the latter as political Zionism (hereafter, when we speak of Zionism, we will be referring to political Zionism).

In 1915, the British government pledged itself, according to the terms of the Hussein-McMahon Treaty, to "recognize and support the independence of the Arabs within the territories included in the limits and boundaries proposed by the Shareef of Mecca." These boundaries upon which Shareef Hussain of Mecca, "as representative of the Arab peoples," and the British government agreed encompassed Palestine. In return, the Arabs under Hussain's leadership pledged to join the Allied forces in World War I in their war with Turkey. The Arabs fulfilled their pledge and fought commendably.[270] In 1919, the French and British governments, in the Joint Anglo-French Proclamation, confirmed the terms of the earlier pact with Shareef Hussein and explicitly guaranteed Arab rule in Palestine and other Arab lands.[271]

Between these two dates, however, the British had concluded two other agreements that were incompatible with the promise made to the

---

[269]Ibid., 9.
[270]Jeffries, *Palestine: The Reality*, 64-87.
[271]Ibid., 238-40.

Arabs. In 1916, the British and French negotiated the Sykes-Picot Treaty, which divided the still unconquered Ottoman empire, including the Arab lands, into British and French "zones of influence." In 1917, the famous Balfour Declaration, in which the British government committed itself to "the establishment in Palestine of a national home for the Jewish people," was issued. The Balfour Declaration reads:

His Majesty's Government views with favour the establishment in Palestine of a national home for the Jewish people, and will use their best endeavours to facilitate the achievement of this object, it being clearly understood that nothing shall be done which may prejudice the civil and religious rights of existing non-Jewish communities in Palestine or the rights and political status enjoyed by Jews in any other country.[272]

This Declaration, which was the proclaimed foundation of British government policy in Palestine for the next thirty-one years, conceals a number of important points. Its brevity suggest that it was drafted hastily, an assumption that is far from the reality. M. Nahom Sakalov, writing about the Declaration in his *History of Zionism*, states that "every idea born in London was tested by the Zionist Organizations in America, and every suggestion in America received the most careful attention in London." Leonard Stein says about the Declaration in his Zionism that "It was issued after prolonged deliberations as a considered statement of policy." Stephen Wise, an American Zionist leader, writes: "The Balfour Declaration was in the process of making for nearly two years."[273]

Another salient feature of the Declaration is its vagueness, all the more remarkable in view of the just-mentioned comments. Certainly, a document drafted so meticulously over a two-year period should have spelled out precisely what was meant by "the civil and religious rights of the non-Jewish communities" and what their not being subjected to "prejudice" would entail. The Shaw Commission, one in a long series of commissions sent by the British government to Palestine in 1930 to investigate continuing and growing racial unrest, complained that the Declaration was open to "a wide variety of interpretations" and recommended that the government should state clearly its policy towards Palestine.[274]

---

[272]Ibid., 170-71.
[273]Ibid., 172.
[274]Ibid., 613.

Along the same lines, the reference to non-Jewish communities in Palestine elicits our attention, since it leaves the impression that the Jews were in the majority in Palestine when the Declaration was issued. The fact of the matter is that at that time 91 per cent of the population was Arab and only 9 per cent was Jewish.[275] Note too that the non-identification of the Arab segment is intentional, for the refusal to recognize the existence of Palestinians was an early Zionist policy that persists until today.[276]

The document's ambiguity was not, according to the Zionist leaders quoted, due to hasty or casual drafting; it could only have been intentional. As Jeffries documents, it was meant to obscure the ultimate Zionist scheme of converting all of Palestine into a Jewish state and the British government's commitment to support this program up to its logical conclusion. In the meantime, the Balfour Declaration was seen as only an intermediary step towards the Zionist ideal.[277]

At the close of the World War I, the Palestinian Arabs anticipated their political independence as promised in the McMahon-Hussain Treaty. In the succeeding years, they discovered that not only did Britain have no intention of honoring its pledge, but that they were to have forced upon them, under the British mandate, a massive immigration of European Jews. In 1914, 9 per cent of the population of Palestine were Jews, while the rest were Arabs. By 1922, the Jewish population had risen to 11 per cent; in 1931 it had increased to 17 per cent; and by 1947 the Jewish share in the population of Palestine was 31 per cent.[278]

Monopolies over the land's natural resources were granted to Zionist companies. Zionist firms were encouraged to buy up cultivable land over the heads of the population from absentee landlords or from "Arab vendors who were in such poverty that they had no recourse but to sell, in order to pay their taxes and meet their wartime debts."[279] The economic impact on the Arabs was devastating. Unemployment skyrocketed and a huge landless class of poor people was created. Palestinian outrage intensified, as would that of American citizens if our government allowed the purchase and colonization of large blocks of the richest American soil by foreigners with the aim of eventually establishing an independent country thereon.

[275] Jeffries, *Palestine: The Reality*, 177.
[276] Wright, *Facts and Fables: The Arab-Israeli Conflict*, 2-5; Edward W. Said, *A Profile of the Palestinian People* (Palestine Human Rights Campaign, 1983), 3-4.
[277] Jeffries, *Palestine: The Reality*, 142-85.
[278] Wright, *Facts and Fables: The Arab-Israeli Conflict*, 4.
[279] Jeffries, *Palestine: The Reality*, 429-55, 704-705.

Throughout the 1920s and 1930s, disorders continued, with a constant stream of Arab delegations traveling to London to present their case, but to no avail. In return, Palestine received an almost equally constant stream of commissions, followed by British government-issued White Papers that sought to evade the findings of the commissions. The Crane-King Commission of 1919, the Haycraft Commission of 1921, the Shaw Commission of 1930, the Hope-Simpson Commission of 1930, and the French Commissions of 1931 and 1932 all concluded that grave injustices were being committed against the Arab Palestinians; that Jewish immigration should be greatly curtailed or suspended indefinitely; and that a government that represented the population should be installed.[280] The record of the British mandate of Palestine was one of thirty-one years of broken pledges, violations of international laws, outright treachery, dishonesty, and deceit. Much of the same, but on a far greater scale, was to be continued with the creation of the State of Israel.

What has been shown thus far allows us to dispel some common American misconceptions on this issue. The average American's understanding is that after World War II, Jewish victims of the Nazi Holocaust began immigrating to a mostly **uninhabited** Palestine with the aim of living peacefully side by side with the **tiny** Arab population, and that a short time later, in response to outbreaks of racial violence, the United Nations partitioned Palestine into an Arab sector and a Jewish sector, which was soon to become the State of Israel. Thus, the reasons for the existence of the State of Israel are believed to have been the Holocaust and the Palestinian Arab hatred of Jews.

But, as we have seen, the Zionist agenda of transforming the whole of Palestine into a Jewish nation was launched long before World War II began. In 1914, Palestine was neither uninhabited nor, as Israel's former Prime Minister Shimon Peres once put it, an "empty desert"; on the contrary, it was the populous homeland, well-known for its fertility and beauty, of a contemporary society.[281] The cause of Palestinian people's outrage was not prejudice, but the result of being cheated out of their promised independence and the subsequent displacement from their land.

The Partition scheme of 1947 was not the reaction of the United Nations to sudden unprecedented civil strife in Palestine, for it was first proposed by the Peel Commission in 1937. While authorities agree that relations between Arabs and Jews in Palestine were on the whole amiable

---

[280]Ibid., 272-95, 420-25, 604-29, 637-51.
[281]Said, *Profile of the Palestinian People*, 2-4.

before the influx of European Zionist settlers, violent clashes between Arabs and Jews began to occur shortly after the Zionist invasion, going as far back as the Jerusalem riots of 1920.[282]

On the eve of the partition, the Jews made up 32.5 per cent of the total population of Palestine and had acquired 5.77 per cent of the total land area. The United Nations' partition granted the Jews sovereignty over 56 per cent of the total land area, ten times as much as they actually owned at the time.[283] Forty-five per cent of the inhabitants of the partitioned territory's Jewish sector were Arabs, a large number of whom were to be expelled through Zionist terror and atrocity in the succeeding months. In 1940, Joseph Weitz, the administrator responsible for Jewish colonization, clearly stated the final goal:

> Between ourselves it must be clear that there is no room for both people together in this country . . . . The only solution is a Palestine without Arabs. And there is no other way than to transfer the Arabs from here to the neighboring countries, to transfer all of them; not one village, not one tribe, should be left.[284]

Massacres by the hundreds of unarmed men, women, and children occurred at Deir Yassin, Ein al Zeitun, Lydda, Safsaf, Saliha, and Duwaima.[285] An Israeli soldier provided the following chilling account of the slaughter at Duwaima: "They killed some eighty to one hundred Arabs, women and children. Their children were killed by smashing their skulls with clubs."[286] An extremely effective Zionist tactic was the broadcasting of frightening radio messages in Arabic, urging Palestinians to flee from their homes for their lives.[287]

The expulsion effort met with considerable success. Between 1 April 1948 and 15 May 1948, four hundred thousand Muslim and Christian Palestinians fled from their homes in the Jewish sector, becoming refugees for the first time in their history. The latter date, 15 May 1948, celebrated the birth of the present-day "State of Israel," after which Zionist tactics became even more ruthless and explicit. The British military historian Edgar O'Ballance wrote:

---

[282]Jeffries, *Palestine: The Reality*, 329-35, 661-69.
[283]Baker, *Theft of a Nation*, 15-16.
[284]Wright, *Facts and Fables: The Arab-Israeli Conflict*, 16-17.
[285]Ibid., 20-21.
[286]Ibid., 21.
[287]Ibid., 18-19.

No longer was there any "reasonable persuasion." Bluntly the Arab inhabitants were ejected and forced to flee into Arab territory, as at Ramleh, Lydda and other places. Wherever the Israeli troops advanced into Arab country, the Arab population was bulldozed out in front of them.[288]

In the ensuing struggle, termed the 1948 War, four hundred thousand additional Palestinian refugees were created, leaving only one hundred sixty thousand Arabs in the Jewish state, and by December the Jews were in possession of 78 per cent of the total area of the country. By 5 June 1967, as a result of the Six Day War, the ranks of Palestinians driven from their homes had swollen to 1.5 million. The government of Israel, in violation of section 11 of UN Resolution 194, has forbidden them to return to their lands or properties.

Since its birth, Israel has fought five major wars with the Arabs and has been involved in additional conflicts and conflagrations, such as the 1978 invasion of Lebanon. The wars occurred in 1948, 1956, 1967, 1973, and 1982. Israeli propaganda claims that the Arabs started all of these, but statements on record of Israeli political and military leaders show that in all but the 1973 war, Israel perceived no threat to its security and was the clear aggressor.[289]

Since the 1967 war, Israel has occupied the whole of Palestine. The West Bank and Gaza Strip are referred to as the Occupied Territories and remain under an oppressive military rule. In 1982, there were almost two million Palestinians living inside Palestine, half of them living inside Israel and the remainder in the Occupied Territories. In the same year, there were just over 2.5 million Palestinians living outside Palestine.[290] The Israeli policy of settling the Occupied Territories with Israeli Jewish citizens continues unabated, despite its being in violation of international law and despite the perfunctory protests of the government of the United States. Such international agencies as UNESCO, Amnesty International, and the Red Cross have been disseminating information for years on such human rights violations as the demolition of Palestinian houses, the seizure of Arab lands, the maltreatment of Palestinian workers, and the torture and illegal detention of Arab prisoners.[291]

Before turning to the Muslim response to the Palestinian tragedy, I wish to address the widely-held notion that Jews have a moral-religious

[288]Edgar O'Ballance, *The Arab-Israeli War* (New York: Praeger, 1948, 1957), 171-72.
[289]Wright, *Facts and Fables: The Arab-Israeli Conflict*, 121-38.
[290]Said, *A Profile of the Palestinian People*, 14.
[291]Said, *The Question of Palestine*, 37-48.

title to Palestine. Undoubtedly Jews have been the victims of terrible persecutions in the past, especially during World War II. Yet the Jews are not the only people to have suffered cruelty at the hands of others, and their past suffering does not entitle them to usurp another nation's land and property.

The wholesale theft of Palestine and the continued violation of the Palestinians' basic human rights will not ease the pain of the victims of the Holocaust. In reality, it only serves to dishonor the great sacrifices that were made and denies the lessons to be learned. Today Zionists are often heard saying that their persecution of the Palestinian people does not compare to the Holocaust. In terms of actual human suffering, that may be granted, but what makes the injustice committed against the Palestinians all the more immoral is that it is perpetrated by those who should so readily and immediately empathize with their affliction. With regard to the so-called Biblical or religious justification, which involves resurrecting already fulfilled prophecies with self-serving interpretations, it is even more despicable, because it implies that God encourages racism and injustice in bringing about His will. This argument not only prostitutes justice and morality, but religion as well.[292]

For every action there is an inevitable reaction, and the global Muslim response to the Palestinian tragedy has by now solidified into the unified conviction that Israel and its supporters are determined opponents of Islam and its adherents. There is no issue that arouses Muslim ire more than the plight of Palestine. This resentment is not engendered only by sympathy for their Muslim Palestinian brethren—the recent Gulf Crisis showed how fragile those bonds of brotherhood actually are—but is much more direct and personal. For Muslims, the State of Israel is the last living vestige of their debasement and dehumanization at the hands of insolent colonialists, a persistent reminder of their exploitation and manipulation by Western imperialists, set in a land which is sacred to them and a place of pilgrimage from which they are debarred. It therefore stands as the supreme example of Jewish and Christian European contempt for Islam. For many others, it is an apocalyptic battle ground heralding the End of Days.

These themes are recited and rehearsed in Friday sermons throughout thousands of American mosques, and Muslim rage festers and strengthens with each passing day. As the oppression of the Palestinians continues, this rage takes on an increasingly ugly side. Jews are categorized as the accursed of God, the initiators of all the sins of mankind, the implacable

---

[292]Baker, *Theft of a Nation*, 58-105; Wright, *Facts and Fables: The Arab-Israeli Conflict*, 164-69.

archenemy of Muslims.[293] Archaic, pernicious Eastern European anti-Jewish propaganda pieces such as the forgery, *The Protocols of the Elders of Zion*, are sometimes cited and endorsed. Not long ago I attended a public lecture in which a Muslim speaker attempted to convince Americans of a global conspiracy by arguing that the Jews control the media, citing Steven Spielberg, Woody Allen, Mel Brooks, and Ted Koppel as proof. An approach of this sort defeats the very cause that it attempts to represent.

The first thing that must be stressed is that not **all** Jews are Zionists and not all Zionists are Jews. Some of the most effective spokespersons against Zionism, from its very earliest days up to the present, have been Jews. Jeffries gives ample testimony to this in his book.[294] There is also the other side of the coin: so-called Christian Zionists. Prominent examples of such people are Jerry Fallwell and Pat Robertson.

Such statements as "the Jews control the media" are exaggerated and prejudicial, giving the impression that all American Jews are collaborating in a vast, illegal manipulation of the press. To be sure, there are very powerful **pro-Israeli** organizations and lobbies in the United States that exercise great influence over the communications industry, as former congressmen Pete McCloskey and Paul Findley testify; but they also point out that, for the most part, these groups operate in compliance with existing American laws.[295] A more pragmatic approach is to expose the extreme pro-Israeli bias of the news media and American foreign policy,[296] as the key to Zionist success has always rested on diffusing a false reality in the West and on keeping the Western public misinformed. Once that is recognized, the task facing Muslims becomes obvious. Muslims in America should organize politically and begin immediately, if only on the local level, to present the truth of the Palestine situation to their fellow Americans. They do not need to voice paranoid exaggerations, but simply to state the facts, which cry out so resoundingly against an enduring injustice.

In the wake of the Gulf crisis, hope among supporters of the Palestinian people has diminished. We often hear pessimistic admissions that time, as many Zionist claim, may be on the side of Israel; that sometime soon, through continued colonization and coercion, Arabs will be driven from the Occupied Territories and the international community will come to recognize all of Palestine as the State of Israel. But if there is any hope for justice for Palestinians, those in the United States who support them must

[293]Lewis, *Jews of Islam*, 185-89.
[294]Jeffries, *Palestine: The Reality*, 112-13.
[295]Paul Findley, *They Dare to Speak Out* (L. Hill Books, 1989).
[296]Said, *Question of Palestine*.

not surrender to despair. Of all the causes dear to America's Muslims, this is the one upon which they can have the most impact.

I disagree with the notion that time is with the Zionists. It is predicted that by the year 2000 the majority of American citizens will not be Caucasian; consequently, it will not be at all surprising if these citizens identify more readily with the Arab Palestinians than with their oppressors. Furthermore, Islam is the fastest growing faith in the West, and it is expected to be the second largest religious community in the United States by the turn of the century. This voice is bound to be heard. Thirdly, American public opinion is already beginning to move away from support of Israel, and the more Americans come to know that their tax dollars are essential to the successful perpetration of heinous crimes against humanity, the faster, I believe, public opinion will change.[297] Finally, America's power, military and economic, is not eternal nor invincible. Signs are that it is already declining, while Muslim nations are becoming stronger. Eventually Muslim governments will undoubtedly yield to democracy and as a result will pay closer attention to the will of the populace, which is more committed to the problem of Palestine than their current rulers.

Today, the Palestinians are advocating what is known as the two-state solution. This calls for the creation of an independent Palestinian state formed from the Occupied Territories. However, in many ways this seems less than equitable, for it delivers only a small fraction of what was promised and what is rightfully owned. But it represents the desire of the Palestinian people, and we should give it our total support. It is hoped that Israel will consider the proposal carefully, before the political pendulum swings in the opposite direction and the opportunity to achieve a peaceful settlement disappears altogether.

Ties of Kinship

I do not remember where the imam of the mosque was driving us in his van, but a few sentences of our conversation have stayed with me ever since.

My dear friend Hamed and I were talking about my parents, and he asked me if they had become Muslims. When I told him that they are very

---

[297]Horrible atrocities have been made possible through American government funding. One terrifying demonstration occurred in Lebanon in September 1983. After the withdrawal of the PLO from the Sabra-Shatila refugee camp in Beirut, the Israeli army surrounding the camps sent in troops of the Lebanese Christian fascist party, known as the Phalange, who proceeded to massacre one thousand Palestinian men, women, and children. The killing continued uninterrupted for thirty-six hours as the Israelis watched.

committed Christians, Hamed reminded me that God is the final judge and that His mercy encompasses all things. I appreciated his concern and openness.

"What is the opinion of the scholars on the fate of Jews and Christians in the hereafter?" he asked the imam.

"Those who died after the time of Muhammad," the imam pronounced coolly, keeping his vision fixed on the road, "are in the Fire."

I was so deeply hurt that I was speechless for the rest of the trip—not because I believed in his statement, but because it was delivered with such utter frigidity and authority. This was exactly that type of thinking that had driven me from religion more than twenty years ago.

During my youth, wherever I went, there was always a crucifix near-by: in every room of our house, hanging from the mirror of the car of the neighbor who drove us to school, above the blackboard in our classrooms, dangling from people's necks, and above the altar at church. It was an omnipresent and woeful image of a man who had just expired, who seconds earlier had sought forgiveness for his persecutors; and, in his death, we found the assurance of forgiveness and love. For us, it was a sign of an impenetrable mystery that held the secret of our existence, our suffering, and our sinfulness. In Catholic schools, the Church doctrines were practically never discussed and, for the children, they required no explanation. We saw in the image on the cross the coming together of God and humanity with all the passion, suffering, and grace that such a symbol entails, and, for us, this tragic death was an eternal sign of our salvation.

When I became an atheist, I discarded the cross. But there was also a sense of personal loss, for our symbols have such power over us that when we lose them, we lose something of ourselves that may not have a ready substitute. After ten years of atheism, I had put the crucifixion far behind me and, when I found fulfillment in Islam, there was nothing in the Qur'an to make me feel the need to believe in the crucifixion again—in fact, quite the contrary.

Perhaps this may pose a greater difficulty for those who converted directly from Christianity. Indeed, the Docetic interpretations of the Qur'an's denial of the crucifixion, which made their way into Islam through heretical Christian channels, probably stem from this difficulty faced by early Christian converts. And even though I am no longer attached to the symbol of the cross, I strongly resent suggestions from any quarter that toss aside, usually insensitively, the Christian experience or, for that matter, anyone's religious experience. Most people do not cling to their beliefs (or disbeliefs) for the sake of mere convenience or out of stupidity, for it is just not that simple, but rather out of feelings of emptiness and desperation. Unless we are ready to approach each other on matters of faith with deep humility and sympathy, it is best to leave that task to others.

It is surprising how many converts to Islam accept the opinion of Muslim scholars on the ultimate destiny of their non-Muslim family members. For while the Qur'an criticizes and corrects the People of the Book on a number of counts, their fate is clearly left in God's hands. As stated earlier, unlike most Muslims, the Qur'an acknowledges that there are true monotheists among them, at the same time warning them that some of their beliefs are misleading and harmful.

Definitely, according to the Qur'an, some of the Jews and Christians are kuffar (rejecters or deniers) and some of their beliefs are incorrect, but it must be stressed that the Qur'an consistently uses the words, "*min ahl al kitab* (among the People of the Book)" in these reprovals. It is one thing to stubbornly reject or avoid confronting truth, but quite another to not be able to see it as a consequence of one's intellectual and cultural limitations, after a genuine attempt to do so. I myself must confess that although I am committed to Islam, the way most Muslims represent their beliefs does not make sense to me because my frame of reference is quite different from theirs.

In addition, we must humbly admit that, in comparison to the wisdom of God, all our knowledge is insignificant and our fates will be determined by how we respond and what we do with what we know, with all our limitations. A fellow Muslim once protested that if he accepted my point of view, he might as well become a Christian so that he would not need to perform the prayers and fasting. "You're missing the point," I told him. "It's because you truly **believe** in Islam that you must submit to it. Otherwise, by leaving your religion, you would be turning your back on what you understand to be true."

In any case, the Qur'an makes it clear in three almost identically phrased passages (2:62; 5:69; 22:17), revealed at three distinct times, that non-Muslims are not automatically excluded from salvation. The early Muslim exegetes sensed a possible conflict here and opined that the Jews and Christians referred to must have been those who lived before the time of Muhammad. However, neither the Qur'an nor the accepted sayings of Muhammad warrant this interpretation.

It is true that the Qur'an insists that no religion finds acceptance with God but Islam (3:19; 3:85), but one must remember that, at the time of the Revelation, the Arabic word *islam* did not yet stand for a thoroughly elaborated system of laws and dogmatic principles. To the Arabs, *islam* meant complete submission or surrender, and in the Qur'anic context it refers to a sincere and willing self-surrender to God, which is the essence of all true worship of God. We are not in a position to determine the extent to which another's faith is based on this intention. On these matters, we have to allow God, in His infinite wisdom and mercy, the final word:

> Those who believe [Muslims] and those who are Jews and the Christians and the Sabians—whoever believes in God and the Last Day and does righteous deeds, for them, their reward is with their Lord, and there shall be no fear on them nor shall they grieve. (2:62)

PARTING THOUGHTS

Grant lived on the outskirts of the Mission District, one of the poorer sectors of San Francisco, where he rented the bottom floor of a small, aging two-story house. It had been his home for over a decade and, thanks to rent control, it was too good a bargain to let go of, even if the neighborhood was steadily deteriorating.

A block from his flat, and from the turnpike, was the San Francisco Islamic Center, which, in more prosperous times, had probably been a warehouse. If one did not happen to notice the small marker above the side entrance, it could still easily be mistaken for one.

Grant walked passed the Center almost every day on his way to the bus stop, so he knew what it was and why Middle Eastern and Indo-Pakistani men clad in traditional attire visited it frequently. His fascination with religions led him to pay his first visit to the Center, which would lead inevitably to his conversion, for he would not be fully satisfied until he actually experienced the religion. Yet he proceeded, as always, cautiously, requiring several visits before he made his Shahadah. "It's better to take your time before deciding," they warned him, "because the penalty for leaving Islam is death."

I met Grant a week after his conversion, which was about three weeks after mine. At that time, he was only the second white American Muslim I had seen. Six months later, he left Islam. He returned to it a year after that, left again to join the Sikhs for a short stint, and then became a Buddhist.

Before Islam, he had tried several other religions: Catholicism, Russian Orthodoxy, and Judaism among them. Now he was in limbo again. "I change religions more often than I change my socks," he used to say. But for Grant it was hardly a joke. Rather it was an admission of one failure after another to satisfy his love for God and to find the community of faith where that love could be realized and lived. "Islam has the best religion, but the worst believers," he would say, quoting a well-known Muslim writer. I did not agree completely, but I had never put much hope in humanity anyway. Yet for Grant, the religious community was at least as important as the religion's ideology.

Through his many conversions we remained friends. Quite often, both before and after I got married we had dinner together, and our conversations were almost exclusively about religion. Our strong friendship, together with his rejection of Islam and his general indecisiveness about religion, had made me question and examine my own commitment continuously and closely. For me, Grant became a spiritual guide, asking questions that I had not thought of but needed to, unintentionally forcing me to explore deeper and deeper within myself. He was my spiritual Khidr, my blue-eyed, sharp and witty, Irish-green pilot into so many contradictions. What was it going to be like without him, I thought, as I veered towards the exit that would take us to his house.

"It is awfully hard to serve God—to truly serve Him!"

My first impulse was to agree with him, because the line between serving God and ourselves is so infinitesimally thin.

"Maybe we're more demanding than He is, Grant. Maybe God only wants us to keep trying."

Darkness takes away distractions; it sensitizes. It was past midnight. I lay in bed on my right side, my right hand tucked under the pillow beneath my head, kept awake by a nagging question on divine justice. Suddenly I was distracted by an eerie sense that something was different. I lay perfectly still, alert to the faintest movement.

The murmur of the night had slipped away, displaced by soundlessness. A strange sensation began to fill me, at first faintly, then radiantly, with no clear transition. I felt I was evaporating into an infinity of tiny atoms, held together by an overpowering tenderness.

I waited for it to subside, but it grew from intensity to intensity, to the point at which I thought this had to be my end. I was consumed by dread and awe and yearning. My body froze, locked in expectation.

The presence seemed greater behind me, over my shoulder. I slowly, timorously reached out with my left hand into the darkness, not daring to turn my head from the pillow to look back. With a surge of power, I was submerged in love, dissolved in inundating kindness. Freed, my resistance dissipating, I thought back to my family. "Please take care of my daughters and my wife!"

Then I reverted to a state of calm. I could hear the buzz of crickets outside my bedroom window and the quiet sound of a car gliding down our street. I tried to interpret what had just happened. I felt protected and fostered and a sense of deep longing—and disappointment in myself. To this day, I have been unable to remember the question I was tackling.

"I do love God, Jeff!"

"I know you do, Grant. I never knew anyone who searched so passionately as you."

Passing the Islamic Center on our left, we made a right onto Ogden Street. I stopped the car in front of Grant's apartment, turning the tires into the curb.

Some people are able to express themselves so effortlessly. They can capture, order, analyze, interpret, and relate what they are feeling in a single breath. I had not planned any parting words. If I had, I probably would have told Grant how glad I was to have known him, how much I had gained from our friendship; that I was looking forward to Kansas—a new place is a chance to grow—but that I would always remember him.

The dream recounted in the first chapter had sustained me through the long turmoil and uncertainties of conversion. I used to recite the story of it to myself and others; I wrote it down so that I would never forget it, so that I could always fall back on it for support. In time, it gave way to my daily reading of the Qur'an, supplanted by its captivating call from Heaven.

Both of them are still important to me, but the experience of God's love in prayer and contemplation now far overshadows them, and yet I am ever more aware of my weaknesses and failings. I know now that if I lose God again, then I have surely lost it all, and I plead, along with Rabi'ah al 'Adawiyah: "O my God, would you really burn this heart that loves you so?" And I find comfort in her answer.

I walked Grant over to the stairway of his apartment. "Take care of yourself and keep in touch," I told him as we shook hands. Something in the moment told me—and I think Grant, too—that we would never see or hear from each other again. Over the years, I tried calling and writing him. I also had friends in the Bay Area try to locate him, but to no avail.

"Al salamu 'alaykum, Jeff," he said, smiling reassuringly.

"Wa 'alaykum al salamu wa rahmat Allah." And may God's peace and mercy be upon you, always.